TOURISM ESSENTIALS: 4

Tourism, Public Transport and Sustainable Mobility

C. Michael Hall, Diem-Trinh Le-Klähn and Yael Ram

CHANNEL VIEW PUBLICATIONS
Bristol • Blue Ridge Summit

Library of Congress Cataloging in Publication Data
A catalog record for this book is available from the Library of Congress.
Names: Hall, Colin Michael, - author. | Le-Klähn, Diem-Trinh, author. |
  Ram, Yael, author.
Title: Tourism, Public Transport and Sustainable Mobility/ C. Michael Hall,
  Diem-Trinh Le-Klähn and Yael Ram.
Description: Bristol, UK: Channel View Publications, 2017. |
  Includes bibliographical references and index.
Identifiers: LCCN 2016043699| ISBN 9781845415983 (hbk : alk. paper) |
ISBN 9781845415976 (pbk : alk. paper) | ISBN 9781845416010 (kindle)
Subjects: LCSH: Tourism—Planning. | Local transit—Planning. |
  Transportation—Planning. | Sustainable tourism.
Classification: LCC G155.A1 H3493 2017 | DDC 388.4068/4—dc23 LC record available at
https://lccn.loc.gov/2016043699

British Library Cataloguing in Publication Data
A catalogue entry for this book is available from the British Library.

ISBN-13: 978-1-84541-598-3 (hbk)
ISBN-13: 978-1-84541-597-6 (pbk)

Channel View Publications
UK: St Nicholas House, 31–34 High Street, Bristol BS1 2AW, UK.
USA: NBN, Blue Ridge Summit, PA, USA.

Website: www.channelviewpublications.com
Twitter: Channel_View
Facebook: https://www.facebook.com/channelviewpublications
Blog: www.channelviewpublications.wordpress.com

The policy of Multilingual Matters/Channel View Publications is to use papers that are
natural, renewable and recyclable products, made from wood grown in sustainable for-
ests. In the manufacturing process of our books, and to further support our policy, preference is given to printers that have FSC and PEFC Chain of Custody certification. The FSC
and/or PEFC logos will appear on those books where full certification has been granted
to the printer concerned.

Typeset by Nova Techset Private Limited, Bengaluru & Chennai, India.
Printed and bound in the UK by Short Run Press Ltd.
Printed and bound in the US by Edwards Brothers Malloy, Inc.

Contents

Boxed Insights and Case Studies

Figures, Tables and Plates

Figures

Tables

Plates

Acknowledgements

This book had its immediate genesis in the Freiburg sustainable mobility workshops at which the authors first met. The workshops provided an excellent base for discussion on issues surrounding public transport and tourism, among other concerns. For this we must thank the organisers Scott Cohen, Stefan Gössling, James Higham, Paul Peeters and Eke Eijgelaar. For Michael the origins also probably go back further, to a time of catching a bus and/or train to school every day and, more recently, the delights of the train and ferry services in Sweden and Finland. It is therefore with some irony that he now lives near a rural community in New Zealand for most of the year, in which the railway was closed down in 1961 and through which the bus stopped coming many years ago – something which is a clear testimony both to the lack of foresight in public transport planning in New Zealand and the related corporatisation of public assets in a neoliberal economy.

We are indebted to a number of people who have supported the research efforts for this book at Ashkelon College, the Technische Universität München and the Department of Management, Marketing and Entrepreneurship at the University of Canterbury. The valuable comments of anonymous reviewers of the manuscript also provided useful suggestions to which we have tried to respond. In addition, we would like to note our deep thanks to Jody Cowper-James for her great assistance in checking the references, the support of all at Channel View and the comments of anonymous reviewers, as well as the invaluable source material on sustainable mobility in Europe provided by Eltis: The urban mobility observatory (http://www.eltis.org).

Michael would like to thank a number of colleagues with whom he has undertaken related research over the years. In particular, thanks to Tim Coles, David Duval, Stefan Gössling, Johan Hultman, Dieter Müller, Paul Peeters, Jarkko Saarinen, Dan Scott, Anna Dóra Sæþórsdóttir and Allan Williams for their thoughts, as well as for the stimulation of Ann Brun, Beirut, Nick Cave, Bruce Cockburn, Elvis Costello, Stephen Cummings, Chris Difford and Glenn Tilbrook, David Bowie, Elvy, Ebba Fosberg, Hoodoo Gurus, Ivan and Alyosha,

Larkin Poe, Vinnie Reilly, David Sylvian, Tango With Lions and *The Guardian*, BBC6 and KCRW – without whom the four walls of a hotel room would have been much more confining. Michael would also like to thank the many people who have supported his work over the years, and especially to the Js and the Cs who stay at home and mind the farm. Yael would like to thank her loving family: Eyal, Niv, Yoav and Yuval as well as her parents: Leah and Mordechai Naor. Diem would like to thank her husband Marco, her parents Vinh and Hieu, her sister Ty and her brother Thang for their support; and to thank her supervisors Michael Hall, Regine Gerike and Jutta Roosen for their guidance during her PhD at the Technische Universität München.

We all look forward to meeting on a train again sometime soon!

Acronyms

ABA	American Bus Association
AVE	Alta Velocidad Española
CONEBI	Confederation of the European Bicycle Industry
DFDS	Det Forenede Dampskibs-Selskab
ECMF	European Citizens Mobility Forum
EFC	European Cyclists' Federation
GHG	greenhouse gas
GIS	Geographic Information Systems
GPS	Geographic Positioning System
HSR	High Speed Rail
ICT	information and communications technology
IRU	International Road Transport Union
ITF	International Transport Forum
km/h	kilometres per hour
NGO	non-government organisation
NHTS	National Household Travel Survey
NMVB	Nationale Maatschappij Van Buurtspoorwegen
OECD	Organisation for Economic Co-operation and Development
P&R	Park and Ride
pkm	passenger-kilometres
RORO	Roll-on Roll-off
UITP	International Association of Public Transport/L'Union internationale des transports publics
UNDESA	United Nations Department of Economic and Social Affairs
UNESCAP	United Nations Economic and Social Commission for Asia and the Pacific
UNHabitat	United Nations Human Settlements Programme
UNWTO	United National World Tourism Organisation
VFR	Visiting Friends and Relations
WEF	World Economic Forum
WHO	World Health Organisation

1 Introduction

Introduction

Transportation, in general, refers to the movement of people, goods, information and/or energy. In this book we are focused on the transportation of people and, in particular, those who are participating in tourism activities. Transport is essential for tourism as, quite clearly, unless an individual is able to move between their home environment and another destination they are unable to be a tourist. Although there is a substantial body of literature on tourism transport (see Duval, 2007; Page & Connell, 2014, for an overview), much of this has been focused on aviation, cruise ships and cars. In contrast, there is much less literature on public transport and tourism despite the important role it plays in moving tourists around and within destinations and its value in moving tourists between destinations (Kagermeier & Gronau, 2015; Le-Klahn, 2015; Le-Klahn & Hall, 2015; Orsi, 2015). This book therefore seeks to address the critical role that public transport plays in tourism with respect to movement, as well as its part in the tourist experience and its significance for destination and tourism sustainability.

Those readers from a tourism studies background will be familiar with the definitional difficulties of 'tourism'. Yet, as discussed below, the concept of public transport is also surrounded by significant definitional issues. This first chapter seeks to outline some of the different ways in which public transport is understood and how this particular volume will use the concept. It also outlines the importance of public transport for tourism and the role that tourism can play in supporting the provision of public transport services. As will be stressed throughout the book, public transport is also important not only for regional sustainability and individual accessibility, but is also increasingly recognised as being significant for developing more sustainable tourism products as well. However, before discussing the role of public transport in the provision of tourism services and products, the chapter will provide an overview of how tourism and public transport are defined.

Defining Tourism

The term 'tourist' is the concept used to describe those consumers who are engaged in voluntary temporary mobility away from their home environment (Hall, 2005). The key conceptual points here are 'voluntary', 'temporary' and mobility (Coles et al., 2004). If involuntarily movement is involved, the individual mobility may be a function of war or disaster and the individual described as a 'refugee', or if the individual is transported by force, then it may constitute a case of 'trafficking'. If an individual moves from one location to another on a permanent basis then they are usually referred to as an 'emigrant' by the country of departure and 'immigrant' by the country of arrival.

The concept of mobility in the context of tourism refers to the capacity of individuals to move from one location to another. In order to be able to do this, individuals need to be able to overcome various economic, social and technological factors that act as constraints on tourism-related mobility (Cooper & Hall, 2016), these include:

Income: sufficient disposable income is required;

Time: the amount of time available to an individual for travel is a key determinant of how far people can travel and also influences destination selection;

Political rights: individual domestic and individual mobility is subject to political and legislative jurisdictions. Under international law there is no right of automatic access to another country for example;

Health: poor health, frailty and/or disability may constrain travel options;

Information and Communication: information influences tourism destination with respect to destination, accommodation and activity selection;

Safety and security: negative perceptions of the potential impacts of criminal, health and political risks affect destination choice and decision to travel;

Legislated holidays: the availability of statutory work and school holidays is a significant influence on travel patterns, although it should be noted that the taking of holidays is also influenced by organisational and national cultures;

Location: the relative location of where someone lives on a permanent basis in relation to transport is a significant constraining factor on travel behaviour because of the relative degree of accessibility. The relative location of transport infrastructure relative to consumers therefore affects both the costs and pattern of travel;

Gender: acts as a constraint on travel because of fears over personal security or cultural issues regarding the appropriateness of travel;

Culture: tourism is understood differently within different cultures, including attitudes towards tourism, particularly when temporary movement away from home is associated with what may be regarded as 'non-essential' behaviours. The cultural context is also extremely important for the influence of family on travel decision making.

There are substantial challenges with respect to the statistical analysis of tourists, and hence tourism, with different definitions often being applied by countries even though the United Nations World Tourism Organisation (UNWTO) and the United Nations (UN) have recommended a common statistical framework (see below). Nevertheless, the principle features that need to be defined in a statistical or 'technical' approach to tourism include:

- The purpose of travel, e.g. the type of travel, such as business travel.
- The time dimension involved in travel, which frames the minimum and maximum periods of time spent away from permanent residence and time spent at the destination.
- Situations in which travellers may not be defined as tourists, e.g. the voluntary nature of their travel, whether they are military or whether people are in transit from one location to another.

With respect to the definition of tourism and tourist the UN Department of Social and Economic Affairs and UNWTO (2010) recommendations on tourism statistics identify three basic forms of tourism:

Domestic tourism, which comprises the activities of a resident visitor within the country of reference either as part of a domestic tourism trip or part of an outbound tourism trip

Inbound tourism, which comprises the activities of a non-resident visitor within the country of reference on an inbound tourism trip

Outbound tourism, which comprises the activities of a resident visitor outside the country of reference, either as part of an outbound tourism trip or as part of a domestic tourism trip. (UN & UNWTO, 2010: 15)

International travel consists of both inbound and outbound travel, and refers to situations in which the country of residence of the traveller is different from the country or countries visited. From this perspective

International tourism comprises inbound tourism and outbound tourism, that is to say, the activities of resident visitors outside the country of reference, either as part of domestic or outbound tourism trips and the activities of non-resident visitors within the country of reference on inbound tourism trips. (UN & UNWTO, 2010: 15)

International visitor: An international traveller qualifies as an international visitor with respect to the country of reference if: (a) he/she is on a tourism trip and (b) he/she is a non-resident travelling in the country of reference or a resident travelling outside of it. (UN & UNWTO, 2010: 16)

From the perspective of the country of reference, a domestic traveller qualifies as a domestic visitor if: (a) s/he is on a tourism trip and (b) s/he is a resident travelling in the country of reference. A domestic trip is therefore 'one with a main destination within the country of residence of the visitor. An inbound or outbound trip is one with a main destination outside the country of residence of the visitor' (UN & UNWTO, 2010: 14). An additional category is that of a same-day visitor or excursionist, for example an international day tripper or excursionist (for example, an international visitor on a cruise ship) should be defined as a

visitor residing in a country who travels the same day to a country other than which he/she has his/her usual environment for less than 24 hours without spending the night in the country visited and whose main purpose of visit is other than the exercise of an activity remunerated from within the country visited. (World Tourism Organisation, 1991)

Insight 1.1: The Kusttram: Belgium's Coastal Tram

The 'kusttram' is a 68-kilometre long tram connection that runs in Belgium from De Panne near the French border to Knokke near the Dutch border every 10 minutes during peak summer months and 20 minutes in winter. It has 69 stops and is the longest tram line in the world, as well as one of the few interurban tramways to remain in operation.

The kusttram was developed by the NMVB (Nationale Maatschappij Van Buurtspoorwegen), the former Belgian public transport provider, which was in charge of connecting regions by tram that would not be connected by train. In 1991 the state-owned organisation was split into two with De Lijn, the Belgian public transport provider, taking over responsibility for operating the kusttram. It is an autonomous government company in which the Flemish local municipalities hold three quarters of the shares. Over 3 million people per year are estimated to take the tram. In July, 2011, 1,839,724 passengers were transported by

---

the tram (59,345 passengers per day). 70% of users in the summer are tourists with up to 70,000 people per day taking the tram in summer. The tram is used for a wide range of tourist purposes and functions as both an inter and intra-destination service as well as providing sightseeing opportunities, although the fact that it is the longest tram line in the world has also made it an attraction in its own right.

Sources:
Eltis The urban mobility observatory: http://www.eltis.org/discover/case-studies/coastal-tram-along-belgian-coastline-focusing-tourism-belgium#sthash.s0BZerFz.dpuf
Kusttram: https://www.delijn.be/en/kusttram/locaties-haltes/
UrbanRail.net (includes map): http://www.urbanrail.net/eu/be/kusttram/kusttram.htm

Defining and Conceptualising Public Transport

The term 'public transport' is typically associated with conventional forms of mass transportation such as scheduled bus, train or commuter ferry services. However, most people would not associate the term with other forms of passenger transportation, such as taxis, shuttles or ride sharing. Yet all of these services share some of the key characteristics of public transport services. (Ministry of Transport, 2016: 3)

There is no widely accepted definition of public transport. Like the tourism phenomenon, the concept of public transport is approached from a variety of perspectives that reflect not only changes in transport technology and how people access them but also the changing role of the state, contemporary governance and the emergence of public-private partnerships. As Glover (2011: 2) observes, 'Understanding what constitutes public transport can assist in understanding the respective roles of public transport and private transport and resolve some of the confusion that arises from efforts to use private transport modes to address public transport problems'.

Drawing on Brändli (1984), Rüetschi and Timpf (2005) note what is likely to be commonly understood by many people when they suggest that public transport is the production of the service 'transport' for masses of people, not just individuals; this service is completely fixed in space and time by means of the timetable; there is always a chauffeur, thus eliminating the need to drive oneself; and trips involve more than one means of transport (including walking), that is, passengers have to change at designated interchanges. 'Based on these properties public transport denotes the set of services for the transportation of people according to a predefined schedule (fixing place and time) and subject to published conditions of use, employing multiple modes of transport' (Rüetschi & Timpf, 2005: 27). However, it should be noted that such conceptions of public transport are being substantially challenged by current changes in transport technology, e.g. the emergence of driverless vehicles, changes in information and communications technology (ICT), e.g. the development of applications that allow an individual to call small scale public transport vehicles to provide pick up, and transport organisation, e.g. public transport services being available on-call rather than fixed by timetable. These issues have also been recognised in a public transport futures project run by the Ministry of Transport in New Zealand

> Many of the changes that are likely to influence the future development of the transport system are driven by technology. In the last few years in particular, we have seen a rapid proliferation of new transport related technologies and business models that are changing the way people travel. Further changes to the transport system are on the horizon. For example, it is now widely assumed that autonomous vehicles will play a role in our future transport system, even if the precise impact that they will have is unclear.
>
> Many of these new transport options do not fit neatly into widely held interpretations of what the terms 'private transport' and 'public transport' mean. While the meaning of these terms has previously been obvious, neither term has been precisely defined. These terms are no longer sufficient to describe the full suite of transport options that are available today. (Ministry of Transport, 2016: 3)

Public transport by mode

Public transport usually serves to describe a group of particular modes of transport, including buses, ferries, light rail, subways, commuter rail and regional or inter-urban rail. For example, for Farag and Lyons (2012) public transport means: train, coach, bus, tram and underground (with taxi and air travel excluded). Similarly, the International Association of Public Transport (UITP) is the peak organisation for public transport authorities, operators, policy bodies and research organisations, with more than 1300 member organisations in 92 countries. The public passenger modes of members include metro/underground, bus, light rail, regional rail, suburban rail and water transport. Barter suggests

> As used here, it refers to passenger transport services which are available to the general public and which are run regularly (or semi-regularly) on fixed (or semi-fixed) routes. It is equivalent in common usage to the North American term, transit.
>
> The word 'public' in public transport need not imply state ownership, nor even public sector management or planning. With this conception of public transport, taxis are excluded but 'jitney' style services by minivans are included. In some cities, shared taxis can straddle a grey area at the boundary between taxi service and fixed-route public transport. (Barter, 2008: 104)

One issue with approaches towards public transport definition by mode is that it often tends to have a very 'Western' focus. For example, Wergeland (2012) notes that in 2009, more than two billion passengers were ferried in about 8 million trips – all ships included, a figure not far behind that of air transport. Asia dominates the ferry passenger market and is responsible for over 40% of the global market. Ferries are an important contributor to multi-modality and carried 252 million cars, 677,000 buses and 32 million trailers in 2009, with about 85% of this market being on roll-on–roll-off services in developed countries (Wergeland, 2012).

However, Glover (2011: 3) suggests that a mode-based approach has limitations, 'there is no uniform relationship between modes and the role of governments; even within one urban transport system there can be a multitude of arrangements and variations of the state's role for a single mode'. Mode-based approaches to definition are nevertheless convenient but raise difficulties when engaging with informal or semi-informal services, i.e. Uber or rickshaw drivers depending on the jurisdiction, or whether all forms of collective/mass transport should be described as public transport. Indeed, the term collective transport as applied to modes and services is widely used in the public transport literature (e.g. Banister, 2005), and often used interchangeably (e.g. McManus, 2005). Rodrigue *et al.* refer to collective transportation interchangeably with public transit and as one of the three broad categories of urban transportation and mobility.

The purpose of collective transportation is to provide publicly accessible mobility over specific parts of a city. Its efficiency is based upon transporting large numbers of people and achieving economies of scale. It includes modes such as tramways, buses, trains, subways and ferry-boats. (Rodrigue *et al.*, 2013: 206)

Collective transportation and shared mobility are therefore distinguished from individual transportation and freight transportation. Given its potential relevance for tourist mobility it is also informative to note how individual transportation is defined:

Includes any mode where mobility is the outcome of personal choice and means such as the automobile, walking, cycling and the motor cycle. The majority of people walk to satisfy their basic mobility, but this number varies according to the city considered. For instance, walking accounts for 88 percent of all movements inside Tokyo while this figure is only 3 percent for Los Angeles. (Rodrigue *et al.*, 2013: 206)

Plate 1.1 Ferry terminal Tallinn, Estonia. The ferry terminal in Tallinn in Estonia is a major transport hub and transfer point with Baltic ferry traffic connecting to taxis, bus services and 'ecocabs' (modern cycle rickshaws).

Plate 1.2 Scandlines ferry entering Helsingborg ferry terminal, Sweden. There are ferry crossings between Helsingborg and Helsingør, Denmark, every 20 minutes. The service is privately owned but functions as a means of public transport.

Public transport by vehicle and system ownership

A widely used approach is to consider public transport as occurring when a service is owned by a government entity and private transport, being that which is privately owned (Glover, 2011). From a governmental perspective, what is defined as public transport depends on the particular jurisdiction (Kübler & Schwab, 2007). However, the notion of a clear-cut divide between government and private entities is completely misplaced given the changing nature of governance, especially in Western societies, and the growth of public-private partnerships (PPPs) as well as the corporatisation of government agencies so that they act like private businesses. PPPs are 'working arrangements based on a mutual commitment (over and above that implied in any contract) between a public sector organisation with any other organisation outside the public sector' (Bouvaird, 2004: 200). This definition highlights the importance of the concept not just referring to cross-sectoral contractual engagement, i.e. via the sometimes controversial contracting out of public services to the private sector, but to the potential for synergies and mutuality in partnership relations, often through the creation of new structures and programs. PPPs are widely used in public transport provision (Burke, 2016; Gordon *et al.*, 2013; Osei–Kyei & Chan, 2016; Tsamboulas *et al.*, 2013). The nature of PPPs is illustrated in Figure 1.1. PPPs can be categorised with respect to organisational form and the mutual dependence that exists in the partnership relationship. Four main categories of partnership are identified from this perspective with joint ventures and networked relationships (i.e. one mode such as train timetabled to connect with another mode such as bus even under different ownership). The PPP concept includes private-NGO partnerships as well as private business-public agency relationships (Mendel & Brudney, 2012). Given the range of mixed and hybrid models of public transport service delivery, partnerships are also possible between all three sectors, as well as

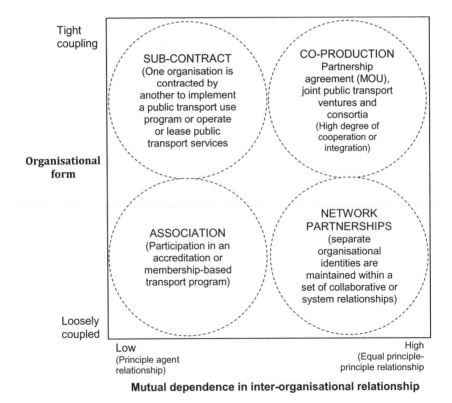

Figure 1.1 Frameworks for public-private partnerships in transport services

intra-sectoral partnerships, i.e. between different public authorities and agencies, sometimes also in different jurisdictions. As Glover (2011) describes, 'the complexity of current transport systems defies such an easy categorization'.

An alternative discussed by Glover is the notion that 'Government officials and those elected or appointed to government bodies express a definition of public transport through the workings of the public policy process' (2011: 4). Under this 'politics as practiced' approach to understanding public transport government understanding of what constitutes public transport can shift over time and between jurisdictions and there may be periods of deliberate or accidental ambiguity over this understanding. However, while such an approach may reflect local circumstances it is not very useful on a macro-scale.

Public transport as an institution

Institutional elements may also be used to distinguish between public and private systems. Criteria include: governance through public policy mechanisms; financial structures for public transport are based in public agencies; and the primary objective of the system operators is the provision of a transport service rather than a corporate goal as for a private operator, such as profits and return on investment (Glover, 2011). From such an approach, even where agencies have a focus on efficiency and cost minimisation the provision of the public transport service is ultimately regarded as a means to achieve a public good rather than a private return. Significantly, in many cases what constitutes public transport is institutionally determined and based on a legal definition of public transport, often stressing its open character (Veeneman, 2002). However, as noted above, the intention of providing transport services may change over time.

Public transport as a common pool resource

Künneke and Finger (2009) and Glover (2011) argue that public transport is a form of common pool resource (CPR) in that by creating public transport systems, governments recognised that the problems that arise from allowing private firms a transport monopoly in particular markets, especially on fixed transport infrastructure such as train lines, represented a monopoly problem, and that an obvious way to addressing the problems of a private monopoly was to either create a public monopoly or to regulate competition. The notion of a CPR 'refers to a natural or man-made resource system that is sufficiently large as to make it costly (but not impossible) to exclude potential beneficiaries from obtaining benefits from its use' (Ostrom, 1990: 30). CPRs have two characteristics: they are goods and services that are diminished by consumption or use and it is difficult to prevent additional users of the good or service (Dolsak & Ostrom, 2003; Ostrom, 1990). In the case of the former, Glover (2011: 8) argues that 'public transport is subject to capacity restraints and to crowding, meaning that users are in competition for a limited resource. In simple terms, users of a service can be added until a limit is reached, such as the capacity of a carriage, bus, or ferry; at this point any potential additional users are in competition with others'. In the case of the second characteristic, Glover (2011) suggests that for those willing to pay the fare there is no rationing of access to the service, while fares are not used as a means of restricting access to the public transport system anyway. However, it should perhaps be noted here that while fares are not used to ration access *in toto*, they are often used to redistribute demand, for example, by lower prices being made available to encourage off-peak travel on certain routes.

Künneke and Finger (2009) suggest that transport infrastructures can be interpreted as common pool resources in relation to four essential functions (system management, capacity management, interconnection and interoperability). They also suggest that given the complexity of infrastructures their governance as CPRs is shifting from vertically integrated organisations under state control towards a more distributed market-oriented governance (see also Laperrouza and Finger (2009) on the regulation of Europe's single railway market). According to Künneke and Finger, infrastructures, including public transport, can be perceived as non-excludable resources for at least three reasons:

> First, infrastructures might be spread through a huge geographical area with difficult to monitor access points, like for instance public road systems. Second, even if the access could be technically monitored, there might be politically motivated universal service obligations, since infrastructures provide essential services like drinking water, energy or means of communication. Third, once the users have entered the network, it might be difficult or even impossible to precisely determine the services they appropriate from the network. (Künneke & Finger, 2009: 5–6)

Glover (2011) suggests that conceptualising public transport as a CPR helps to differentiate between public transport which is the responses of government to market failures in free markets for mobility, and informal transport which is a manifestation of particular types of market failure, such as the inability of the public sector to provide mass transport services. For Glover (2011) state ownership and control of the public transport system is necessary in order to protect the resource itself, but the development of public transport in recent years has resulted in neo-liberal reforms that has seen service provision increasingly provided by private corporations (Haughton & McManus, 2012; van de Velde, 2015). The different regulatory and competitive structures for such a situation are illustrated in Figure 1.2 (see also van de Velde (2015) who relates these positions to different approaches to public transport reform), while Figure 1.3 illustrates the potential links between institutions, organisational forms and technologies. Accordingly, 'Public transport services can be defined, therefore, as those where governments act to resolve CPR problems' (Glover, 2011: 12).

Glover's (2011) approach to defining public transport as CPR undoubtedly provides some useful insights into the governance of public transport as well as the rationale for the role of the state. However, as Figure 1.3 suggests, and as noted earlier in this discussion, the notion of public transport and its

	DIRECT COMPETITION BETWEEN OPERATORS	INDIRECT OR NO COMPETITION BETWEEN OPERATORS
PUBLIC TRANSPORT REGIMES BASED ON MARKET INITIATIVES Operators are free to take initiatives to provide public transport services	**Market deregulation** There is direct and "daily" competition between different operators and service providers. "Informal" public transport providers operate.	**Competitive regulation of monopolistic operators** Public/private operators are regulated on the basis of performance comparisons (benchmarking)
PUBLIC TRANSPORT REGIMES BASED UPON AUTHORITY INITIATIVES A public transport authority organises services and/or assigns a right to an operator	**Operational rights are competitively tendered** There is periodic competition between operators for temporary rights to provide services	**Public operator governance** Performance incentives are used to encourage publically owned operators to provide good services

Figure 1.2 Regulatory and competitive structures for public transport as a common pool resource

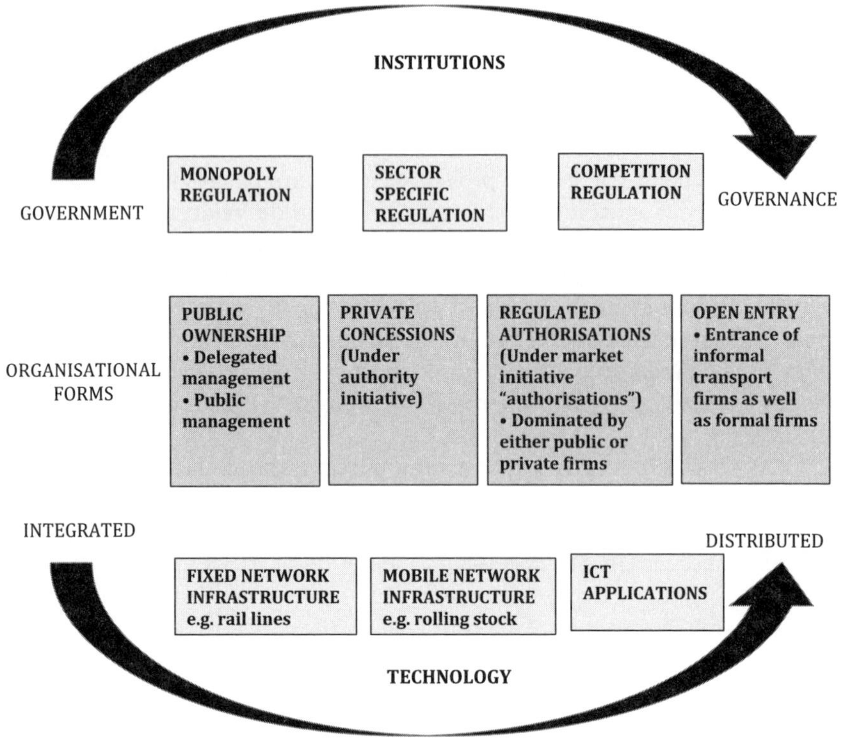

INSTITUTIONS

GOVERNMENT

| MONOPOLY REGULATION | SECTOR SPECIFIC REGULATION | COMPETITION REGULATION |

GOVERNANCE

ORGANISATIONAL FORMS

| PUBLIC OWNERSHIP • Delegated management • Public management | PRIVATE CONCESSIONS (Under authority initiative) | REGULATED AUTHORISATIONS (Under market initiative "authorisations") • Dominated by either public or private firms | OPEN ENTRY • Entrance of informal transport firms as well as formal firms |

INTEGRATED

DISTRIBUTED

| FIXED NETWORK INFRASTRUCTURE e.g. rail lines | MOBILE NETWORK INFRASTRUCTURE e.g. rolling stock | ICT APPLICATIONS |

TECHNOLOGY

Figure 1.3 Relationships between institutions, organisational forms and technologies

intersection with institutions, organisational structures and technology is always changing. Therefore, while providing for a further understanding of the role of the state and the 'public' in public transport, its broader application is likely to remain restricted.

Public transport as a designed environment

Wayfinding is navigation with a focus on its cognitive component. Rüetschi and Timpf (2005) focus on public transport as an environment for wayfinding. They argue that public transport constitutes a designed environment, which can be looked at from at least these two perspectives:

- the designer's perspective (how is it conceived?);
- the traveller's perspective (how is it perceived?).

These design influence observations are significant as they do highlight the issue of positionality in defining public transport. However, Rüetschi and Timpf (2005) are more interested in the system properties of public transport. They suggest that public transport is mostly organised according to the line operation principle, which is the publically accessible servicing of a fixed sequence of stops with predefined departure times. They argue that it is also subject to four 'bindings' that influence how the traveller interacts with the system:

(1)   the network of roads, contact wires or tracks;
(2)   the lines, which use the road, track or contact wire network;
(3)   the stops; and
(4)   the timetable.

The various elements of a traveller's journey are indicated in Figure 1.4. The access, transfer and egress nodes (together with interconnections, lines, tariffs, schedule and services) are part of the public transport system. Importantly, the public transport system is part of a broader transport system. As a result of how they define public transport (see above), Rüetschi and Timpf (2005) suggest that because of the bindings that affect how travellers interact with the system: with respect to stops people have to access (and leave) the system using some other mode of transport, such as private care, walking or cycling. In the case of binding to lines, transfers are inevitable for most trips, while because of the binding to a timetable, passengers are unlikely to access the system at arbitrary times. Instead, as they observe, travellers 'have to plan in advance, look for services and connecting services, and try to optimise travel time, travel cost, route complexity... and other criteria' (Rüetschi & Timpf, 2005: 27). These points are particularly significant for tourists who are, by definition, outside of their home environment, and in order to access public transport need to be able to understand and access the system in an unfamiliar environment and, for many tourists, often in a different language.

The different elements of a trip are also similar to those by which tourism is often understood though, especially at the destination level, at a different scale. Nevertheless, many of the elements that influence tourism decision making with respect to destination and activities at the macro-scale are often repeated at the micro-level with respect to public transport. Furthermore, even once the decision to use public transport has been made significant issues arise. These are recorded in Figure 1.4 as consumer actions and reasoning processes and may be particularly stressful until learning and

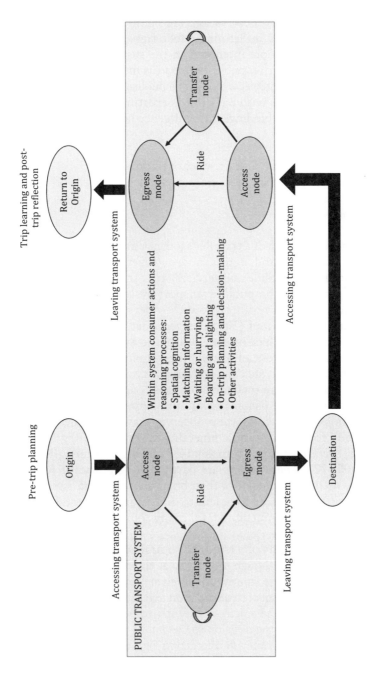

Figure 1.4 Elements of a return journey using public transport

experience reduces the stress of travelling in an unfamiliar transport system over time. Some of the means by which access to the system and its use may be improved are noted later on in this book.

Synthesising a definition of public transport services

Several key items can be identified from the above discussion. First, public transport is a service that is usually of a pre-defined availability in space and time that is open to everyone (i.e. public) and usually excludes driving your-self. Second, it is designed to transport large numbers of people between a relatively limited number of locations. The New Zealand Ministry of Transport (2016) suggests that public transport services share a number of common characteristics: public subsidies, passive users, hire and reward, shared transport, open to the public and fixed routes and schedules. However, as they note, 'none of these characteristics are exclusive to public transport and none of them are universally accepted as defining features of public trans-port' (Ministry of Transport, 2016: 5). Khisty and Lall (2003) also identify another characteristics of public transport that is that it provides transporta-tion for those who are not able to have their own private transport. This point is extremely significant with respect to rationales for state involvement in public transport delivery, especially in peripheral regions as well as areas with low levels of personal car ownership. However, it also raises significant issues as to how tourism can assist with such delivery, especially in peripheral and rural areas that may have less public transport access than in cities.

Importantly, the core element of public transport is that it is a service in which the passenger is transported and that it is open to everyone. 'The system might not be available everywhere and always; network density and operating hours limit availability, but not accessibility' (Veeneman, 2002: 28). Because it is open to everyone also means that it is a shared or collective service. This means that services restricted to specific groups, such as a tour group, are not public transport although we may still be interested in use of collective transport for reasons of sustainability, whereas use of, for example, scheduled public train services by tourists clearly constitutes a form of public transport. In many jurisdictions taxis are also therefore not regarded as public transport, although shared systems are. However, the growth of on demand and sharing services, means that depending on the location, and especially areas of limited demand, taxis may increasingly be taking on some of the characteristics of a public transport service. Veeneman (2002: 29) therefore defined public transport as simply as possible: 'passenger transport services open to everyone'. The nuances to this definitional approach will come from the purpose(s) to which any definition will be used.

Why Should We Be Interested in Tourism and Public Transport?

An obvious question to be asking is, why should the relationship between tourism and public transport be of interest? This can be responded to in several ways. Perhaps the most obvious being the economic significance of tourism and the scale of tourist flows.

According to the UNWTO (2011, 2012, 2015), the number of worldwide international tourist arrivals is expected to increase by an average 3.3% a year from 2010 to 2030 (Table 1.1). Over time, the rate of growth is forecast to gradually slow down, from 3.8% between 2010 and 2020 to 2.9% from 2020 to 2030. However, the actual rate of growth between 2010 and 2015 has been over 4.5% on average (UNWTO, 2016). In absolute numbers, international tourist arrivals are forecast to increase by some 43 million a year, compared to an average increase of 28 million a year during the period 1995

Table 1.1 International tourism arrivals and forecasts 1950–2030 (millions)

Year	World	Africa	Americas	Asia & Pacific	Europe	Middle East
1950	25.3	0.5	7.5	0.2	16.8	0.2
1960	69.3	0.8	16.7	0.9	50.4	0.6
1965	112.9	1.4	23.2	2.1	83.7	2.4
1970	165.8	2.4	42.3	6.2	113.0	1.9
1975	222.3	4.7	50.0	10.2	153.9	3.5
1980	278.1	7.2	62.3	23.0	178.5	7.1
1985	320.1	9.7	65.1	32.9	204.3	8.1
1990	439.5	15.2	92.8	56.2	265.8	9.6
1995	540.6	20.4	109.0	82.4	315.0	13.7
2000	687.0	28.3	128.1	110.5	395.9	24.2
2005	799.0	34.8	133.3	153.6	440.7	36.3
2010	940.0	50.2	150.7	204.4	474.8	60.3
2015*	1184.0	53.1	190.7	277.0	609.1	54.1
Forecast						
2020	1360	85	199	355	620	101
2030	1809	134	248	535	744	149

*Preliminary figures.
Source: WTO (1997); UNWTO (2006, 2012, 2016).

to 2010. At the projected rate of growth, international tourist arrivals worldwide will reach 1.36 billion by 2020 and 1.809 billion by the year 2030, after exceeding 1 billion for the first time in 2012. By 2030, the UNWTO (2012) suggest that 57% of international arrivals will be in emerging economy destinations (versus 30% in 1980) and 43% in advanced economy destinations (versus 70% in 1980). In regional terms the biggest growth is expected to be in the Asia Pacific, where arrivals are forecast to reach 535 million in 2030 at an average growth rate of 4.9% per year. Table 1.2 shows growth in international tourist arrivals by region per 100 population 1995–2030.

Although there is no internationally consistent and comprehensive set of data for domestic tourism the UNWTO estimated that in 2005, 5 billion arrivals were by same-day visitors (4 billion domestic and 1 billion international) and 4.8 billion from arrivals of tourists staying overnight (4 billion

Table 1.2 International tourist arrivals and estimates by region per 100 population 1995–2030

(sub)region	1995	2010	2030
Western Europe	62	81	114
Southern/Mediterranean Europe	47	71	103
Northern Europe	42	63	80
Caribbean	38	48	65
Central/Eastern Europe	15	25	47
Middle East	9	27	47
Southern Africa	9	22	46
Oceania	28	32	40
Central America	8	19	38
North Africa	6	15	28
South-East Asia	6	12	27
North America	21	21	26
North-East Asia	3	7	18
South America	4	6	13
East Africa	2	4	7
West and Central Africa	1	2	3
South Asia	0	1	2

Note: figures are rounded off.
Source: After UNWTO (2011).

domestic and 800 million international). Taking into account that an international trip can generate arrivals in more than one destination country, the
number of trips is regarded as somewhat lower than the number of arrivals.
Therefore for 2005 the global number of international tourist trips (i.e. trips
by overnight visitors) was estimated at 750 million corresponding to 16% of
the total number of tourist trips, with domestic trips representing 84% or
4 billion tourist trips (Scott *et al.*, 2008). The figures for international and
domestic overnight tourist arrivals in 2005 are illustrated in Table 1.3
together with extrapolations for 2010, 2020 and 2030. Some time between
2015 and 2017, the total number of visitor arrivals by international and
domestic overnight visitors will exceed the world's population for the first
time (Hall, 2015).

Economically, tourism is estimated to be worth 9% of global GDP
(including direct, indirect and induced impact). This equates to approximately US$1.5 trillion or 6% of world exports (30% of services exports) in
2014 (UNWTO, 2015). Importantly, tourism is estimated to account for one
in every 11 jobs once direct, indirect and induced impacts are included
(UNWTO, 2015). The employment generating capacities of tourism is also
becoming of increasing importance given the loss of jobs to technological
change in other sectors. The economic and employment benefits of tourism
are, as with tourist flows and patterns, uneven over time and space (Cooper
& Hall, 2016). Nevertheless, the majority of countries around the world focus
on tourism as a means of economic development while even for those

Table 1.3 Global international and domestic tourist arrivals 2005–2030

	Year/billions			
	2005	*2010*	*2020*	*2030*
Actual/Estimated number of international visitor arrivals	0.80	0.94	1.36	1.81
Approximate/Estimated number of domestic tourist arrivals	4.00	4.7	6.8	9.05
Approximate/Estimated number of total tourist arrivals	4.80	5.64	8.16	10.86
Approximate/Estimated global population	6.48	6.91	7.67	8.31

Note: Actual and estimated forecasts of international visitor arrivals based on UNWTO (2012); 2005
approximate figures based on Scott *et al.* (2008); Approximate and estimated global population
figures are based on United Nations Department of Economic and Social Affairs Population Division 2010 revisions.

countries in which leisure tourism is not significant, tourism related business travel is integral to international trade. However, with respect to transport, international tourism is becoming increasingly dominated by air travel. In 2014, slightly over half of all overnight visitors travelled to their destination by air (54%), while the remainder travelled by surface transport (46%) by road (39%), rail (2%) or water transport (5%) (UNWTO, 2015). These figures are a challenge to the public transport sector but they also pose a serious challenge with respect to emissions and climate change (Scott *et al.*, 2016a, 2016b, 2016c).

Insight 1.2: A Shuttle Bus Service in Order to Reduce Car Access to Campo di Dentro Valley, South Tyrol

In the Summer of 2009, the municipality of Innichen (Italian: San Candido) in the South Tyrol in northern Italy introduced a shuttle bus service in order to reduce car access to Campo di Dentro Valley, one of the main access routes to the 'Tre Cime di Lavaredo' (three peaks of Lavaredo), part of the Dolomites World Heritage site and one of the most well-known mountain groups in the European Alps.

The project is the result of a 2007 feasibility study aimed at improving the accessibility to the valley while, at the same time, reducing car traffic access. Several strategies were adopted:

- delocalisation of car parks spaces from the end of the valley to the entrance of it;
- improvement of public transport services connecting the surrounding towns;
- enhancement of exchange car/bus at the entrance of the valley;
- implementation of shuttle bus service that allows people to reach the end of the valley;
- limitation of car access to the end of the valley.

The project required two years from the feasibility study phase to the complete realisation phase. During 2009 a new car park was built and a new bus stop installed at the entrance to the Campo di Dentro Valley. With only 80 parking spaces, the car park was designed to encourage tourist use of public transport. The new bus stop connected the entrance of the valley with the surrounding towns and the shuttle bus stop. The service connects the new car park to the Antoniusstein Valley, one of the most important access points to the Dolomites, every 30 minutes. The first shuttle is at 9.10 am and the last one at 6 pm. Access to the valley is also not allowed in summer from 9 am to 6 pm with the only exception of employees and farmers working in the area.

Over the two month period in 2009 in which it was introduced the shuttle bus carried up to 400 passengers a day, roughly a third of them (60–110 people) used public transport to travel to the entrance of the valley. A carbon footprint analysis indicated that, as a result of the initiative, emissions at Campo di Dentro Valley decreased by 3.7–6.5 tonnes of CO_2e (Carbon Dioxide equivalent). A third of the visitors now use public transport from Sesto, Moso, Dobbiaco or San Candido to reach the entrance of Campo di Dentro Valley. Depending on the number of shuttle users this represents a decrease of 4.1 tonnes CO_2e (300 users) or 10.4 tonnes CO_2e (400 users).

Sources:
Berg Hotel, walk to the little rocca of the Baranci peak: http://www.berghotel.com/en/hiking/rocca-baranci/
Eltis The urban mobility observatory: http://www.eltis.org/discover/case-studies/discovering-dolomites-without-car-san-candido-italy#sthash.Fd3WfEZe.dpuf
South Tyrol region tourism website: http://www.three-peaks.info/en/holiday-region-in-south-tyrol.html

A UNWTO *et al.* (2008) examination of the tourism sector contribution to global CO_2 emissions estimated that in 2005, tourism transport, accommodation and activities contributed approximately 5% (1304 Mt) to global anthropogenic emissions of CO_2. Most CO_2 emissions are caused by transport, with aviation accounting for 40% of tourism's overall carbon footprint, followed by car transport (32%) and accommodation (21%). A World Economic Forum (WEF) (2009) study produced similar results, but also estimated that cruise ships generated 19.2 Mt CO_2, account for around 1.5% of global tourism emissions. The WEF (2009) estimated that of land transport emissions arising from tourism in 2005 car emissions contributed 418 MtCO2 as compared to 71 $MtCO_2$ from bus and 28 $MtCO_2$ from rail. According to the WEF (2009):

- North America, Europe and Asia Pacific combined contribute to ~90% of travel and tourism land transport emissions.

- North America accounts for almost half of car emissions, followed by Europe and Asia Pacific (25% & 18% respectively).
- Europe and the Asia Pacific use significant amounts of mass transit for travel and tourism, whereas North America's overall use of mass transit is significantly lower (13% in bus and 5% in rail).
- On a global level, 16–20% of total passenger miles in car transport are estimated to be for travel and tourism;

A more recent model of tourism sector energy use from transport, accommodation and activities estimated sectoral emissions at 1101 Mt CO_2 in 2010 (Gössling & Peeters, 2015). This analysis excluded daytrips, which UNWTO *et al.* (2008) had included, and therefore produced a lower estimate of emissions.

The WEF (2009: 5) suggested that the most promising tourism and travel sector-specific emissions mitigation measure was to 'Encourage modal-shift from cars to mass-transit systems (bus and rails)'. Nevertheless, at the same time, the WEF forecasts for 2035 suggest an increase in travel and tourism related land transport emissions to 938 $MtCO_2$.

Cars will continue to be the dominant land transport mode for travel and tourism under business-as-usual assumptions. In fact, the share of emissions from cars will increase to 85% by 2035 from 81% in 2005. It's important to note that under business-as usual assumptions emissions from buses will actually decrease from 14% in 2005 to 9% in 2035. The declining carbon contribution of buses is largely driven by a drop in traffic, the result of their general lack of popularity as a means of travel and tourism in most developed countries. (WEF, 2009: 16)

However, it is important to understand that while emissions have a global impact with respect to climate change, and public transport can be part of the adaptive and mitigative responses to promote more sustainable leisure and tourism mobility, people's experiences of transport is immediate and local. In a study of European tourism transport, Peeters *et al.* (2007) found that road transport has the greatest impacts on air quality while rail, coach and ferry represent almost 20% of all trips but have a very limited environmental impact due to relatively low emissions on a per passenger basis. With many cities now facing the problem of growing populations, high motorisation and increasing congestion, more urban planners are therefore looking towards public transport as a response to traffic and pollution problems (Le-Klähn & Hall, 2015). However, the overall contribution of transport to leisure and tourism related mobility clearly creates a massive challenge for tourism and public transport because at the same time that the environmental benefits of public transport are being promoted in general, if trends remain unchanged the actual relative use of public transport by international tourists, for example, appears likely to decline. Therefore, from a low carbon mobility transition perspective, there is a substantial need to encourage greater tourism use of public transport together with local inhabitants as part of modal change towards lower emission transport and therefore lower emissions per trip (Scott *et al.*, 2016a, 2016b).

In addition to public transport's role in encouraging sustainable mobility from an environmental perspective, the relationship between tourism and public transport can also have substantial economic and social benefits. The economic significance of tourism has been long recognised (Cortés-Jiménez, 2008; Cortes-Jimenez & Pulina, 2010; Candela & Figini 2012), but public transport is also an important direct and indirect contributor to regional economies. The UITP (2014a: 1) note that, 'Public transport operators and authorities represent significant levels for the local economy as they offer green local jobs that cannot be off-shored or moved out of the local area and are therefore less affected in the event of an economic downturn'. Furthermore, investing in public transport 'creates from 50% to 100% (i.e. twice) more jobs per Euro invested than investing in other areas, such as roads' (UITP, 2014a: 2). In Europe public transport operators are the largest employers in Amsterdam, Barcelona, Brussels, Dublin and Genoa and are among the top five employers in Madrid, Paris, Porto, Tallinn and Turin. Overall, investment in public transport is regarded as generating up to three to four times the value of the initial investment, including wider economic benefits such as the impact of increased connectivity on the regional economy (UITP, 2014a).

Good quality public transport, along with many of the attributes and services that also attract tourists to destinations, is regarded as integral to high quality-of-life amenity environments that are also attractive to skilled migrants, businesses and capital (Caragliu & Del Bo, 2012; Carvalho *et al.* 2012; Herrschel, 2013; Hockey *et al.*, 2013; Niedomysl, 2008). This is not only because of the physical accessibility that public transport provides but also because of contribution to cost of living. For example, the UITP (2014a: 1) claim that 'the cost of urban transportation for the community is 50% lower (as % of urban GDP) in cities with higher shares of public transport, walking and cycling'.

Plate 1.3 Electric-hybrid bus, Oxford Bus Company, UK

Plate 1.4 Green tramline, Freiburg, Germany. By having a grass, earth and gravel base rather than concrete or bitumen water is able to percolate through. The tramway not only looks good it also helps ensure that water is not lost from the urban system.

Insight 1.3: Local Public Transport Services in the EU28

- 57 billion passenger journeys per year by public transport.
- 190 million passenger journeys in the average working day.
- Public transport ridership in the EU has increased on average by 1% per year between 2000 and 2012.
- There are 1.2 million jobs with public transport operators and around 2 million jobs in the entire supply chain (supply industries, authorities, operators).
- The contribution of public transport to the EU economy is between €130 and €150 billion per year, representing 1–1.2% of the EU's GDP.
- Average annual investment in public transport is about €40 billion (i.e. about 0.5% of the EUs GDP).
- Average modal split in EU metropolitan areas: 15% public transport, 30% cycling and walking and 55% private motorised vehicles.

Source: UITP, 2014a, 2014b

Public transport plays an important role in tourism development, especially in urban areas, although it is also of significance for particular tourist activities in rural and peripheral regions. But this does not only benefit the local residents. Cities with effective and extensive public transport networks are potentially more attractive to tourists (Mandeno, 2011; Yang, 2010), including with respect to connectivity between intra-destination transport and long-distance transport (see Insight 1.4). Hong Kong is a good example of this situation. At the same time that Hong Kong is an important aviation hub Hong Kong around 80% of all trips in the territory are made by public transport, increasing to 90% if taxis are included in the definition of public transport (Cullinane, 2003). In some cases public transport may even be critical for destination image and identity and be a tourist attraction in its own right. For example, trams are an important element of tourism in Melbourne, Australia, as well as other destinations, such as Christchurch, New Zealand (Pearce, 2001). Similarly, ferries are often not only critical for connectivity in coastal areas but may be important tourism resources in their own right. For example, coastal ferries to the Scottish Isles (Butler, 2011; Scott *et al.*, 2005).

In some cases iconic public transport for tourists may constitute a form of public transport heritage (Halsall, 2001), for example, cable cars in San

Francisco or Wellington, New Zealand. In other cases, the role of public transport as specific attractions may be enhanced by association with film and television. The West Highland Line in Scotland from Glasgow to Mallaig via Fort William has been made famous as a result of the *Harry Potter* movies. However, contemporary public rapid transit systems are also significant attractions, such as the London Underground or 'Tube' (Hadlaw, 2003) (although only about 45% of the system is actually underground in tunnels) and London's buses (to which can be added the black taxi cab), while the Japanese bullet trains are also iconic tourist attractions as well as a way of moving around the country.

Tourists' experience with public transport services may also influence their satisfaction with a destination (Thompson & Schofield, 2007), especially as public transport is not only a way to see the destination but also enables social contact with local people as well. Also of significance is that income from tourism can also providing funding for public transport development and service improvement (Albalate & Bel, 2010).

Plate 1.5 Stornoway Ullapool ferry, Scotland. The ferry, here arriving at Ullapool, is one of the main means of access to Stornoway on the Isle of Lewis and Harris in Scotland's Outer Hebrides.

Plate 1.6 Melbourne Airport, Victoria, Australia. The drop-off and pick-up points for the arrivals and departures area of Melbourne Airport can be seen with lanes and stops dedicated to taxis, public buses, airport shuttles and private cars.

Insight 1.4: From Airport to the City: Compulsory Inter-Destination and Intra-Destination Travel with Public Transportation

Most major airports are located outside or on the outskirts of the metropolis they serve. Heathrow Airport, for example, is located 22 km west to central London and Beijing Airport is located 32 km northeast to Beijing city centre. In other words, the travel between airports and cities is a form of 'compulsory' inter-destination travel for the incoming tourists. Many times this compulsory inter-destination travel involves using public transportation.

A comparison study was conducted to learn more about the public transportation services to and from airports. In this study, the public transportation services from the 16 busiest airports (Airport Council International, 2014) were tested, using both airport website information and Google Maps. The time of testing was identical in all cases – 12:00 noon at Monday 8 February 2016 and the destination point was identical in all cases, the main tourist information centre in the nearby metropolis. For all airports, timetables, travel times, the number of exchanges and walking times were reported. The table shows airports from three continents: America, Europe and Asia.

From the 16 busiest airports that were analysed, six were also nominated in the list of 10 best airports that was published by the Skytrax organisation (Skytrax, 2016). Several of the 39 criteria in the Skytrax ranking method refers to public transportation services: getting to and from the airport, ease of access public transport options, efficiency and prices and taxi availability and prices.

Table 1.4 presents the findings of the analysis of public transportations services provided by the 16 busiest airports. All six airports that were also nominated as best airports (Beijing Capital, London Heathrow, Tokyo Henada, Hong-Kong International, Amsterdam Schiphol and Singapore Changi) provide very useful public transportation services from airports to central tourist information office. These airports offer the arriving tourists a frequent public transportation service with no more than one exchange of trains and minimum of walking distance. Three of the best airports: Beijing Capital, Heathrow Airport and Tokyo Henada also provide detailed and easy to use information on their websites, including direct links to updated timetables. None of the other airports provided direct links to transport information and schedule at the time of writing (January 2016).

Three airports, Dallas/Fort Worth, Frankfurt and Soekarno-Hatta, provide public transportation that is less regular, and the tourist may have to wait more than 15 minutes. Additionally, in two American airports tourists may have to walk more than eight minutes to get the tourist information, a significant walking time and distance in a new location, especially if carrying luggage and/or children. In Jakarta, Indonesia the walking time rises to more than 20 minutes. The six airports noted here were not mentioned in the list of the best airports.

Google Maps did not provide public transportation information for two destinations: Paris and Istanbul. In both cases, the airport websites did not provide useful information either. Therefore, tourists using these

Table 1.4 Analysis of public transportation services provided by the 16 busiest airports

World's busiest airports					Information about public transportation using Google map (date – 8/2; time – 12 pm)					A direct link to PT time-table from airport web-page*
No.	Airport	Location	Number of passengers (2014)	Best airport award (2014) according to Skytrax** ranking	Close main city (tourist information office)	Waiting time	Travelling time	Walking time	Number of exchanges	
1.	Hartsfield-Jackson Atlanta	Atlanta, Georgia, US	96M	–	Atlanta	6 min	26 min	8	0	No
2	Beijing Captial	Chaoyang – Shunyi, China	86M	7th	Beijing	10 min	100 min	4–11 min	1	Yes
3	London Heathrow	Hillingdon, Greater London, UK	73M	10th	London	Up to 7 min	48–65 min	None	1	Yes
4.	Tokyo, Henada	Ota, Tokyo, Japan	73M	6th	Tokyo	Up to 6 min	36 min	4 min	1	Yes
5.	Los Angeles	Los Angeles, California, US	71M	–	Los Angeles	Up to 10 min	90–100 min	9–11 min	1–2	No
6.	Dubai International	Garhoud, Dubai	70M	–	Dubai	Up to 6 min	7–10 min	5–10 min	0	No

#	Airport	Location								
7.	O'hare International	Chicago, Illinois, US	70M	–	Chicago	10 min	63 min	8 min	1	No
8.	Paris-Charles de Gaulle	Roissy-en-France, Val d'Oise, France	64M	–	Paris	Google map does not provide public transportation service from airport to tourist information office				No
9.	Dallas/Fort Worth	Dallas-Fort Worth, Texas, US	64M	–	Dallas	18 min	69–74 min	3–8 min	1–2	No
10.	Hong Kong International	Chep-Lap-Kok, Lantau Island, Hong Kong	63M	4th	Hong Kong	Up to 7 min	58–62 min	1–3 min	1	The website was shut down
11.	Frankfurt	Flughafen, Frankfurt, Germany	60M	–	Frankfurt	15 min	20 min	5 min	0	No
12.	Soekarno-Hatta	Cengkarent, Banten, Indonesia	57M	–	Jakarta	Up to 25 min	180–240 min	21 min	1	No
13.	Istanbul, Ataturk	Yesilkoy, Bakirkoy, Turkey	57M	–	Istanbul	Google map does not provide public transportation service from airport to tourist information office				No
14.	Amsterdam Schiphol	Haarlemmermeer, North Holland, Netherlands	55M	5th	Amsterdam	Up to 4 min	21–33 min	0	0–1	No
15.	Guangzoh, Baiyun	Baiyun – Hunadu, Guangzhou, Gungdong, China	55M		Guangzhou	7 min	80–90 min	5–7 min	1	No
16.	Singapore Changi	Changi, East region, Singapore	54M	1st	Singapore	9 min	50 min	3 min	0	No

Note: Analysis undertaken Monday 8/1/16

*Two clicks or less were needed to find the public transportation relevant information

**http://www.worldairportawards.com/main/about_skytrax.html

airports may face problems when trying to use public transportation modes. With or without connection to these difficulties, these two airports were not nominated in the best airports list.

In sum, public transportation is an important aspect of airport services. It is also often the first interface between the tourist and the public transportation system in the destination, with corresponding implications for destination and trip satisfaction. Tourists depend on public transport services to get from the airports to the cities (and back). Airports and public transportation authorities have to provide the tourists with useful service and information. It an essential service to tourists, and when presented properly, it may become a competitive advantage for airports and destination.

Sources:
Skytrax World Airport Awards: http://www.worldairportawards.com/main/about_skytrax.html
Airports International Council: http://www.aci.aero/Data-Centre/Annual-Traffic-Data

Examining Public Transport and Tourism

This book is interested in tourist use of passenger transport services open to everyone. However, how we understand this issue depends on the perspective we take. In examining the relationships between tourism and public transport we are interested in how tourists consume public transport and the challenges that this can pose for uptake as well as the advantages and disadvantages of such use. From the public transport production side we are interested in how tourism 'fits in' to the overall provision of public transport and how this may potentially benefit both the locations in which the public transport is based (the destination) as well as public transport provision overall? Furthermore, from a wider perspective how does tourism use of public transport potentially contribute to economic and social development – given that where tourists go must also effect where they spend – and how does this intersect with other businesses, including tourism and hospitality?

Figure 1.5 provides a visual representation of some of the issues that the book examines. Most important is the intersection between the public transport system and the tourist. From a consumer perspective we are concerned with the tourist experience of public transport services. From a service producer perspective we seek to understand the planning, marketing and management strategies that enable tourist use of public transport. The relationship between these two foci can provide insights into how experiences and tourist use of public transport might be improved. However, the relationship between tourism and public transport also has wider implications for sustainable mobility which we understand not only with respect to the environmental dimensions of tourism mobility, as important as that is, but also its broader contribution to economic and social wellbeing and equity. In the case of tourism this particularly means the economic contribution of tourism to destinations in a manner that is socially equitable. This may also include the way in which tourist use of public transport acts as a means to maintain services to areas that may otherwise be regarded as uneconomic. Something which may be extremely important for rural and more peripheral areas that have otherwise lost permanent population. In such cases, tourist use of public transport enables continued access to services by destination residents who otherwise do not possess the means for personal mobility.

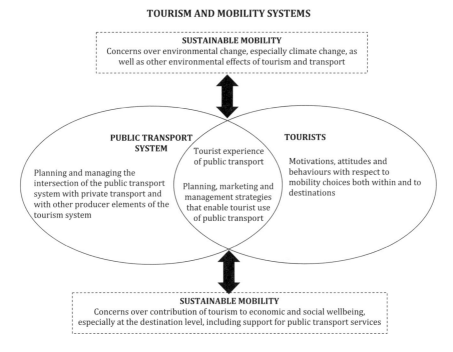

Figure 1.5 Examining the interrelationships between tourism and public transport

Insight 1.5: The Scope of Paratransit Transport Services

The term 'paratransit' was developed in the 1960s to describe the range of land-based transport services that fall between the private car and the passenger bus (Cervero, 1997, 2000; Orski, 1975). The term means 'alongside transit' (Lave & Mathias, 2000). Paratransit services combine the flexibility of a car, by connecting multiple places within a region, with the economic and environmental benefits of buses by being an efficient user of energy resources and roads because of higher than average loads (Orski, 1975). Paratransit ranges from a small bus or taxi service that runs along a defined route or within a defined range and stops to pick up or discharge passengers upon request. At the other end of the range of service flexibility, paratransit systems may offer on-demand call-up door-to-door services from any origin to any destination in a given service area, what is also referred to as full demand responsive transport. Paratransit services also have a significant role as a special transport service for people with disabilities and those with impaired mobility, and the aged. These services are often provided as a supplement to fixed-route rail and bus passenger services provided by public transport agencies and/or local and regional government. Table 1.5 provides a typology of different paratransit services.

From a tourism perspective paratransit is primarily an intra-destination urban form of public transport, and in developed countries it is especially important for tourists with disabilities (Darcy & Dickson, 2009), although airport shuttle services which are an important aspect of intermodal tourism transit in some locations are also a significant paratransit service. In the US jitney are significant, these are small passenger vehicles for hire that are intermediate between a taxi and a bus, although in some regions the term is used to refer to unlicensed taxis. In the US jitney use is highest in significant urban tourism destinations such as Atlantic City, Atlanta and Miami. As Chapter 4 discusses a public transport development which also bears some of the hallmarks of paratransit is the growth in curbside intercity buses which have provided a significant boost to long-distance bus travel in the US (Klein, 2015).

In developing countries paratransit is an extremely significant form of transport operated as part of the informal sector (Cervero & Golub, 2007; Tangphaisankun et al., 2010) with Phun and Yai (2015), in their review of paratransit transport services in Asia, describing them as

Table 1.5 Typology of paratransit transport services

Category	Route	Schedule	Typical seat capacity
Motorised Services			
Motorcycle taxi (habal-habal, ojek)	flexible	flexible	1–2
Auto rickshaw (bemo, tuktuk, trishaw)	flexible	flexible	2–4
Motorcyle rickshaw (motorela, Philippines)	flexible	flexible	2–6
Motorcycle rickshaw (remork, Cambodia)	fixed	flexible	12–20
Shared-ride taxis	flexible	flexible	3–4
Specialised dial-a-ride	flexible	flexible	6–10
Airport shuttles	flexible/semi-fixed	flexible/semi-fixed	6–10
Jitneys (circulators)	fixed	fixed route	6–15
Jitneys (transit feeders)	fixed	semi-fixed	6–15
Jitneys (areawide)	fixed	flexible	6–15
Microbus (angkot, songtaew)	flexible	semi-fixed	4–14
Minibus (jeepney)	fixed	semi-fixed	12–24
Commuter vans	semi-fixed/fixed	semi-fixed/fixed	10–60
Shared/pooled services			
Shuttle (Employer sponsored)	fixed	fixed	15–30
Car/vanpools	fixed	fixed	6–15
Non-motorised services			
Bicycle taxi	flexible	flexible	1–2
Pulled Rickshaw	flexible	flexible	1–2
Animal cart	flexible	flexible	2–6
Cycle rickshaw (becak)	flexible	flexible	1–2

Source: Cervero, 1997, 2000; Phun & Yai, 2015; Shimazaki & Rahman, 1996.

'indispensible'. However, as cities achieve greater levels of economic growth and develop mass transit systems so the relative importance of paratransit falls, although in some cities and in tourism resort areas paratransit, e.g. cycle and auto rickshaws, may be an attraction in its own right. In cities such as Bangkok, Jakarta and Kuala Lumpur buses carry more than half of public transport passengers (Shimazaki & Rahman, 1996). Paratransit modes such as silor lek (microbus), motorcycle taxis, samlor (three-wheeled bicycles) in Bangkok, Thailand and becak (cycle rickshaw) in Jakarta, Indonesia, act as feeder services to public transport. In Manila, the largest urban centre of the Philippines, jeepney carry almost three-quarters of public transport passengers although this number is gradually declining, here tricycles act as a feeder service (Guillen & Ishida, 2004). In Chiang Mai in northern Thailand and Phuket in the south, samlor, silor lek and songthaew [truck bus]) are an important part of tourism transport and are featured in tourist promotion. For example, in Phuket songthaew are promoted to tourists as a good way of getting around:

Phuket Songthaew Bus
Songthaew is the local bus service used by both Thai locals and tourists.
Songthaew means two rows, which refers to the two wooden benches that run down either side of the bus, which have been converted from pick-up trucks.
There is no actual bus stops, to get on a songthaew, you just wait along the roadside until one approaches and you wave it down.
These buses are the cheapest way to get from all the main tourist beaches into Phuket Town, costing around 35 - 50 baht, the trip will take around 30 minutes.
When you want to get off the bus you need to press a buzzer to signal the driver to stop.
This bus service is good for getting into Phuket Town for shopping and back to the beach but they do not go from one beach to another.
In Phuket Town the buses depart from Ranong Road opposite the Thai airways ticketing office and they run from 7.00 am to 6.00 pm. The main destinations include Patong, Chalong, Karon, Kata, Kamala, Makham Bay, Nai Harn, Nai Yang, Rawai, Surin and Thalang. (Phuket-Travel-Secrets.com, 2016)

In south Asia paratransit is dominated by cycle rickshaws although as economic growth occurs the development of bus services and greater rates of personal car ownership together with ongoing use of the railway system means that paratransit transport services are declining as a means of transport. Paratransit is extremely important as a domestic and tourist passenger service in developing countries, especially in earlier stages of destination development. Although their informal nature at times means that such transport is often not well-maintained and can be polluting and lead to urban congestion, there is substantial awareness in its potential contributions to sustainable mobility as a result of its flexibility and capacity to support the scheduled public transport, while the development of cheaper and longer lasting batteries has potential for new forms of low-carbon services.

In examining public transport and tourism this book focuses on particular types of transport. In keeping with most approaches to collective public transport, as well as membership of the UITP, the primary mechanised forms of transport we discuss are transit/metro and light rail (including tramways), regional and suburban railways, bus services and waterborne transport, such as ferries. Taxis are not usually considered public transport because they are not shared by people without private arrangement, although they may be integral to transport offerings in some urban centres. However, the growth of share taxis that offer on-demand services and paratransit means that the notion of public transport is undergoing significant change. Therefore, the book does note the role of taxis within urban transportation systems (Table 1.6). As well as mechanised public transport the book also includes a discussion of non-mechanised transport in the form of cycling and walking. These forms of transport are increasingly recognised as having an important role to play in sustainable urban mobility and design for cycling and walking is often closely integrated with public transport services. However, there are substantial variations in the provision and use of such services (Table 1.6). This may be because of built and urban form, the specific types of transport services that are available, transport culture and/or other socio economic factors.

The book is divided into six chapters. This chapter has provided details of some of the different approaches to conceptualising public transport as well as introducing the reader to the significance of the interrelationships between tourism and public transport. The following chapters will now look into these issues in greater depth. Chapter 2 provides an overview of tourist

Table 1.6 Passenger transport mode shares in select cities

City	Country	Population (mn)	Area (km²)	Walk & Cycle (%)	Walk (%)	Cycle (%)	Paratransit (%)	Taxi (%)	Public Transport (%)	Bus (%)	Rail (%)	Private Transport (%)	Others (%)
Ahmedabad[a]	India	6.1	466	32	–	–	–	–	30	–	–	38	–
Bangalore[a]	India	8.6	1831	35	32	3	7	–	27	–	–	31	–
Barcelona[a]	Spain	1.6	102	44	–	–	–	–	35	–	–	21	–
Beijing[a]	China	12.3	1368	14	–	14	–	6	44	27	17	33	3
Berlin[a]	Germany	3.5	892	42	29	13	–	–	26	–	–	32	–
Bogotá[a]	Colombia	7.4	1587	14	12	2	–	3	53	–	–	25	5
Chicago[a]	USA	2.7	590	20	19	1	–	1	16	11	5	63	1
Delhi[a]	India	16.3	1114	41	35	6	5	–	31	27	4	23	–
Guangzhou[b]	China	11.2	3842	–	–	–	–	11	49	–	–	40	–
Hong Kong[b]	China SAR	7.2	1104	–	–	–	–	6	81	51[c]	30	12	1
London[a]	UK	8.4	1595	35	32	3	–	1	27	15[c]	12	38	–
Madrid[a]	Spain	3.3	604	30	–	–	–	1	39	18	21	26	4
Mumbai[a]	India	12.7	603	33	–	–	–	–	52	–	–	15	–

Osaka[a]	Japan	2.7	223	48	24	24	–	38	2	36	15	–
Paris (main city)[a]	France	2.3	105	50	47	3	–	34	–	–	16	–
Prague[a]	Czech Republic	1.2	496	24	23	1	–	43	–	–	33	–
São Paulo[a]	Brazil	20.0	7944	32	31	1	–	37	–	–	31	–
Seoul[b]	South Korea	10.4	605	–	–	–	7	65	27	38	23	4
Shanghai[a]	China	16.4[d]	2141	47	27	10	–	33	–	–	20	10[d]
Singapore[b]	Singapore	5.5	718	–	–	–	7	50	29	21	43	–
Stockholm[a] (Metropolitan)	Sweden	2.2	6526	31	27	4	–	25	–	–	44	–
Sydney[e]	Australia	4.8	12368	18	18	–	–	12	6	6	68	4
Taipei[a]	Taiwan	2.7	272	20	15	5	2	35	19	16	43	1
Tokyo (23-Ward)[a]	Japan	9.1	623	37	23	14	–	51	3	48	12	–
Toronto[a]	Canada	2.6	634	8	–	–	–	26	–	26	65	1
Vienna[b]	Austria	1.8	415	33	27	6	–	39	–	–	28	–

[a]Based on the number of journeys by main mode of transport.
[b]Based on the number of journeys by main mode of motorised transport.
[c]Bus figures combined with tram.
[d]Other figure is for e-bikes, which is added to the total figure for bicycles and walking.
[e]Based on the number of unlinked trips, except for trips by walking only, includes all modes for all purposes.
Source: Journeys (2014).

demand for public transport. Chapter 3 examines intra-destination transport and Chapter 4 looks at long distance public transport services. Chapter 5 examines marketing and planning approaches that can be used to encourage greater tourist use of public transport. The final chapter discusses some of the potential futures for public transport, taking into account the need for sustainable transport and tourism initiatives in light of the negative environmental externalities that arise for tourism mobility.

Further Reading

A useful introduction to tourism and transport in general is

Duval, D.T. (2007) *Tourism and Transport: Modes, Networks and Flow.* Clevedon: Channel View Publications.

While a useful concise overview is to be found in

Page, S. and Connell, J. (2014) Transport and tourism. In A. Lew, C.M. Hall and A. Williams (eds) *The Wiley Blackwell Companion to Tourism* (pp. 155–167). Chichester: Wiley.
For statistical information on transport in general as well as the issues associated with sustainable transport and mobility refer to the web site of the International Transport Forum (ITF): http://www.itf-oecd.org/

For overviews of the tourism and public transport relationship see

Le-Klähn, D.-T. (2015) Public transportation. In C.M. Hall, S. Gössling and D. Scott (eds) *The Routledge Handbook of Tourism and Sustainability* (pp. 440–449). London: Routledge.
Le-Klähn, D.-T. and Hall, C.M. (2015) Tourist use of public transport at destinations – a review. *Current Issues in Tourism* 18 (8), 785–803.
Several chapters on tourist use of public transport in protected areas can also be found in Orsi, F. (ed.) (2015) *Sustainable Transportation in Natural and Protected Areas.* Abingdon: Earthscan by Routledge.

On accessible tourism in general see

Darcy, S., and Dickson, T.J. (2009) A whole-of-life approach to tourism: The case for accessible tourism experiences. *Journal of Hospitality and Tourism Management* 16 (01), 32–44.

For a discussion on informal and paratransit transport see

Cervero, R. and Golub, A. (2007) Informal transport: A global perspective. *Transport Policy* 14, 445–457.
Guillen, M.D.V. and Ishida, H. (2004) Motorcycle-propelled public transport and local policy development: The case of "tricycles" and "habal-habal" in Davao City Philippines. *IATSS Research* 28 (1), 56–66.
Phun, V. K. and Yai, T. (2015) State of the art of paratransit literatures in Asian developing countries. *Proceedings of the 13th Eastern Asia Society for Transportation Studies*, 11–14. See http://www.dynamicglobalsoft.com/easts2015/program/pdf_files/1169.pdf

2 Tourism Demand for Public Transport

Introduction

This chapter discusses the nature of tourism demand for public transport. It first examines tourist use of public transport before examining its role as part of tourist behaviour, motivations, decision-making and satisfaction. A number of cultural constraints in the use of public transport are also noted which potentially creates difficulties for some public transport users.

Tourists' Transport Modes at Destination

Types of transport mode

The mobility of tourists is supported by various transport modes including ground transport (also known as land or road transport), marine transport, and air transport (Duval, 2007). The choice of transport modes depends on various factors such as time budget, financial budget, accessibility and availability. Air transport is popular for longer distance travel from origin to tourism destinations. However, the main mode of domestic tourists is usually land transport (Peeters *et al.*, 2007), which accounts for the most energy used (81%) in the transport sector (Chapman, 2007). This section discusses the land transport modes use at destinations.

Motorised transport

Land transport comprises of several different modes ranging from car, bus, coach, rail to cycling and walking (Page & Connell, 2014). In Europe, the car is most widely used for travelling, especially for day trips and trips to the countryside (Gronau & Kagermeier, 2007; Guiver *et al.*, 2008; Regnerus

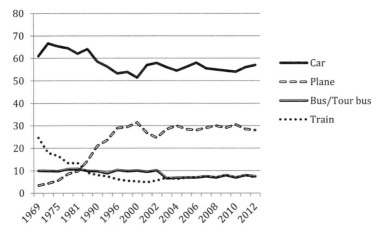

Figure 2.1 Mode of transport by Austrian tourists for main holidays 1969–2012
Source: Statistics Austria, 2013.

et al., 2007). In Austria, for example, the car has constantly been the most dominant travel mode since 1969 (Figure 2.1) (Statistics Austria, 2013). More than half of holiday trips in Austria are made by car every year (57% in 2012). The plane had a minor share in earlier times (3.4% in 1969) but quickly became the second major mode, representing almost one-third of trips (28%) in 2012. Air travel has increased at the expense of the train for longer distance travel. From a major mode accounting for a quarter of trips in 1969, the train has dropped in popularity since the 1970s. Over the last decade, trains together with buses have accounted for small shares, with each representing under 10% of total holiday trips made.

Other motorised transport modes such as motorcycles, scooters or mopeds are also used by tourists, especially the younger ones (Blackman & Haworth, 2013). However, the number of holiday trips by these transport modes is comparatively small.

Public transport

Tourists travelling without automobiles have to rely on alternative transport modes in which case public transport systems play an important role. The choice of public transport types e.g. train and bus varies in different countries. Train is relatively well favoured by tourists in Europe, probably because of the available network as well as public commitment to its use. Tourists travelling in coach tours, which in many cases replaced passenger traffic on existing train routes, form a considerable segment in New Zealand and Australia tourism, where many train lines previously used for passenger traffic are now only used for freight or have been closed down altogether (Becken, 2005), with government investing disproportionately more into the road system than rail. Nevertheless, public transport still accounts for a minor share of holiday trips. Even in Germany where there is a well-established train network, only 5% of holiday trips are by public transport (Gronau & Kagermeier, 2007).

Non-motorised transport

Non-motorised transports are the forms of transport that are not powered by engines and include walking, cycling, wheeled carriages and animals (Lumsdon & Tolley, 2004). Together with motorised transport and public transport, non-motorised modes provide tourists with more options for travelling at destinations. Relatively little is known about this mode of transport in terms of overall use by tourists, even though it is part of a growing interest in the concepts of 'slow travel' and 'slow tourism' (Dickinson & Lumsdon, 2010) (see Chapter 6 for further discussion of the relationships between the Slow Movement and sustainable mobility).

One of the reasons for the lack of detailed information on non-motorised transport could be the difficulty in determining the type of trips and visits that are eligible to be counted (Lumsdon & Tolley, 2004). As both a form of transport and an activity that requires skills, motivation and interests, non-motorised transport is therefore often regarded as a 'tourism transport experience' rather than simply a transport mode. However, given the growing interest in encouraging low carbon tourism greater statistical recognition of non-motorised transport is likely to be required.

Insight 2.1: Offering Bicycles to Tourists and Expanding the Visitor Season in Riccione, Italy

The city of Riccione is a major tourism destination, with over 400 hotels, many tourist flats, lots of bars, restaurants, nightlife and entertainment. The city attracts approximately 690,000 arrivals annually accounting for 3,350,000 tourist nights, with a peak during the summer season. Approximately 70% of tourists arrive by car, which is in significant contrast to the local modal split for residents.

The local government wanted to encourage more 'active mobility' (cycling and walking), while discouraging car use and had a goal to increase the share of active mobility from 8–9% in 2011 to 20% within five years. At the same time local government seeks to change mobility patterns, hotels in Riccione are facing heavy competition from other hotels along the northern Adriatic coast. In an attempt to attract more guests and to expand the tourist season to spring and autumn, many hotels began to offer bicycles for rent to their guests. By offering bicycles to tourists, the hotels of Riccione are therefore simultaneously diversifying the activity and mobility base of tourism as well contributing to creating a better urban environment, in keeping with the strategy of the local government.

Riccione is a compact city, situated on a strip of the Adriatic coast, where the main services and attractions can be reached within a radius of 5 km. The Bike Hotels (a consortium of 14 hotels specialising in offering specific services to cyclists (www.riccionebikehotels.it) constitute one of the many initiatives that aims to promote cycling to tourists. Others include events such as the 'Glam Bike' (a fashion show on bikes), shops offering special discounts to buyers arriving by bike, and the creation of a cycling/walking map.

Results from a survey conducted in 2011, revealed that many hotels (294 out of 391 hotels) were offering bicycles without extra charge to their guests:

- 54% of 1 star hotels;
- 68% of 2 star hotels;
- 91% of 3 star hotels; and
- 100% of 4 star hotels.

As figures indicate, the percentage of hotels offering bicycles increases with the quality of the hotel, suggesting that hoteliers consider the offer of bicycles as a key component of the quality of their hotels and that higher quality hotels seek to gain most from the positioning of the destination in terms of biking.

Source:
Riccione bike hotel web site: www.riccionebikehotels.it
Eltis The urban mobility observatory: http://www.eltis.org/discover/case-studies/ offering-bicycles-tourists-boost-eco-mobility-riccione-italy#sthash.EhLvbYN4. dpuf

Statistics on Tourists' Transport Modes at the National Level

Statistics on local tourism transport are not regularly and systematically collected in most countries (Peeters et al., 2004). In many cases, data before the year 2000 are not available online. It is also difficult to draw cross-national comparisons due to the inconsistencies in trip definition, data collection method and study subjects. Intra-destination transport modes are usually reported for domestic tourists through surveys such as household travel surveys. For foreign tourists, modes of arrival are documented instead, often by immigration offices. While national statistical offices are often the main information source, in many cases, data were collected and published by other authorities such as national tourism administrations, ministries of transport, immigration agencies or even economic development departments. As a result, tourism transport data tend to come in different formats depending on the information source. In general, tourism transport data should be used with caution. Some points to notice when looking at these statistics are:

(1) Type of tourist: domestic, foreign or for total tourists.
(2) Type of trip: business, leisure or visiting friends and relatives (VFR).
(3) Trip duration: day trip, overnight trip, short trip or long trip.
(4) Definition of transport mode: in some cases all transport modes were collected (multiple responses), whereas in others only the main mode was reported. For international tourists, mode of arrival should be clearly differentiated with mode of local transport.
(5) Data collection period: total trips in the year or one main trip of the year.

Transport modes at destinations: Domestic vs. foreign tourists

An online search was conducted to collect data on tourists' transport mode with the aim to identify the patterns of tourist transport modes over time. The sample initially consisted of the top three most visited countries in each UNWTO region (UNWTO, 2012). However, due to ease of access, availability of data, and language constraint, some countries were removed and replaced by the next most visited ones. Owing to largely missing data, top destinations in Asia (e.g. China, Malaysia and Hong Kong) and Africa (e.g. Morocco and South Africa) were removed (Table 2.1). Data were available for most European countries from which five were included.

Domestic tourists

The countries in the study sample were selected due to their data availability. It was however impossible to organise a comparison of data at the same point of time. In most cases, time series data were not accessible while data was also only available for certain years. With the aim to have an overview of changes in transport modes used by tourists at the national level, data were recorded for three different time periods: (1) 1990–1999,

Table 2.1 Countries for which data are available

Region	Rank	Country	Visitors arrivals in 2011 (million)
Europe	1	France	79,500
	2	Spain	56,694
	3	Italy	46,119
	4	Turkey*	29,343
	5	UK	29,192
	6	Germany	28,352
Americas	1	USA	62,325
	2	Mexico*	23,403
	3	Canada	15,976
Oceania	1	Australia	5875
	2	New Zealand	2601
	3	Guam*	1106
Asia	1	China*	57,581
	2	Malaysia*	24,714
	3	Hong Kong*	22,316
Africa	1	Morocco*	9288
	2	South Africa	8074
	3	Tunisia*	6902

Source: UNWTO (2012).
*Data on tourists' transport mode were not available online and were thus excluded from the sample.

(2) 2000–2009 and (3) 2010–2012. Restricted by data availability, each time period could be presented by statistics of only one year, preferably the most recent ones (i.e. 1990 and 2000 instead of 1999 and 2009). Figure 2.2 and Figure 2.3 show the transport modes used by domestic and foreign tourists respectively in selected countries across five continents in three periods. Regardless of countries, the car is the main mode of transport for domestic trips, accounting for at least half (and in most cases three-quarters) of the total number of holiday trips. Information for the period 1990–1999 was only available for the US and Canada, whereas data for the other two periods were available in most countries.

Comparing the latest data (i.e. period 2010–2012), Canada has the highest number of trips by car (2010: 92.4%), following by New Zealand (2012: 92%) and Spain (2010: 81.2%). This reflects no or minor changes in car use

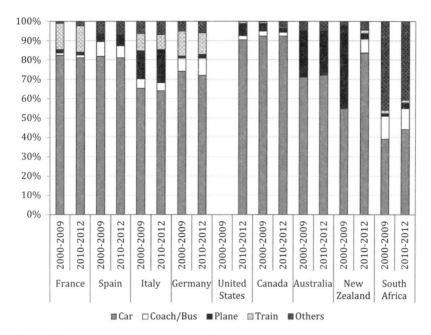

Figure 2.2 Mode of transport by domestic tourists

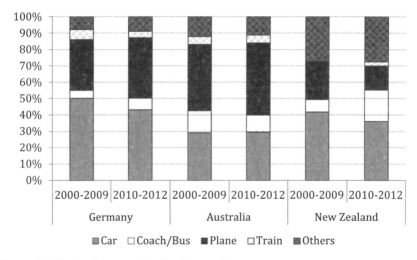

Figure 2.3 Mode of transport by foreign tourists

for holidays by residents of most countries compared to period 2000–2009. In countries where the share of car trips has slightly decreased (e.g. France and Germany), the train plays a relatively important role, accounting for at least 10% of total trips made, a much higher number compared to other countries. In 2010, France and Germany have the highest percentage of trips by train (13.7% and 11% respectively). Outside Europe, the train is little used (below 2%). In most cases, the proportion of domestic holiday trips by plane is relatively small (around 5% or lower). Australia is the exception where the plane is responsible for almost a quarter of the total trips made in 2012. It is, however, not surprising considering Australia's geography.

Foreign tourists

Data on local transport modes used by foreign tourists are difficult to find. Most often it is not clear whether what is indicated as tourists' transport mode is mode of arrival or mode of travel within the destination. Figure 2.3 includes only statistics which were explicitly stated as transport mode for travelling within a country. Germany, Australia and New Zealand are the few countries in which these data were available in two different time periods. Car is the main mode of transport for foreign tourists in Germany though the proportion has decreased over the last years (from 50% in 2007/2008 to 43% in 2010/2011). The number of trips by plane, campervan, and bus has increased at the expense of train and car. Foreign tourists in New Zealand tend to use car or van as the main mode of transport. In Australia, travelling by plane is most common (more than 40% in 2008 and 2012), following by car (under 30%). Coach and bus tour appear to be more popular in both New Zealand and Australia than in other countries. In general, though car is also basically the number one mode by foreign tourists (except in Australia), the proportion of car trips taken by foreign tourists is considerably lower than that of domestic tourists.

Table 2.2 shows the mode of arrival by tourists across different selected countries. Generally, the number of trips by plane has increased over the last decades while car and train trips have slightly declined. The exceptions are New Zealand, Hong Kong and Taiwan. Nevertheless, the reduction in the number of plane trips in New Zealand and Taiwan are negligible. Hong Kong, however, saw a shift from plane to car, probably due to the fact that a large part of Hong Kong visitors are from mainland China (Hong Kong Tourism Board, 2015). Europe has extensive and developed rail systems yet the proportion of trips by train is small (under 10%) and has reduced over time.

In general, data on tourism transport at destinations are limited despite the fact that transport plays an important role in destination development. There is need for systematic data on local tourist transport for a better picture of tourist use of transport modes at destinations. Figures 2.2 and 2.3

Table 2.2 Tourists' mode of arrival (%)

Country	Air 1990–1999	Air 2000–2009	Air 2010–2012	Sea 1990–1999	Sea 2000–2009	Sea 2010–2012	Land 1990–1999	Land 2000–2009	Land 2010–2012	Rail 1990–1999	Rail 2000–2009	Rail 2010–2012
France		2.0	13.7		0.8	5.2		83.2	78.2		13.7	2.8
Spain		72.7	78.7		2.6	2.5		24.2	18.5		0.5	0.2
Italy		20.0			6.0			66.0			7.0	
Germany		27.0	30.0		2.0			62.0	63.0		10.0	7.0
UK	70.8	70.7	73.5	29.2	17.1	14.6		14.6	11.9			
USA	14.3	15.2	17.3	0.9	0.8	0.2	84.8	84.0	82.5			
Canada	68.5	85.5	86.5				31.5	14.5	13.4			
Mexico	5.3	7.6	14.3	1.0	3.8	7.0	93.7	88.6	78.7			
New Zealand	98.8	99.3	99.0	1.2	0.7	0.1						
Hong Kong		41.6	24.0		15.1	9.7		43.3	66.4			
Taiwan		99.2	97.2		0.8	2.3						
Singapore		71.3	77.0		15.6	10.0		13.2	12.9			
South Africa	24.0	21.7	30.0	1.0	2.0	0.1	75.0	76.3	69.9			

indicates the dominance of the car as a travel mode. However, it should be noted that the sample included only developed countries. In less developed countries, especially where car ownership among residents is relatively low, bus and train are more significant as travel modes (Vo, 2013).

Insight 2.2: Electric Vehicle Service for Disabled Tourists, Córdoba, Spain

Disabled and reduced mobility tourists are a significant part of the tourist market. The need for the adaption of public transport services to meet the requirements of this market are also growing given an aging population in many countries around the world as well as greater emphasis on access in many tourism centres. Paratransit is one of the most recognisable forms of public transport for the disabled. Although many passenger transport services are being designed or modified to enable access for the disabled and the mobility impaired, substantial issues still remain in some heritage attractions where the nature of the environment mitigates modification of historic lanes and access ways.

In the city of Córdoba in southern Spain an electric vehicle service has been developed that allows tourists with disabilities and reduced mobility to explore the sights of its World Heritage listed historic city centre. Three different kinds of electric vehicles are now available for people with reduced mobility and run on 10 tourist routes throughout the centre. All of the vehicles are outfitted with a Geographic Positioning System (GPS) tracking system with information on their location constantly fed to a traffic coordinator and mobility team to provide assistance if required. Users are also taught how to operate the vehicles and have an opportunity to test them before setting off on their tour.

Source:
Eltis The urban mobility observatory: http://www.eltis.org/discover/news/cordoba-launches-ev-service-disabled-tourists-spain#sthash.4GftEIvK.dpuf

---

Tourist Behaviour, Decision-making and Satisfaction

Tourists' use of public transport: A model of decision-making

Consumers' decision-making is a complex process and is influenced by several factors. Factors affecting consumer buying behaviour are generally categorised into (1) consumer characteristics, (2) product characteristics and (3) situational context (Peter & Olson, 2009). Similarly, in the case of the tourist as a consumer, factors influencing the purchasing process include tourist characteristics (e.g. demographic, social and psychological factors), characteristics of the object (e.g. destination or activity) and external factors (e.g. environmental factors, marketing, and other influences) (Fesenmaier & Jeng, 2000; Jeng & Fesenmaier, 2002). Several tourist decision-making models have been proposed in the literature, however, most of these models examine tourist choice of destination (e.g. Hsu *et al.*, 2009; Moore *et al.*, 2012; Seddighi & Theocharous, 2002). Transport mode is an important component of the tourists' travel choice (Dellaert *et al.*, 1998), yet little has been explored about how tourists make their decisions regarding which transport mode to use at destinations (Masiero & Zoltan, 2013).

As a part of tourists' travel planning, transport mode choice is a sequential, multi-facet, and multistage process (Fesenmaier & Jeng, 2000; Jeng & Fesenmaier, 2002). Several factors influences tourists' transport mode choice, namely (1) personal characteristics, (2) trip characteristics, (3) destination features, (4) travel motivations and (5) mode quality evaluation (Hergesell & Dickinger, 2013; Koo *et al.*, 2010; Pettebone *et al.*, 2011; Vo, 2013). The personal characteristics and travel motivational factors represents 'tourist characteristics', mode quality and destination features represents 'product characteristics', and trip characteristics reflects the 'situational context' (Peter & Olson, 2009).

As travel planning is a sequential process, decisions made in earlier stages are considered to be more important than those made later (Bansal & Eiselt, 2004; Fesenmaier & Jeng, 2000; Jeng & Fesenmaier, 2002). It is critical, therefore, to know when a tourist makes his/her decision on the transport mode so as to understand how important the mode choice is in tourists' travel planning. Motivations play an important role in tourist behaviour (Fodness, 1994). Tourists may or may not use public transport for several reasons. Knowledge of tourists' motivations for public transport use and non-use is necessary to understand tourist transport behaviour. Finally, to provide tourists with better experiences, transport providers need to be aware of how tourists perceive their services. Measuring tourist satisfaction with public transport services is needed to provide feedback for public transport operators for service improvement. Transport infrastructure (including public transport systems) as a component of the destination features, plays an important role in destination attractiveness (Ashworth & Page, 2011; Khadaroo & Seetanah, 2007). An improved public transport system influences the destination attractiveness to tourists and enhances tourists' mode quality evaluation, consequently affects tourists' transport mode choice.

Figure 2.4 describes the tourists' experience with public transport use (Le, 2014). In this process, whether or not public transport is selected is determined by a number of reasons including educational levels, 'Push' motivational factors for visiting the city/destination, length of stay, number of previous trips, importance of price in mode quality evaluation and ownership of a valid driving license. The role of transport mode choice was highlighted given that most tourists searched for information and determined their mode before arriving at the destinations. Obtaining public transport information is important for tourists and the most common information channels are train stations, the internet, word-of-mouth, accommodations and tourist centres. Motivations for using public transport are their drive-free benefits, traffic reduction, advantages of local public transport and car unavailability. On the other hand, public transport's relative inconvenience and restrictions, the lack of information, the disadvantages compared to private modes and personal preferences are discouraging factors. The satisfaction level of public transport services are affected by attributes such as information, ticket price, service frequency, ease-of-use, cleanliness of the vehicle and space on the vehicles. The following sections discuss further the public transport users' profile and their behaviour while various aspects of mode choice are also discussed in the following two chapters.

The user of public transport

Users of public transport include local residents and tourists, who exhibit distinctive travel behaviour from each other. Tourists tend to be more concerned with the provision of information and reliability of service and place less emphasis on traditional aspects of Public Transport (PT) such as service quality and safety (Kinsella & Caulfield, 2011). Conversely, for local users, punctuality, frequency and waiting times are highly important (Fang & Zimmerman, 2015). In general, the tourist users of public transport are diverse and consist of several groups, among which substantial differences exist between users in urban and rural areas.

The majority of public transport users in rural areas are relatively older (above 50-years-old) and in retirement. An example is the patronage of the Wayfarer, a multi-modal ticket for day excursions to the countryside in the UK (Lumsdon et al., 2006). Users of rural tourism buses can be the 'sightseer' or the 'activity seeker' (Lumsdon, 2006). Representing the largest user segment of the tourism bus network in the UK, the 'sightseer' uses the bus mainly for scenic rides. However, they are also driven by other motivations such as avoiding parking fees and driving in unfamiliar places, or looking for social contact with others. Most sightseers are around 40-years-old plus,

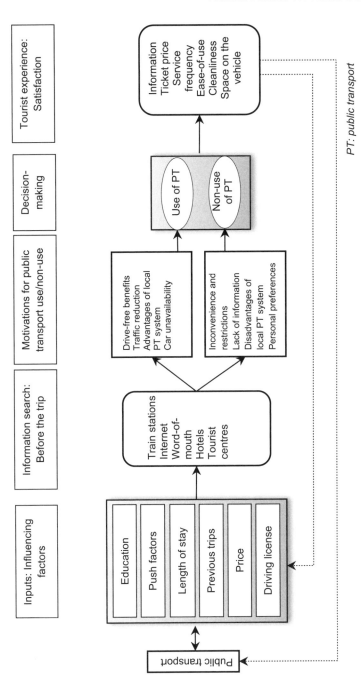

Figure 2.4 Tourist use of public transport: A decision-making model
Source: Le (2014).

travel solo or as a couple, but there are also a sub-segment of older women who looked for social contact and a sub-segment of young backpackers travelling without the car. The 'activity seeker', as described by the name, are mostly older tourists whose main purpose are to take part in activity at destinations. This group of users take the bus to carry the equipment for their activities such as walking, cycling, and surfing.

Likewise, train users can be classified into different groups. Visitors taking the train to St Ives (UK) include 'road regulars', 'public transport reliant' and 'train enjoyers' (Dallen, 2007b). 'Road regulars' include family groups who are regular car users, yet travel by public transport mostly to avoid road congestion and because of recommendations from friends and relatives. The 'public transport reliant' are in younger age group (16–34 years old) and less likely to possess a driving license and a car. This group includes mostly regular public transport users and international visitors. Conversely, the 'train enjoyers' are older tourists (45–54 years old), who appreciate scenic and relaxing train rides. Similarly, the visitor users of the train in The Looe Valley (UK) consisted of the 'train devotees', 'infrequent enthusiasts', 'train tolerators', 'consented car users' and 'last resort riders' (Dallen, 2007a). The 'train devotees' tend to have strong preferences for using the train although they could afford a car. The 'train tolerators', nonetheless, do not desire for the train but simply do not have another choice due to their inability to drive.

In contrast to rural areas, in cities, the profiles of public transport tourist users are little uncovered. Most users of public transport are well-educated and relatively young (under 35-years-old) (Le-Klähn et al., 2014a; Thompson & Schofield, 2007). As expected, the majority of tourists who use public transport in cities are independent travellers (Chang & Lai, 2009). Tourists who use public transport at destinations tended to have experience similar systems in other countries or at their home residence. They are also likely to travel on holiday, either alone or with family and friends (Chang & Lai, 2009; Le-Klähn et al., 2014b).

Motivations for public transport use and non-use

Motivations for using public transport

Tourists use public transport for multiple reasons, which include both the factors deriving from the tourist's motives and those reasons deriving from the transport system (Dallen, 2007a, 2007b; Guiver et al., 2007; Stradling et al., 2007). Le-Klähn and Hall (2015) summarised the motivations for public transport use and non-use in several cases (Table 2.3). In general, motivations for using public transport differ substantially between rural and urban areas. For visitors of several national parks in the UK, environmental concern is a

Table 2.3 Reasons for tourist public transport use/non-use

Study	Methods	Context	Reasons for public transport use	Reasons for public transport non-use
Urban				
Edwards and Griffin (2013)	GPS tracking, semi-structure interviews	Tourists in Melbourne and Sydney, Australia		1. Lack of information
Kinsella and Caulfield (2011)	Online survey	Newcomers (visiting students) in Dublin, Ireland		1. Lack of information
Le-Klähn et al. (2014a)	Intercept survey	Visitors in Munich, Germany	1. Drive-free benefits 2. Traffic reduction 3. Advantages of local public transport 4. Car unavailability	1. Inconvenience and restrictions 2. Lack of information 3. Disadvantages of public transport 4. Personal preferences
Malhado and Rothfuss (2013)	Intercept survey	Tourists in Manaus, Brazil		1. Lack of information 2. Preference for convenience and comfort
Rural				
Dallen (2007)	Intercept survey	Visitors of the St Ives Bay Line, Cornwall, UK		1. Lack of information 2. Personal preferences
Guiver et al. (2007)	Intercept survey	Tourists in different rural areas and natural attractions in the UK	1. Desire for a walk 2. Avoiding driving in unfamiliar places 3. Environmental concerns	
Lumsdon (2006)	In-depth interview	Experts who involved in planning and designing of tourism bus networks in rural UK	1. Scenic ride 2. Avoid the hassle of parking and congestion, etc. 3. Avoid driving in unfamiliar places 4. Facilitating other activities such as walking and cycling	

Source: Le-Klähn and Hall (2015).

major motivating factor for a shift to bus (Guiver *et al.*, 2007; Lumsdon, 2006). People having no car available were more likely to be concerned with environmental impacts than those having a car. Car owners took the bus mostly for the walks yet they also wanted to avoid damaging the nature. Other motivations include avoiding parking fees and driving in unfamiliar places, reducing the number of car use, and looking for social contact and for a scenic ride (Dallen, 2007b). While destination features matter, personal characteristics also play an important role in tourist transport behaviour. Most users in rural areas are of older age group, whose ability to drive a car decreases with increasing age. It is understandable that older people may be more reluctant to drive in unfamiliar places and thus more likely to use public transport. Motivations for using public transport could also be related to trip purposes. Visitors to national parks, rural, and remote areas tend to look for nature experience and sport activities. Nature tourists take the bus to avoid crowding the parks with cars and contribute to less emission. Where buses are appropriately designed sport tourists can transport their equipment, such as bicycles, on the bus for activities at the destination.

In urban areas, tourists are more likely to be motivated to use public transport because of the traffic and the complexity of an urban setting. In Munich (Germany) for example, tourists used public transport because of the drive-free benefits, traffic reduction, car unavailability and advantages of local public transport (Le-Klähn *et al.*, 2014a). *'Drive-free benefit'* describes the benefits of a drive-free experience in which visitors can do other things on board as opposed to concentrating on driving the car. The *'traffic reduction'* motivation refers to traffic related reasons such as avoiding traffic jam and contributing to less traffic. *'Car unavailability'* indicates an absence of the car either not owning or renting. These first three motivations could be categorised as 'push' factors whereas the last motivation, *'Advantages of the local public transport system'*, is a 'pull' factor (Dann, 1981). The well-developed public transport systems in Munich were attractive to the visitors, which suggested that if the public transport is good enough, people would use it. However, as motivations for use of public by visitors in urban areas have not been extensively discussed, further studies are needed for a more comprehensive understanding of the effect of 'pull' factors on visitor motivations for public use.

Motivations for not using public transport

Unlike the motivations for use, the reasons for not using public transport are more straightforward: personal preferences or lack of information. Specifically, what discourages visitors from using the bus in Edinburgh are feeling unsafe, preference for walking or cycling, problems with service provision, crowded buses, preference for car use, cost, disability and discomfort, and self-image (Stradling *et al.*, 2007). In St Ives, visitors did not use the train due to a lack of awareness of a train service, unsuitable train connections or simply because of preferences (Dallen, 2007b). Non-users of the train in Dallen's (2007b) study included the 'anti-rail riders', the 'content car drivers' and the 'train tempted'. 'Anti-rail riders' are those of higher socio-economic occupational background who have strong preference for a car for independence and convenience. The 'content car drivers' are familiar with train travel but are indifferent about whether it is an enjoyable mode. The last group, the 'train tempted' is believed to have the greatest potential to switch to alternative mode. This group consists of mostly visitors over 55 years old, retired and likely to be male.

In metropolitan areas, public transport is more likely to be used than in the villages, yet visitors cited several discouraging factors of public transport such as inconvenience and restrictions, lack of information, disadvantages of public transport and personal preferences (Le-Klähn *et al.*, 2014a).

In general, there have been few studies on the socio-psychological benefits associated with public transport (Lumsdon, 2006). Understanding tourists' motivation for public transport use and non-use is important. From that transport policies and marketing strategies can be planned so as to attract more public transport non-users to become choice users.

Insight 2.3: Public Transport, Religious Imperatives and Gender Segregation

The links between public transport and religious imperatives are complicated. In several countries, the public transport system follows the local religious imperatives. In other cases, the public transport system does not allow passengers to obey their religious imperatives. In both cases, tourists should know the local norms and rules and how this affects public transport use, especially in terms of time of service, dress code and gender segregation issues.

Public transport in Israel, including buses and trains, is suspended almost entirely from Friday afternoon until Saturday night (Shabbat time). Tourists and locals must use private cars, rental cars, taxis and private transport services. However, rental cars, taxis and private transport services may also be limited on Saturdays. The same is true for all Jewish holidays. In addition, gender segregation is still enforced by bus lines in ultraorthodox population neighbourhoods (Ilan, 2015), even though this form of discrimination is not acceptable among the vast majority of the Israeli population (Freedman, 2009) and was officially declared as unlawful by the Israeli High Court of Justice in 2011 because of its discriminatory nature (Ilan, 2015).

In Saudi Arabia, religious gender segregation is a state law under sharia and is obeyed in all public spheres, including public transport (Merriman, 2009; Al-Atawi & Saleh, 2014). As a consequence, women have to use a separate entrance to public transport and sit in a back section reserved for women. However, the bus companies with the widest coverage in Riyadh and Jeddah do not allow women at all. In Iran's local buses, men and women sit separately, even if related, although this is not the case in most of Iran's trains and long-distance buses, where men and women sit together. According to the Iranian norms, women are advised to sit next to other women and sit in the back in taxis. The dress code, especially for women, is also part of the constraints of public transport use in religious countries. In contrast, the Netherlands (Agence France-Presse, 2015), Belgium and France banned the Islamic veil in public transport for security reasons.

Interestingly, the call for gender segregation comes recently from women groups that argue that women-only public transportation will be safer for female passengers. In Malaysia, Egypt, Taiwan, Thailand, Japan, Brazil, Indonesia, India and Mexico women are allowed to take a women-only carriage in trains for safety purposes (Sommers, 2015), this can also be used by female tourists who want to use public transport safely and avoid harassment (issues of safety and security on public transport are further discussed in Chapter 5). The question as to why this segregation is considered differently from gendered religious segregation is still an open debate and calls for further investigation.

Sources:
Hostelbookers.com, Women's travel in the Middle East: http://www.hostelbookers.com/blog/travel/womens-travel-in-middle-east/.
Touristisrael.com. Transport in Israel: http://www.touristisrael.com/public-transport/.

Satisfaction with public transport services
The local user
Understanding customer satisfaction is critical for all products and services providers. A happy customer will return and recommend the product to her friends and family; the unhappy one will do just the opposite.

To collect regular feedback from customers, survey is among the most common methods. If well designed, surveys can provide companies with valuable information, such as what aspects are important for customers and which areas should be improved. In transport services, many public transport operators conduct passenger surveys on a regular basis to update their users' perception of the provided services.

In Europe, the annual transnational public transport customer satisfaction survey in nine European cities (Stockholm, Barcelona, Copenhagen, Geneva, Helsinki, Vienna, Berlin, Manchester and Oslo), provides interesting comparison between these cities' public transport systems (Fellesson & Friman, 2008). Four service dimensions, namely system, comfort, staff and safety were found to be important factors on passenger satisfaction. Variations between the cities in the sample, however, suggest public transport services were evaluated inconsistently among users of different systems. Several factors contribute to the diversity of customer perceptions including those related to management (how the services were provided) and personal group (culture and tradition).

A study of five transit systems in Athens and Thessaloniki (Greece) confirmed the differences between customer perceptions of several transit operators. The most important satisfaction attributes across transit operators were service frequency, vehicle cleanliness, waiting conditions, transfer distance and network coverage. Nevertheless, the rating of each of these dimensions varied across different transit systems. For metro (subway) services, vehicle cleanliness, staff behaviour and ticketing system were more emphasised. On the other hand, customers stressed service frequency, vehicle cleanliness and network coverage when evaluating bus operators. A well-coordinated and reliable transportation environment was strongly preferred by all users (Tyrinopoulos & Antoniou, 2008).

In Switzerland, passenger satisfaction with public transport was found to be related to behaviour and habits (Abou-Zeid et al., 2012). Those who switched to public transport tended to be more satisfied than those who did not. Conversely, Italian passengers' satisfaction of services and their frequency of use were not correlated (Diana, 2012). Public transport received greatest use in city centres, followed by towns of above 50 thousands inhabitants. However, satisfaction levels tended to be highest in smaller towns and lowest in metropolitan areas. As often found in customer satisfaction studies (e.g. Song et al., 2012; Tribe & Snaith, 1998), expectation is also a factor influencing satisfaction with public transportation experience. Level of satisfaction with the services decreased with increasing travel time (Gorter et al., 2000), longer waiting time, and crowded or unreliable services (Cantwell et al., 2009).

The strong growth of the Asian economy has led to the development and extension of several public transport networks. Though being relatively new, the network in Asia accounts for a large part of world's total public transport systems (UITP, 2015). Similar to users in other continents, passengers in Indonesia valued public transport for its advantageous qualities, which can be classified into 'soft' and 'functionality' (Budiono, 2009). The 'soft quality' factor includes security issues and comfort while the 'functionality quality' consists of frequency, travel time, punctuality and time, with the latter being the more influential on levels of the customer satisfaction. In Kaohsiung (Taiwan), passenger emphasised service quality and perceived value in rating their satisfaction with the metro systems (Lai & Chen, 2011).

The tourist user

Tourists make up a substantial segment of public transport passengers at urban destinations e.g. 8% of the total number of daily passengers in Munich (Plantsch et al., 2010). Given their distinctive behaviour, expectations and perceptions from the local users, separate investigations of tourist satisfaction with public transport services are necessary.

Tourists are heterogeneous, which explains their diverse perceptions and attitudes towards transport (Dallen, 2007b). Like the local users, tourists' satisfaction and perceptions depend on multiple factors, among which cultural background has an important effect (Kozak, 2001). British tourists who were on summer holidays in Turkey and Mallorca, for instance, were generally more satisfied with the local transport services than their German counterparts. Dimensions of service attributes were also perceived differently. Attributes such as comfort, cleanliness, information and driver helpfulness were highly rated by the tourist users of bus services in the rural areas in the UK (Guiver et al., 2007). Conversely, poor service delivery, unreliability, poor information, bad driving or inferior vehicles, and above all frequency of services were areas that required improvement.

In Munich, four service dimensions were found important to tourist satisfaction, which are 'travelling comfort', 'service quality', 'accessibility' and 'additional features' (Le-Klähn et al., 2014b). 'Travelling comfort' referred to the features required for a comfortable trip such as space on the vehicle, cleanliness, seat availability and safety. Service qualities such as efficiency, punctuality, reliability, frequent services, convenient schedule and good network connection are important to tourists. Accessible stations and transport vehicles are essential for the improvement of customer penetration. Additional features such as driver, staff, ease-of-use and information availability contribute to tourists' evaluation of public transport services. As tourists are new to the areas, a user-friendly public transport system plays an important role in motivating use (Chang & Lai, 2009;

Le-Klähn *et al.*, 2014a, 2014b; Thompson & Schofield, 2007). Additional critical aspects include reliability, service frequency and punctuality (Kinsella & Caulfield, 2011).

Transport at destinations is an integral part of the tourist experience and public transport is thus an additional tourism product (Duval, 2007). Tourists' experience with public transport can also influence their satisfaction with the destination (Thompson & Schofield, 2007). However, the number of studies on tourists' use of public transport in general and their satisfaction in particular are still modest. Most studies on visitor motivations for public transport use were in rural context, whereas the majority of studies examining factors influencing tourist transport choice and satisfaction were in urban destinations. These studies tended to adopt an applied approach that was directed towards the improvement of local public transport operators. The coordination between transport and tourism management (e.g. destination management organisations) was not examined, an issue returned to in Chapter 5.

Insight 2.4: Tourist Choice of Transport Mode in Munich

The context

Munich is the third largest city in Germany and the capital of the Bavaria state. The city is world famous for its annual beer festival, the Oktoberfest, as well as its plentiful activities, museums and access to the Bavarian Alps. As a major tourist destination, e.g. 6.3 million tourist arrivals in 2013 (City of Munich, 2014), it is important for the city to have an effective transport solution, especially during peak times. For this reason, a survey was conducted in November and December 2013 to examine tourists' choice of transport in Munich (Le-Klähn *et al.*, 2015).

The study sample

The sample included 474 respondents of which slightly more than half is men (52.5%) (Table 2.4). Younger respondents are the majority with 41.4% being 18–29 years old and 24.7% are of 30–39 years of age. There is only a small group of seniors (3%) in the sample. Respondents of the study appeared to be well-educated (61% completed college/university or graduate studies). This is not surprising as younger and more educated people tend to be more willing to participate in survey as compared to other groups. Around half of the survey participants (52.1%) reside in Germany as opposed to 47.9% came from abroad.

Table 2.4 Respondent profile

Characteristics	Categories	% (n = 474)
Gender	Male	52.5
	Female	47.5
Age group	<18	1.5
	18–29	41.4
	30–39	24.7
	40–54	22.4
	55–64	7.2
	65 and above	3.0
Educational level	College/University and post graduate	61.0
	Others	39.0
German residence	Yes	52.1
	No	47.9
First trip to Munich	Yes	27.2
	No	72.8
Length of stay in Munich	One day	21.5
	2–3 days	45.8
	4–7 days	26.7
	8 days and more	6.0
Travel partner	Alone	47.9
	With partner	52.1
On holiday trip	Yes	31
	No	69

Regarding trip characteristics, most respondents are returning visitors in Munich (72.8%). Those had been to Munich 1 to 5 times before represent 44.5% of the sample, followed by those with 6 to 10 times (11.7%). Very frequent visitors (21 times and more) account for a relatively small group (8.5%). Visitors tended to have short to medium stay with the majority (45.8%) spent 2 to 3 days in the city and only 6% of the respondents stayed for eight days or more. About one fifth of the respondents (21.5%) were day-trippers in Munich, who were more likely to travel from nearby cities. Slightly less than half of the respondents (47.9%) were travelling alone, whereas the rest (52.1%) were with their family, friends, or colleagues. One third of the participants (31%) were on a holiday trip in Munich while the others primarily visited their family or relatives or were on business trip. A large part of the sample (60.3%) arrived in Munich from a direct departure point in Germany as compared to 39.7% of respondents coming from overseas. This could be related to the high proportion of German residents in the sample as explained above.

Tourists' transport behaviour characteristics
Decision-making

The majority of the respondents (91.5%) indicated ownership of a valid driving license (Figure 2.5). Nevertheless, 35.5% stated that they used public transport almost every day and 26.6% are casual users at their home place. The largest group (38%), however, rarely or never used public transport. The decision on which transport mode to be used tended to be made well before the arrival in Munich. Thirty-eight percent of the respondents made their transport decision more than two weeks before coming to Munich and 23.9% finalised the choice within two weeks ahead of the trip. The rest (23.7%) of the respondents chose their intra-transport mode during their time in the city.

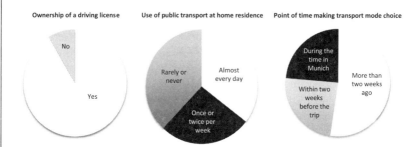

Figure 2.5 Transport behaviour characteristics of the respondents ($n = 474$)

Transport mode evaluation

Respondents were asked to evaluate the importance of transport mode quality in their mode choice on a scale of 1 (least important) to 5 (most important). A list of eight attributes was chosen with inputs from transport studies. Figure 2.6 shows that all eight attributes were rated as being between somewhat important and very important with the top three most important are best priced (M = 3.93), safe (M = 3.88) and accessible (M = 3.87). 'Eco-friendly' is perceived relatively least important (M = 3.20) compared to other qualities. This challenges the concept

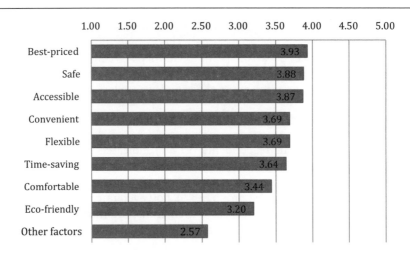

Figure 2.6 Importance of mode quality attributes in tourists' choice of transport mode

of green branding by tourism and transport providers: people may not be as interested in how the mode benefits the environment as they are in their personal benefits. Marketing of public transport should highlight the attractiveness of public transport system such as cost-effective, safe, accessible and comfortable to travel with, rather than on its eco-friendly features (which is not, of course, to say that they should not have environmentally friendly features!).

Tourists' transport mode choice

Respondents were asked to indicate where they went and which transport mode they used during the time in Munich. Answers for transport mode were then grouped into those used public transport at one point during the visit and those did not at all use public transport. Figure 2.7 shows that the majority of visitors (78.5%) used public transport during their trip in Munich. While this number is large, it is not surprising considering the study sites which excluded tourists travelling by car to Munich (train station, bus station and airport). On the other hand, this is similar to what was found in previous study (Le-Klähn *et al.*, 2014a, 2014b). In terms of extent of places, however, city tourists account for 57.6% as compared to 42.6% who extended their visit beyond the city. This could be related to the fact that a large part of survey participants are returning visitors to Munich.

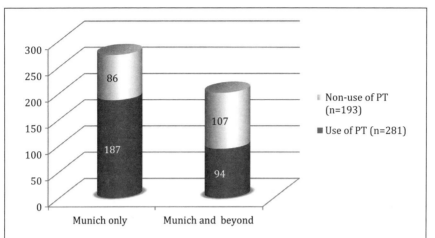

Figure 2.7 Tourists' transport mode choices and places visited

The user of public transport in Munich

Analysis of respondents' profiles indicated that the users of public transport in Munich are overnight international tourists travelling for holiday purposes. First time visitors in the city are also the potential customers of public transport services. The majority of visitors who used public transport owned valid driving licences, which suggested that public transport was a choice even though several factors may lie behind it.

Demand for public transport and sustainable mobility

Public transport is an environmentally friendly travel mode, which contributes to sustainable mobility (Peeters *et al.*, 2007; Orsi, 2015). Travelling by public transport also provides social engagement and interaction opportunities (Stradling *et al.*, 2007). Yet demand for public transport in tourism in the future is unclear. Despite the benefits, shifting to public transport is not an easy task for most people. Leisure journeys to or within rural areas are mostly by car (Dickinson & Dickinson, 2006; Dickinson *et al.*, 2009; Dickinson & Robbins, 2007; Guiver *et al.*, 2007). Similarly, visitors showed strong preferences for private modes in national parks and ski resorts and would not be easily influenced to change modes (Eaton & Holding, 1996; Reilly *et al.*, 2010). The car is also often used for short distances even when there are alternatives such as walking or buses (Dickinson & Robbins, 2007). Outside metropolitan areas, public transport may be relatively poor and often negatively perceived. Its potential as car replacement is therefore arguably only possible for shorter-distance travels (Dickinson *et al.*, 2004).

Certain disadvantages of public transport compared to private modes such as limited routes, fixed scheduled or waiting times may hinder modal shifts. However, personal characteristics, mobility habits and attitudes towards environment are also important factors. Understanding tourist response to climate and environmental change is thus necessary to predict changes in tourism demand (Gössling *et al.*, 2012b; Scott *et al.*, 2016a, 2016b). Tourists are more likely to accept traffic problems and are reluctant to pay for costs such as car use and parking charges, despite acknowledging their impacts on the environment (Dickinson *et al.*, 2009; Dickinson & Robbins, 2007). They are unwilling to change their behaviour during holiday travel and are less supportive in shifting to alternative transport modes (Barr & Prillwitz, 2012; Hall, 2014). More than a third of visitors experienced congestion (Dickinson *et al.*, 2004). Yet in response to congestion, tourists tend to opt for timing adjustment rather than route diversion (Shailes *et al.*, 2001). In most cases, people strongly prefer private modes for leisure trips (Reilly *et al.*, 2010). In the majority of developed countries the private car is the most popular chosen mode for travelling to as well as within destinations (Barr & Prillwitz, 2012). However, if sustainable mobility is to be enabled in tourism this pattern of use must change.

Insight 2.5: Park and Ride

Park and Ride (P&R) is a transport system in which cars and bicycles are left in car parks in the suburbs or on the outskirts of a city and travel to a city centre, major transport hub (i.e. airport) or a major attraction on public transport, usually train or bus. The modal interchange is made either because the traveller wishes to use the public transport service as the primary mode for the journey, but a private car or bicycle is judged the most effective way to access the public transport network, or, conversely, the car or bicycle is the preferred primary mode for the journey, but advantages, such as cost or ease of access, are perceived if the final part of the journey is made by public transport (Parkhurst & Meek, 2014). Although often framed as being targeted at commuters the approach is also often utilised in tourism destinations and attractions, such as heritage areas and national parks, to reduce traffic congestion and improve air quality (Dijk *et al.*, 2013; Clayton *et al.*, 2014). In a study of P&R in the Netherlands and the United Kingdom, Parkhurst and Meek (2014) found that only a portion of P&R users' car trips were shortened and therefore overall increases in car use occurred, combined with overall reductions in public transport use, and in some cases less active travel. They concluded that implementation of P&R interventions were generally successful where they were explicitly for providing more parking for economic growth or traffic management reasons, such as in the case of heritage city centres, rather than to enhance sustainable mobility per se (see also Dijk & Parkhurst, 2014). Parkhurst and Meek (2014) argue that strategic sub-regional integrated parking and public transport strategies are essential to create the conditions for traffic reduction. This requires the early interception of car trips as well as ensuring that public transport services are attractive over all access modes.

Case studies of P&R:
Aarhus, Denmark (Park and Bike): http://www.eltis.org/discover/case-studies/
    denmarks-first-park-and-bike-terminal-aarhus
Bristol, England: http://www.eltis.org/discover/case-studies/park-and-ride-bristol
Warsaw, Poland: http://www.eltis.org/discover/case-studies/reducing-congestion-
    warsaws-park-and-ride-system-poland

Chapter Summary and Conclusion

Public transport has not been popular for tourism purposes since car ownership became widespread and its potential as a replacement travel mode remains a major challenge in the absence of fundamental economic and social change. However, growing concerns over emissions and air quality as well as the encouragement of more active experiences in tourism and recreation provide significant points of departure for new public transport policies and initiatives as well as new patterns of tourist behaviour. The potential for change therefore likely depends on whether public transport is for use to destinations and/or within destinations, the different behavioural dimensions of which may have considerable implications for both the supply and demand for public transport by tourists. Nevertheless, public transport is a significant contributor to tourism in many destinations, while as the following chapters highlight many policy makers realise the importance of influencing consumer attitudes towards the use of public transport in developing more sustainable cities and regions.

Further Readings

On tourist use of specific forms of public transit with respect to light and conventional rail

Chang, H.H. and Lai, T.Y. (2009) The Taipei MRT (Mass Rapid Transit) tourism attraction analysis from the inbound tourists' perspective. *Journal of Travel and Tourism Marketing* 26 (5–6), 445–461.

Dallen, J. (2007) Sustainable transport, market segmentation and tourism: The Looe Valley Branch Line Railway, Cornwall, UK. *Journal of Sustainable Tourism* 15 (2), 180–199.

Dallen, J. (2007) The challenges of diverse visitor perceptions: rail policy and sustainable transport at the resort destination. *Journal of Transport Geography* 15 (2), 104–115.

On bus transport see

Guiver, J., Lumsdon, L., Weston, R. and Ferguson, M. (2007) Do buses help meet tourism objectives? The contribution and potential of scheduled buses in rural destination areas. *Transport Policy* 14 (4), 275–282.

For more information about the research on tourist use of public transport in Munich see

Le-Klähn, D.-T., Gerike, R. and Hall, C.M. (2014) Visitor users vs. non-users of public transport: The case of Munich, Germany. *Journal of Destination Marketing & Management* 3 (3), 152–161.

Le-Klähn, D.-T., Hall, C.M. and Gerike, R. (2014) Analysis of visitor satisfaction with public transport in Munich, Germany. *Journal of Public Transportation* 17 (3), 68–85.

For information on visitor use of public transport in London see

Transport for London (2013) Visitor Segmentation Presentation. Available: http://content.tfl.gov.uk/visitor-segmentation-research-report.pdf

3 Local and Intra-Destination Public Transport

Introduction

This chapter will examine the use of public transport within tourism destinations and is primarily concerned with the short or secondary trips that occur as a result of tourist activities within the destination. Inter-modal transfer that is part of longer distance travel to accommodation at the destinations is dealt with in the following chapter. The present chapter is organised via the examination of different modes of transport. However, before going through the different modes we will commence with a discussion of the different factors that influence tourist choice of transport modes at destinations.

Factors Affecting Mode Choice at Destination

Transport plays an important role in destination development. While inter-destination transports, e.g. aviation and private automobiles, have been well examined, intra-destination tourist mobility behaviour has received relatively less attention (Le-Klähn & Hall, 2015; Lew & McKercher, 2006; Prideaux, 2000). Tourists have several options for travelling within a destination and the choice of transport mode depends on several factors (e.g. Koo *et al.*, 2010, 2012; Le-Klähn *et al.*, 2015; Lew & McKercher, 2006; McKercher *et al.*, 2006) (see also the discussion of tourist behaviour in Chapter 2). Factors influencing tourists' mode choice can generally be categorised to five groups: (1) visitor characteristics, (2) trip characteristics, (3) destination features, (4) travel motivations and (5) mode quality evaluations.

Visitor characteristics

Tourists' demographic characteristics such as gender and age are often important factors of their travel behaviour. However, these two factors do not tend to have a major influence on tourist transport mode choice (Koo *et al.*, 2012; Le-Klähn *et al.*, 2015; Masiero & Zoltan, 2013). Instead, educational level and country of origin have been found to be more influential. Well-educated visitors tend to travel farther (Wynen, 2013), and are more likely to use public transport than others (Le-Klähn *et al.*, 2014a; Le-Klähn *et al.*, 2015). Likewise, cultural background (or country of origin) influences mode choice: Irish tourists are much less likely to use a train in comparison to Belgians and the Swiss (van Goeverden, 2009). American and Asian tourists in New Zealand also appear much more likely to take domestic flights and less likely to travel by train than their Australian and European counterparts (Becken, 2005). Income is also a contributing factor to mode choice. Given the options of plane, train and bus, tourists with higher income are likely to choose plane or train for better service qualities (Vo, 2013).

Trip characteristics

How long a tourist plans to stay at a destination appears determined by the choice of transport mode. Extended stay visitors in New Zealand are more likely to travel by rental vehicles and private transport (Moore *et al.*, 2012). On the other hand, day visitors in Canada, who had high income, preferred private modes (Kelly *et al.*, 2007). In Germany, public transport users are also more likely to have longer stays at destinations than the non-users (Le-Klähn *et al.*, 2014a; Le-Klähn *et al.*, 2015). Travel partners are also an additional factor that influences tourists' mode choice. Single tourists or those travelling in a large group (of at least nine people) appear to have a higher probability to use alternative transport modes (Van Middelkoop *et al.*, 2003).

Destination features

Each destination has its own geographical characteristics, morphology, tourism, and transport infrastructure (Hall & Page, 2014; Lew & McKercher, 2006). The geographic characteristics of a destination influence the spatial patterns of tourists (Hwang & Fesenmaier, 2003), whereas transport infrastructure and the availability of the public transport influence the mode choice (Thrasher *et al.*, 2000).

Insight 3.1: Explore the Cotswolds by Public Transport

The Cotswolds are a UK Area of Outstanding Natural Beauty and a significant domestic and international tourism destination. In order to help reduce road and parking congestion and improve the quality of the visitor experience since 2007 the Cotswolds Public Transport Guides have promoted sustainable transport options to visitors and residents, using the network of trains and rural buses. *Explore the Cotswolds by Public Transport* is a package of promotional publications and website pages produced annually designed to promote environmentally sustainable tourism and travel to, and within, the Cotswolds area. An additional 20-page guide, *Walk and Explore the Cotswold Way by Public Transport* was also produced using an identical format to the other timetables. A series of publications, listing visitor and heritage attractions in the area accessible by public transport were devised, along with suggestions for attractive 'Taster Days' undertaken on foot, by cycle or bus. These were linked to maps to simplify the network into a series of colour coded maps, all of which relate to services within three zones.

Sources:
Eltis The urban mobility observatory: http://www.eltis.org/discover/case-studies/
    walk-and-explore-cotswolds-public-transport-guide-uk#sthash.TzWHR7mj.dpuf
Escape to the Cotswolds: http://www.escapetothecotswolds.org.uk/visitor-info/
    gettinghere/
Welcome to the Cotswolds Area of Outstanding Natural Beauty: http://www.cots-
    woldsaonb.org.uk/

Travel motivations

Psychographic characteristics are important factors in tourist behaviour yet their influences on tourists' choices of transport mode at destinations have not been extensively researched. The effects of 'pull' and 'push' factors seemed to be reverse in this case. Visitors who were more motivated by 'pull' factors such as a destination's attractions and landscape are more likely to use private transport (Le-Klähn et al., 2015). This probably connects to the desire to travel to a larger spatial extent. Conversely, those who had been activity-driven (push factors) tended to use public transport, perhaps for ease and convenience of participating in activities.

Mode quality evaluation

Tourists' choice of transport modes is limited by what is available at destinations. Nevertheless, mode qualities can also play a relevant role.

Factors such as price, travel time, flexibility, comfort, safety and convenience are important in mode evaluation (Fellesson & Friman, 2008; Redman et al., 2013). However, these mode qualities are perceived differently among different groups of people, yet in most cases, cost and time are often cited as most important (Chang & Lai, 2009; Hergesell & Dickinger, 2013; Le-Klähn et al., 2015; Redman et al., 2013). The shorter the trip, the more likely tourists chose private transport modes (Kelly et al., 2007). Day visitors are particularly sensitive due to their limited time budget. Conversely, the probability that tourists use private transport modes decreases if there is an increase in fuel cost (Kelly et al., 2007). Likewise, ticket price can strongly influence tourist's use of public transport (Le-Klähn et al., 2015). Obviously lower ticket prices can attract more users (issues of pricing are subject to more detailed discussion in Chapter 5).

Insight 3.2: Public Transport Ridership in Europe

Public transport plays an important role in Europe's urban transportation. It carried almost 57 billion journeys, about 182 million trips on an average working day in the European Union in 2012 (UITP, 2014b). The majority of public transport trips (56%) were made by urban and suburban buses, followed by metros (16%), tramways (14%) and suburban railways (14%). On average, a city-dweller in Europe travelled 150 journeys per year or 3 trips weekly by public transport. Despite some slight declines in 2009 and 2010, ridership of public transport in Europe has increased since 2000. It is estimated that public transport will grow by 1.6–4.4% per year up to 2050 (Dubois & Aliaga, 2014).

Railways, Trams and Light Rail

Public transport at the destination includes railway, bus, tram and light rail. Metropolitan railway (or metro) is an electric train system, which is independent from traffic, roads, and pedestrians. Metro is characterised by high capacity and high frequency (UITP, 2009). Metro requires substantial investment yet it is essential for many cities with large population to reduce traffic congestion. Over 160 million passengers are transported by metro systems everyday worldwide (or 50 billion per year), accounting for 11% of public transport journeys (UITP, 2015), with many metros being iconic tourist attractions in their own right as well as an important means of getting around cities.

Plate 3.1 Riverside tram system as part of the revitalisation of the Bilbao waterfront, Spain

Plate 3.2 Southern Cross Railway Station, Melbourne, Victoria, Australia. The station, which is managed as part of a public-private partnership, is of major importance to domestic tourism as it is the terminus of the state's regional railway network and inter-state services from Adelaide and Sydney.

Insight 3.3: World Metro Statistics

In 2014, 549 metro systems were in operation worldwide. These systems had over 9200 stations, and covered a total length of 11,300 kilometres (Figure 3.1). As of 2009, there are 46 metro systems in Europe, the majority of them (78%) are in the EU-15 country group (UITP, 2009). The Europe metro systems carry almost 10 billion passengers per year. France tops the list in terms of annual passengers (2 billion), followed by Germany (1.5 billion) and Spain (1.3 billion). At the city level, Paris has the highest number of yearly passengers (1.5 billion), followed by London (1.1 billion), and Madrid (700 million).

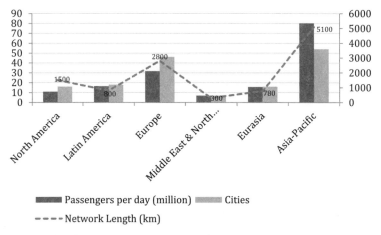

Figure 3.1 Metro networks worldwide in 2014
Source: Derived from UITP (2015).

Tram (tramcar, streetcar or trolley car) is typically electrically-powered rail vehicle which runs on tracks alongside streets for cars in cities. Light rail or light rail transit (LRT) is similar to tram but usually operated on high platform, has higher capacity, and exclusive right of way. Most large cities (at least 300,000 inhabitants) with a strong economy can offer a light rail system to reduce pressure on road traffic (Knowles & Ferbrache, 2015). Investment in an LRT system can positively impact the city's economy by providing accessibility to previously less reachable areas and reducing transport constraints. From a tourist perspective light rail can be an important means to visit attractions outside of the immediate city centre while it can also make a very important contribution to multimodality, especially in combination with cycling and walking activities.

Insight 3.4: The TRAM for Tourists in Alicante

A regional tramline called TRAM covers the coast and the urban area of Alicante, Spain. The use of the TRAM by tourists is important, with passenger numbers doubling during the summer months. More than half of the TRAM users travel on the service for leisure reasons, including shopping and sightseeing, and nearly 20% are foreigners. The Valencia Government Railway company (Ferrocarrils de la Generalitat Valenciana (FGV)) and the Provincial Association of Hotels and Accommodations (Asociación Provincial de Hoteles y Alojamientos Turísticos de Alicante) have a formal collaborative agreement in place in order to promote the use of the Alicante tramway of Alicante to their customers. More than 70 members of the Association offer detailed information to their guests on the different services, tariffs, timetables and promotions of the TRAM. To encourage greater use the FGV offers TRAM tickets for 24, 48 or 72 hour periods. In the future, TRAM is also planned to connect to the intermodal station of Alicante, the university and the airport.

Source:
Eltis The urban mobility observatory: http://www.eltis.org/discover/news/tram-transport-mode-tourists-alicante-spain-0#sthash.KSv713An.dpuf

---

Bus

The bus is a type of public transport that can be easily found in most areas with some basic level of infrastructure development. Buses play an important role in transporting tourists to attractions within destinations or for long-distance inter-destination routes. Buses are also often used for traditional package tours. Apart from specially designed tourism buses (e.g. city sightseeing or hop-on/hop-off buses) and those provided by tour operators, tourists can use the bus network originally built for utility purposes. While the design of the residents' buses may not be optimised for tourists' needs, in some cases, using the local bus becomes part of a tourist's 'must-do' activities. For example, sitting on an overcrowded local bus on a bumpy ride in Thailand is an authentic and exciting experience for many tourists (Howard, 2009). Likewise, in a much less dangerous way, taking the iconic double-decker is among tourists' favourite activities in London.

Bus systems move around 50–60% of all transit passengers (30 billion per year) in the EU. This pattern changes from around a 50% share in large cities with multimodal networks up to 100% in smaller towns and medium-size cities (Corazza *et al.*, 2015). Buses are highly efficient passenger transport modes with low levels of fuel consumption and therefore contribute to the reduction of transport-related CO_2 and other greenhouse gases (GHG) emissions. Buses are also a relatively safe form of transport, with very low accident rates if compared to other passenger transport modes (Eurostat, 2013; Corazza *et al.*, 2015). Nevertheless, there is substantial variation in levels of satisfaction with bus transport. 'Dissatisfaction stems from poor performance such as regularity, punctuality, speed, comfort and design, which all contribute to the general modest attractiveness of this mode, if compared to other transit options' (Corazza *et al.*, 2015: 2). In some urban places, residents are not interested in buses because of their personal feelings and preferences (Stradling *et al.*, 2007). Travelling by bus was perceived to be uncomfortable and associated with less favourable self-image. Though these reasons are not totally relevant for tourists, a complicated system, especially when coupled with insufficient information can put off the (potential) tourist users (Le-Klähn *et al.*, 2014b).

The bus generally cannot compete with the train in urban areas in terms of popularity among independent tourists due to their relatively complicated network, and in many cases, relatively unreliable services. However, even in areas where they are the only public transport option available (e.g. in rural areas, national parks or remote resorts), buses also did not appear to be appealing to tourists (Dickinson & Dickinson, 2006; Dickinson & Robbins, 2008). To successfully attract tourists, rural bus providers need to emphasise two aspects (1) reliability and (2) driver quality (Lumsdon, 2006). Reliability reflects the bus service quality, which encompasses aspects such as frequent services and punctuality. Tourists valued a reliable bus service, and also the role of the bus driver. Bus drivers are expected to be friendly and cooperative. They also need to have some local knowledge and good driving skills. However, as there is a lack of data on the users of buses for leisure, transport planners should consider undertaking monitoring programs and market research on tourist demand and motivations on a regular basis in order to successfully encourage a modal shift.

Hop-on hop-off bus

A common transport mode (as well as activity for tourists) at destinations is the sightseeing bus. These buses are often run by bus tour operators (with the largest franchise being City Sightseeing) and were designed especially to cater to tourists' needs. A typical hop on hop off bus is an open top double-decker bus, providing passengers with the city view. Bus routes connect major landmarks and attractions within the cities and nearby. By buying the bus ticket, tourists can get on and off the bus as often as they want during a certain period of time specified in the ticket. In some cities, access to the hop-on hop-off bus is included or combined with other attractions in one bundle package such as the Go San Francisco Card and the London Pass.

Insight 3.5: Jurassic CoastlinX53 – The Jurassic Coast Bus in Devon and Dorset, UK

Jurassic CoastlinX53 is an all year round double decker bus service operating between Exeter, Poole and Bournemouth, parallel to the Jurassic Coast World Heritage Site. It serves a large number of towns and villages along the 95 mile long coast as well as both the East Devon and Dorset Areas of Outstanding Natural Beauty. The service uses a fleet of low floor, high profile Jurassic Coast branded vehicles that augment the existing bus service and importantly the majority of these services also cater for wheelchairs and buggies.

Service X53 was originally introduced in October 1998, using a Rural Bus Subsidy Grant. The service provided a new link between Exeter, East Devon and West Dorset, which had not previously existed. Passenger numbers grew strongly, increasing from 29,797 in the first year of operation to 52,972 in 2001/2002 and 124,738 in 2004/2005. In 2005/6, this figure more than doubled to 267,993 with further spectacular growth in 2006/7 to 392,996. 2007/8 showed a further 3.7% growth in relation to 2006/7. The service also became one of the principal services in the developing Jurassic Coast World Heritage Site transport strategy, serving one of the anchor towns and seven of the gateway towns. The bus service provides easy access to popular sections of coastal paths in the South West for local people and tourists. Key partners include the Devon and Dorset County Councils, First Bus and the Jurassic Coast World Heritage Steering Group.

Significantly, although the bus service was designed to attract large numbers of day visitors and tourists it also provides a year-round bus services for local people that facilitate daily journeys for work, education and leisure, it was also envisaged that the service would form an essential part of the area's green tourism infrastructure and be a major attraction on its own.

Very prominent branding to create a high level of awareness of the Jurassic Coast service was planned from the start. The service was given the name/logo 'CoastlinX53 Jurassic Coast'; developed by Devon County Council using the service number, and the World Heritage site's corporate colours and ammonite symbol. The logo was also designed so that it could be used as branding on publicity material, bus stops and vehicles alike. For the 2003 summer period 150,000 full colour timetable leaflets were produced, which include details of tickets, other bus links and an introduction to towns and sights to see along the coast, 120,000 leaflets were produced for the winter services. The leaflets have been widely distributed to local outlets including Post Offices, Tourist Information Centres, libraries, holiday accommodation and bus stations. For summer 2004, three full colour days out brochures were produced for Weymouth, Seaton/Beer and Lyme Regis, providing suggestions for days out, including sample times and fares. Ten thousand copies of each version were produced and distributed to local outlets along the route. These have now been supplemented by online material (see source material below).

Market research was conducted on users and non-users in September 2004. Among users of the service there was an approximate 50/50 split between regular local users and visitors. Of the visitors 29% were using the service for the first time. Satisfaction with the service was high with the buses, drivers and reliability scoring particularly strongly. Awareness of the service was also high, especially the specially branded buses. Non-users recorded a slightly lower level of awareness of the service (and the World Heritage Site), although the service was still seen as an attractive proposition. In-depth interviews with 'front of house' staff, i.e. those with direct contact with the public, at accommodation providers, tourist attractions and Tourist Information Centres indicated a high level of recommendation to visitors.

Sources:
Devon County Council (CoastLinX53 – Jurassic Coast Years 1 and 2 Report, June 2003 to May 2005: http://www.devon.gov.uk/x53-annual-report2003-5.pdf
Devon County Council, Journeydevon your guide to public transport: https://www.journeydevon.info/great-journeys/featured-trips/jurassic-coast/
Eltis The urban mobility observatory: http://www.eltis.org/discover/case-studies/jurassic-coastlinx53-jurassic-coast-bus-devon-and-dorset-uk#sthash.SsFnVbGR.dpuf
Jurassic Coast Dorset and East Devon World Heritage Site: http://jurassiccoast.org/discover/travel-information/x53-and-x51-jurassic-coaster-bus-services/

Plate 3.3 Tram, bus and taxi, Stockholm, Sweden. Dedicated lanes and pick up points make it easy to access public transport downtown in Sweden's capital.

Plate 3.4 Luna Bus transport, Flic en Flac, Mauritius. As a tropical island in the Indian Ocean that is often promoted as a 'tourist paradise', Mauritius would seemingly be an ideal candidate for sustainable mobility planning. However, its public transport system is not easily usable by tourists. Mauritius has a bus network of over 200 bus lines in an island of just over 2000 km², but with no island-wide inter-operator ticket.

Taxi

A taxi, also referred to as a taxicab or cab, is a vehicle with a driver provided for hire, often used by a single or a group of passengers for their specific transport need, typically for a short period of time. As a shared transport mode, taxis are sometimes considered as part of a city's public transport system, which can contribute much to urban transportation (Aarhaug, 2014; Grünig, 2012). Taxi may refer to different services across countries yet there are generally four types of taxis:

- taxis for public hire or street taxis;
- taxis for private hire with pre-booking;
- taxi-buses i.e. on-call public transport services operated on pre-set routes; and
- limousine services.

Because of its flexibility, accessibility and speed, the taxi is popular among tourists. In some large cities, taxis have even become an integral part of the city image. For example, it would be hard to imagine the streets in New York without its famous yellow cabs or London with its black cabs. However, taxis are relatively expensive compared to other modes and hence only tend to be used for short distances, or for specific routes such as city-airport (Castillo-Manzano, 2010; Wang et al., 2015). Exceptions are when passengers need to travel with heavy and bulky luggage or due to time constraints or safety reasons.

In recent years taxis have been at the forefront of change as a result of new information and communication technologies, mobile phone applications (or 'apps') have gradually replaced traditional phone booking systems to facilitate the process of finding and booking taxis. These apps match a passenger with a driver based on the information of their locations to optimise waiting times and routes. A few simple steps on a smart phone will summon a taxi to the caller's location. Cashless payment is enabled in many cases making it another big advantage of the system. As many app development companies operate worldwide, app-users who travel to other destinations can continue using the services without any hassle. Table 3.1 lists some of the largest companies providing app-based on-demand ride services.

Uber and Lyft

Since its foundation in 2009, Uber, a Silicon Valley transport network company has greatly affected the world's taxi industry and brought new

Table 3.1 Examples of taxi-booking mobile phone applications

	Didi Dache	EasyTaxi	GrabTaxi	Gett	Hailo
Year Founded	2012	2011	2012	2011	2011
Origin/ Headquarters	China	Sao Paulo (Brazil)	Malaysia/ Singapore	Tel Aviv (Israel)	London (UK)
Driver	1.5 million	400,000	60,000	35,000	50,000
Apps User	154 million	17 million	500,000	–	1 million
Bookings/ Second	–	–	3	1	–
Cities	300	420	22	57	16
Countries	1	30	6	4	8
Employees	–	–	500	350	150
	http://www. xiaojukeji.com	http://www. easytaxi.com	http://www. grabtaxi.com	http://gett. com	https://www. hailoapp.com

Note: Information as of January 2016.

concepts to ridesharing. While other app-based companies noted above (see Table 3.1) partner with existing taxi companies to match passengers and drivers (Tay, 2014), Uber has its own network of drivers. Any driver with a car, who passes background checks, can join Uber network to provide private transportation. The company has aggressively extended its network to 68 countries and more than 300 cities worldwide as of Jan 2016 (https://www. uber.com). Services provided by Uber include:

- *Uber Black* is the company's original service, provides rides in black cars, primarily for business clientele.
- *UberX* is Uber's most budget option, provides low cost everyday rides for up to four people. For a larger group, the alternative UberXL can transport six people or more.
- *UberSUV* provides an SUV (Sport Utility Vehicle) with seating up to six passengers.
- *UberLUX* is Uber's most expensive service, providing transport in limousine or luxury vehicles.
- *UberTaxi* provides services by taxis which partner with Uber and operates much like ordinary taxis (except that payment is charged on users' credit card).

Lyft (founded 2012) is another ridesharing apps-based company from San Francisco (https://www.lyft.com). Unlike Uber, Lyft has so far focused only on the American market, operating in more than 65 cities. International expansion is projected in coming years.

The development of app-based companies such as Uber and Lyft has significantly affected the way people use taxi, public transport and overall vehicle travel. While most rides by Uber and Lyft replaced taxi trips, a significant portion also replaced other modes such as public transport or private vehicle (Rayle *et al.*, 2016). Compared to traditional taxis, app-based on-demand transport services have certain advantages regarding ease of payment and/or booking and wait time. The technological advantages make the services attractive to younger and well-educated users, who require short wait times and fast services. Like traditional taxis, ride-sharing transport service can also be used when the consumer wants to avoid the hassles of finding parking space or dealing with traffic congestion.

Ride-sharing transport services provide more mobility options for people, especially where public transport is insufficient. Given the growing number of concerns over environmental and urban problems, and economical reasons, ride-sharing services are expected to increase their share in the transportation market in the future. However, amidst their growth, Uber and Lyft have faced challenges from local governments and ordinary taxi drivers in several countries. There is a lack of legal framework for the management of this relatively new form of business. Different countries and jurisdictions also have different regulations regarding driver training, service and knowledge levels. Drivers can easily join the network to start earning money without the need to have a taxi-driver license. Facing fierce competition, taxi drivers have regularly protested to call for equal regulations for taxi booking services (Nguyen, 2015). Until a legislative framework is confirmed, Uber's legal status varies from country to country. As of late 2015 it was fully or partially banned in several cities in the US, Germany, Japan and Australia (Khosla, 2015).

Insight 3.6: Public Transport in Singapore

Singapore is a small island state (718 km²) with one of the highest population densities in the world (7987 people per km²). Having a strong economy and increasing disposable income per capita, Singapore has been facing growing levels of private motorisation. To reverse the increasing trend of private car usage, the Singaporean government is promoting public transport as a key element in transport policies, having set an aim to achieve 75% of trips during peak hours made on public transport by 2030 (Singapore Land Transport Authority (LTA), 2014). Although a relatively new system, the mass transit system already accounted for 44% of total journeys in 2011 (LTA, 2011). Singapore's public transport network is mostly land-based and includes the MRT (short for Mass Rapid Transit), LRT (Light Rail Transit) and buses. There are also ferryboat services connecting the main island with the nearby smaller ones.

Singapore is among the most visited destinations in Southeast Asia and is an important aviation hub. In 2014, 15.1 million tourists visited Singapore (Singapore Tourism Board, 2015), a number about three times the size of the total population. To facilitate tourist use of public transport and enhance their experience, a collaboration arrangement between the Singapore Tourism Board and the Land Transport Authority was formed. As a result of this, a Singapore Tourist Pass and a public transport guide for tourists (*Travel with Ease*) were introduced in 2007. The Tourist Pass offers tourists with unlimited travel on Singapore's public transport system for a specified duration (typically for one, two or three days). Upon expiration, the Pass can be topped up and then works as a normal smart transit card. The *Travel with Ease* guide provides tourists with the information on modes, routes, and places of interests in Singapore. Network map and key bus services around tourist areas are also included. From the Guide, tourists can get useful information for their navigation and route planning, whereas with the Pass, tourists can conveniently and extensively travel by public transport.

The Singapore Tourist Pass and Travel with Ease Guide were meant to make tourist use of public transport easy, yet like other tourist passes (Le-Klähn, 2015), its effectiveness is unknown. From the user's view, one needs to make several trips to make the pass (priced at 10$ SGD/day) worth buying. On the other hand, little is known on whether or not the Tourist Card contributes to encourage tourists' use of public transport and their experiences. This is especially interesting considering the wide implementation of such cards in many parts of the world.

Sources:
Singapore Tourism Board, Your Singapore, Getting Around Singapore: http://www.yoursingapore.com/about-singapore/traveller-information/travelling-around-singapore.html
Singapore Tourist Pass: http://www.thesingaporetouristpass.com.sg/

Ferries and Waterborne Transport

Ferries and other forms of waterborne transport, such as water buses and taxes, are playing an increasingly important role in many urban and regional centres with sufficiently large water bodies. Sydney, Brisbane, Stockholm, London, New York and Bangkok already have significant linear urban ferry services while water taxis and ferries are also significant in cities such as Vancouver and Helsinki. In Istanbul, more than 100 ferries and sea buses carry up to 2100 commuters per trip with many routes served by eight departures an hour. The Istanbul Deniz Otobusleri (IDO) or Istanbul Sea Bus company, the largest maritime transport corporation in the world, carried 47 million passengers around the city in 2014, with a similar number using other ferry companies in the city (Starr, 2015).

Sydney Ferries Limited became the world's largest ferry operator shortly after the Sydney Harbour Bridge opened on 19 March 1932. Unfortunately, the opening of the Sydney Harbour Bridge saw ferry travel drop from 30 million passengers a year to 13 million passengers a year. Nevertheless, the iconic Sydney Harbour ferry services is an integral public transport service for visitors to the region as well as locals. In 2011–12, 173,329 ferry services were scheduled, carrying 14.7 million passengers. Circular Quay is the hub of the network, providing access to 37 other wharves ranging from Manly at the northern end of Sydney Harbour, through to Eastern and Lower North Shore suburbs, suburbs adjacent to the Parramatta River, the Balmain peninsula and Darling Harbour. Although their spatial reach is limited, a critical aspect of both the Istanbul and Sydney ferry services is that they are integrated with other public transport modes. For example, even with appropriate development of piers and riverside development delivery it is expected that ferry traffic would account for only 20 million of the current 3.5 billion annual journeys taken in London (Starr, 2015).

In February 2015, New York City Mayor Bill de Blasio announced that a new ferry service for the city is to begin operating in 2017. New York is 'the ultimate coastal city', he said, and plans to spend $55 m (£36 m) linking Brooklyn, Manhattan, Queens and elsewhere by a ferry service. As in Istanbul, De Blasio's plan would see ferry fares the same as bus and subway, and outlying districts are expected to enjoy increased service (Starr, 2015). However, at the time of writing, a number of ferry stops, such as New York's Pier 11 at Wall Street, have no bus or mass transit connections. In contrast, in Kadikoy on the Asian shore of Istanbul's, only 20 steps separate ferry stations from the entrance of a 16-stop metro line that stretches to the city southern limits. A two-minute walk brings commuters to a major bus terminal (Starr, 2015). Although the ferry service is facing challenges from new public transport connections such as the Marmaray train line that takes passengers under the Bosphorus Strait, the ferry service remains an important part of the city's transport culture and is also a tourist attraction in its own right.

In contrast in some locations ferry services may play a major role as a visitor oriented public transport service. For example, ferries provide a major linkage between Stockholm and the Stockholm archipelago which is important for day-trips and second homes (Marjavaara, 2007). Similarly, the ferry services from Helsinki are the main means of access to Suomenlinna or Sveaborg which is a World Heritage listed inhabited sea fortress dating from the 18th century built on six islands off the coast of Helsinki. The islands are important as a day-trip leisure destination, including for picnicking and swimming in summer, for local residents as well as being a significant heritage tourism attraction.

An indication of the potential of ferry services as a means of tourist public transport was the reintroduction of waterbuses to the Scottish tourist destination of Loch Lomond, which has been a significant tourist destination for over 200 years and is now part of The Loch Lomond and Trossachs National Park (http://www.lochlomond-trossachs.org/waterbus/). The park authority's intention behind the introduction of water buses was to improve community and tourism links across the loch, cut down road use and reduce harmful emissions, which were all seen to be in keeping with the park's character. In addition, the water buses were perceived to have significant economic impact because of their capacity to disperse visitors to a wider number of villages.

Insight 3.7: Dortrecht Waterbus

Dordrecht is a 120,000 inhabitant Dutch city located in an island 20 kilometres southeast of Rotterdam. It is also an important junction of railway lines, motorways and rivers, and is the centre of the Drechtsteden region. Dortrecht has the second largest water-borne public transport system after Venice. With private car use reaching its limits in urban areas because of severe congestion a waterbus system that links Dordrecht with the adjacent towns and feeds to a fast ferry system that links the region with Rotterdam was developed with the objective of reinstate a modern version of the traditional ferry.

Waterbus was launched in 1999 as an experimental project, and became a permanent service integrated in the regional public transport network in 2002. By 2003 1.3 million and 600,000 passengers per year were estimated for Waterbus and Fast Ferry respectively. The 15 minutes frequency service is also integrated with the bicycle network, and 70% of passengers carry their bikes on board. The operator is a private company in which the City of Dordrecht and the regional transport operator participate for 50% each, and the province of South-Holland is the client. The Waterbus gets 40% of its income from ticket sales and two-thirds of the remaining deficit is financed by the province of South-Holland and the rest by Drechtsteden. It is estimated that the service contributes to the reduction of 400,000 private car trips.

Source:
Eltis The urban mobility observatory: http://www.eltis.org/discover/case-studies/waterbus-public-transport-over-water-dordrecht#sthash.CLaQKXk7.dpuf

Plate 3.5 Waterbus, Vancouver, British Columbia, Canada. Established in 1986, Aquabus Ferries are a privately owned and operated ferry service that provides commuter and tourist services to locations all along False Creek in Vancouver.

Plate 3.6 Bicycles for rent, New York City, USA

Cycling

Cycling has become increasingly popular with a sharp increase in the number of bikes sold, public bikes and bike-sharing programmes all over the world (Lamont & Buultjens, 2011; Oja *et al.*, 2011; Fishman *et al.*, 2013). In many European cities such as Copenhagen and Amsterdam, bicycles are the major mode of transport, accounting for at least one-third of total daily trips (Pucher & Buehler, 2008; Gössling, 2013). Much cycling is obviously undertaken by local residents for commuting or recreational purposes and longer distance cycle tourism is discussed in Chapter 4. However, there also appears to be growth in the number of tourists who travel to destinations via one mode of transport and then are interested in using their own bicycle or hiring one at the destination.

Offering more public bikes for sharing near train or bus stations or in the city centres that are often a focal point for tourist activity would be a potential plus to attract visitor use. In addition some hotels and accommodation providers are now including the possibility for bike hire. Public transport operators could also provide the bike programme themselves as in the case of Deutsche Bahn's 'Call-A-Bike' in Germany. However, while some public transport operators have specifically designed services to carry bikes (see Insight 3.8), this is not always possible, particularly in urban environments when there is already considerable overcrowding in the passenger sections of trains. Alternative strategies include enhanced (and reduced cost) cycle hire at stations and for local use the retention of a cycle at both rail stations – see for example (Sherwin *et al.*, 2011). Local authorities could also collaborate with sponsors to provide the bikes for rent (or for free). Multiple bike-sharing programmes have been proven successful (e.g. Copenhagen's City Bikes) (Gössling, 2013).

Insight 3.8: Integrating Cycling into the Public Transport System of South Moravia, Czech Republic

An important aspect of encouraging cycling within destinations is the development of intermodality capacity with other means of transport such as bus and train. One example of where this has occurred is in South Moravia in the Czech Republic where bicycle touring is an increasingly popular recreation and tourism activity. In April 2012 the South Moravian County and the Integrated Public Transport System of the South Moravian Region launched a new project to improve the attractiveness of the region by making rail and bus services more compatible with bicycle use. The objective of the project was to enable tourists to travel by bike combined with railway and/or bus in one of the most attractive regions of South Moravia. Although the region's railways had already been offering bicycle transport for some years there was a lack of capacity to carry cycles on the region's buses, run by three different operators.

Measures used to encouraging greater cycle tourism included:

- On five existing bus routes, buses were equipped with trailers to allow transportation of bicycles on weekends over the summer season (from the end of April until the end of September);
- bicycle transportation by railway was expanded with more compartments for bicycles and two new train connections for bicycle transport on weekends in the summer season;
- better connections were made between the bus routes and the railway;
- a new tariff was introduced for bicycle transport on railways and buses.

Source:
Eltis The urban mobility observatory: http://www.eltis.org/discover/case-studies/ integrating-cycling-public-transport-system-south-moravian-region-czech#sthash. MwoELsHo.dpuf

Walking

A person who walks can be viewed as a wheel-less 'transportation unit' (Hamid, 2014). Solnit (2000) described it as a functional mobility behaviour that takes a person between two sites. However, walking can also become more than an automatic physical activity (Alfonzo, 2005). For Solnit (2000), the ideal walking is when the walking turns to a 'state in which the mind, the body, and the world are aligned' (Solnit, 2000: 5). In the context of tourism, walking can serve both definitions, first as a functional mobility mode and second as a deep and meaningful experience. However, it is important to note that the two definitions are not mutually exclusive.

Walking is very popular leisure activity, in Germany, it is estimated that about 60% of the population hike sometimes (Statista, 2015). In the US, 30 million people participate in hiking activity (about 10% of the population) (Statista, 2014). Table 1.6 showed that for those cities that collected data on walking as part of passenger transport modes, walking's share of all passenger transport ranged from lows of 12% (Bogotá, Colombia) and 18% (Sydney, Australia) to highs of 47% (Paris, France) and 35% (Delhi, India).

In terms of tourist walking in urban destinations, a study of Manchester in the UK indicated that about 30% of tourists walked in the city while staying there (Thompson & Schofield, 2007). When analysis has been combined with use of public transportation, the percentage of walking (and public transport use) rose to 60% of visitors to Munich, Germany (Le-Klähn et al., 2015). However, the two studies were conducted in different destinations and periods and therefore are not directly comparable.

Creating engaged tourists

The concept of the 'tourist gaze' (Urry, 2002) focuses on the visual dimension and the differentiation of the tourist experience from ordinary life. This 'gaze', according to Urry (2002), creates a distance between tourists and locals that is filled by socially constructed images. The walking tourist provides a challenge for this concept. First, walking involves more than the visual sense. Hamid (2014) argued that three different senses are activated while walking: seeing, hearing and touching. To these three senses we can easily add the sense of smell and in some cases – taste. Furthermore, there is no differentiation between walking as an everyday practice and as a tourist behaviour, the physical exercise is the same. Hence, walking, together with cycling and other forms of more immersive mobility, can be viewed as an alternative to the appreciable tourist gaze, creating an engaged tourist that not only uses the 'gaze' of the destination but 'experiences' it first-hand.

Walking and cycling, as physical activities, relates to a potentially more meaningful tourist experience than passive traveling by motorised transportation means as active participation can contribute to a greater sense of engagement with the environment and people within it. Furthermore, walking can support a sense of authenticity because it can engage all the senses. For example, Ujang and Muslim (2014) found that the engaged walking urban tourists developed a sense of place attachment to the destination. Similarly, Kyle *et al.* (2003) identified relationships between hiking and place attachment.

The walkable city 'supports and encourages walking, by providing for pedestrian comfort and safety, connecting people with varied destinations within a reasonable amount of time and effort, and offering visual interest in journeys throughout the network' (Southworth, 2005: 248; see Forsyth 2015 for a discussion of different notions of walkability). When a city is not walkable, because of comfort or security concerns, many tourists may not enjoy walking. Rotem-Mindali and Shemesh (2013), for example, reported that about 10% percent of the tourists that participated in their study did not enjoy walking in Tel Aviv. However, the notion of what constitutes a walkable destination, or at least satisfying walking in a destination, may vary with market segment. Timothy and Boyd (2015), for example, argued that well maintained trails be may favoured by the majority of travellers, but not necessarily by wilderness hikers. These two examples nevertheless suggest that the tangible dimensions of the walking facilities influence walking experience, both in urban settings and natural surroundings (Pikora *et al.*, 2003; Ewing *et al.*, 2006).

Physical dimensions and facilities for walkable urban destinations

Ujang and Muslim (2014) summarised the physical criteria for a walkable urban tourism city. Based on their study in Kuala Lumpur, Malaysia, they identified accessibility, connectivity, comfort, safety, attractiveness and pleasantness as leading criteria. Connectivity refers to the continuation of the sidewalks and proximity to transit points and public transportation. Comfort is defined as the minimisation of effort needed to perform walking and, in the context of urban tourism, it refers to pedestrian facilities (such as benches and shades), the physical condition of pavements, walking routes signage and the ability to walk freely with less obstruction. Pleasantness of walking and attractiveness refer to aspects of touristic appeal, such as atmosphere, vibrant surroundings, attractive visual appearance, cultural heritage and diversity of people and activities.

Similar criteria were found in an experimental study that identified the predictors for walkability decisions in Japan (Samarasekara *et al.*, 2011). According to this study, safety, comfort, shades and visual appearance can be perceived as positive cues for walking decisions. The experiment yield two more variables that positively predict walking decisions. The first is the potential for activity and the second is the potential for exploration. However, these two predictors are intangible and thus cannot be directly included as physical dimensions of walkability.

Cities, as walking spaces, were developed for their citizens around two forms of walking facilities – streets and what Solnit (2000: 177) described as 'anti-streets', meaning parks, gardens and promenades. While the 'streets' reflect everyday life and before the 18th century were seldom used for pleasure, the 'anti-streets' were, from the mid-19th century on, built solely for the pleasure and recreation of the citizens and designed to reflect a high-class aesthetic (Solnit, 2000). However, this division is increasingly breaking down in many urban environments as streets become designed to accommodate cycling, walking and the provision of greenspace, as cities attempt to become more sustainable by reducing carbon footprints and create attractive living environments. Nevertheless, the reduction of road capacities to increase pedestrian areas is an extremely challenging and under-utilised transport strategy in many parts of the world. For example, in Turkey, as in many other countries, many local governments believe that restrictions on traffic access may have a negative effect on local businesses. However, in contrast, the city of Eskisehir has transformed a number of its main roads in the city centre into tram-only or pedestrian-only corridors. The main city centre corridor is now open only to pedestrians and the street tram, while the streets running along the banks of the rehabilitated Porsuk River have also been closed to motorised traffic. As a result of the closures and the introduction of new street infrastructure, both the tram-only corridor and the riverside pedestrian streets have become major destinations, attracting shoppers, tourists and students from the two universities in the city. This has gone hand-in-hand with the opening of several cafes and restaurants, radically altering the face of the city centre and improving its overall attractiveness. The creation of pedestrian-only road corridors in retail areas can also be managed by restricting access to delivery vehicles to early morning periods (Quak & de Koster, 2009). For example, one of the main pedestrian streets in Stockholm, Drottninggatan, which is also a major tourist shopping area, manages its deliveries in this way.

Insight 3.9: Combining Hiking and Trains in the Gorges de la Loire, France

Since 2000 the Local Committee for Hiking of Haute-Loire and the National Federation of Hiking have been trying to encourage greater integration and cooperation between hiking and the regional train of the Auvergne in the Loire, France. This has been done with goals of both enhancing tourist mobility and improving destination image and has been undertaken in cooperation with five communities of joined municipalities, the Urban Community of Le Puy en Velay, local authorities of Haute Loire and the Etablissement Public Loire. Hiking trails have been redesigned so that they are closer to the eight local train stations, with both the regional train and the walking trails running along the banks of the river Loire.

The idea of the project was to encourage hikers to reach the starting point of their hikes without using their cars. The long-term goal is to establish a route on which people could hike from one station to another in one afternoon, with the total route taking eight or nine days. An additional objective of the project is to increase the occupancy of local accommodation facilities, via encouraging both local visitors and domestic and international tourists. An information strategy has been central to the project. In the train stations, signage indicates the hiking trails directly guides hikers to the beginning of the trail.

The significant increase in hiking in the gorges of the Loire is evidenced by service providers and the Tourist Information Centres of the area and has also contributes to an increase in patronage of the line TER Auvergne Saint Etienne – Le Puy-en-Velay as well as tourism development in the region. Further discussion of inter-modal schemes can be found in Chapters Four and Five.

Sources:
Eltis The urban mobility observatory: http://www.eltis.org/discover/case-studies/combining-train-and-hiking-paths-gorges-loire-france#sthash.Acb8yMrp.dpuf

Physical dimension and facilities for walkable natural settings

Physical dimensions and facilitation of walking at natural settings are often regarded as visitor management issues. Frost and Laing (2015) identified three essential components: the first is the level of access, if the walking trail is open to anyone or is limited, to protect the environment and/or the visitors. An additional aspect of access is linked to physically challenged people and the barriers they face in engaging in outdoor activities. The second criteria addresses protection (or safety) where visitors may need to be protected from dangers while walking, including falls and land slips. In addition, the natural surrounding has to be protected from damage by visitors. The third component is the interpretation that can help provide meaning and understanding for visitors from their walking experience.

Learning from a sample of on-site visitors in a natural park, Pan and Ryan (2007) identified a number of physical facilities and infrastructure that assisted the walking experience, among them were clear directional signage (with an accurate walking time indicators), good condition and uncrowded hiking trails and emergency communication facilities along the trail. Interestingly, they also commented on the importance of clean toilet facilities. This kind of infrastructure is rarely included in the study of walking spheres, urban or natural, despite it's significant importance. An exceptional case is a study from the Sultanate of Oman, where a GIS study was conducted as a part of governmental policy to improve the facilities for tourists. The focus was to improve the accessibility and service that is provided by public toilet facilities (Langer & Car, 2014). However, this dimension is likely to get more important as populations age.

Insight 3.10: Walkability and Visitor Attractions: The Case of Montreal, Quebec

The events and attractions of the city of Montreal in Quebec, Canada, attracted about 27 million visitors in 2014, of which 9 million people stayed in the city at least one night (Montreal Tourism Organization, 2015). These visitors and tourists were added to the local population of 1.6 million people that live, shop, eat and visit the points of interest in Montreal. Travelling around the city requires a good transport network and sufficient conditions for walking. Theoretically, more accessible attractions should attract higher numbers of visitors.

This case study aims to explore the links between accessibility (by walking) and the number of visitors to attractions in Montreal. It indicates patterns and trends and also presents how the shortcomings of current sets of data limit our knowledge regarding the contribution of walkability to urban tourism. Therefore, future directions and recommendations are presented as well.

Direct estimation of the number of visitors to urban attractions

The exact numbers of visitors to urban attractions in Montreal were provided by the Montreal Tourism Organization (2016). This database includes information on visitation to Montreal's attractions. Some of the major attractions of the city, such as Mont-Royal or the Underground City, are excluded from the list while others that were included attract only a very limited audience (for example, Musée Stewart had 17,000 visitors in 2014). As a consequence, only 18 attractions were included in the list, all of them were located in the urban area of Montreal, and attracted more than 50,000 visitors in 2014.

Indirect estimation of the number of visitors to urban attractions

To address the popular visitor attractions in Montreal, including the ones that were excluded from the 'Montreal list', the top attractions of the TripAdvisor application were also considered, using the numbers of reviews as a proxy for popularity. Three conditions were employed to put together a list of TripAdvisor top attractions:

(1)   to be on the first page of the top attraction for Montreal;
(2)   to reflect a physical location (and not the offer of a 'guided tour' for example);
(3)   to have more than 500 reviews, for eliminating biases that are caused by small number of reviews.

Eighteen attractions met all these conditions, but interestingly, only seven of these were also included in the 'Montreal list'.

Walkability scores

The Walkscore.com application was used for indicating a walkability points of each of the attractions, from both lists. This application (available at https://www.walkscore.com/) provides a numeric index, between 0–100 to any location, based on the walking possibilities for dining, shopping, daily errands, schools, parks, culture and entertainment. All analyses and calculations were done in March 2016, and reflect the information that was accessible at that time.

Results

Tables 3.2 and 3.3 present the attractions from Montreal's list and TripAdvisor's list alongside the numbers of visitors and the number of reviews respectively, and Walkscore points. Seven attractions are present in both tables. No correlation was found between Walkscore points and the number of visitors (Figure 3.2) but the correlation between Walkscore points and the number of reviews (Figure 3.3) formed a defined U-shape curve. Both figures suggest that very popular and unpopular attractions alike share high Walkscore points. In the case of TripAdvisor reviews, both less popular and very popular visitor attractions share higher Walkscore points than mid-popular ones. Both figures show that the most popular attractions are also very walkable.

Discussion

The scattered pattern of Figure 3.2 together with the U-shape curve of Figure 3.3 suggest that for a single attraction, the assumption of 'more walkability – more visitors' could be misleading. The results show that high walkability is also associated with less popular visitor attractions. This could happen when visitors can walk easily from one attraction to the other, and as a consequence select to visit only a few attractions. In other words, walkability may cause a cannibalisation effect. However, it is important to note that even if the walkability cannibalisation is

Table 3.2 Montreal Tourism Organization list of attractions (Montreal list)

	Attractions (Montreal's List)	# of visitors	Walkscore
1	Atrium Le 1000 de La Gauchetière	86,159	100
2	Basilique Notre-Dame	538,514	98
3	Casino	816,779	24
4	Centre Bell	2,132,880	95
5	Centre canadien d'architecture	65,900	99
6	Cosmodôme	131,361	66
7	Biodôme	832,835	58
8	Jardin botanique	742,692	68
9	Planétarium	281,832	97
10	Maison Saint-Gabriel	99,569	69
11	Marché Bonsecours	699,863	98
12	Musée Marguerite Bourgeoys	169,355	100
13	Musée McCord	125,257	100
14	Musée d'art contemporain	261,979	100
15	Musée des beaux-arts	1,009,648	100
16	Parc olympique	213,150	52
17	Pointe-à-Callière	350,910	98
18	Vieux-Port de Montréal	6,265,614	98

Table 3.3 TripAdvisor's Montreal Top Attractions (TripAdvisor list)

	Attractions (TripAdvisor)	TripAdvisor # of reviews	Walkscore
1	Basilique Notre-Dame	7810	98
2	Biodôme	2695	49
3	Cathedral of Marie-Reine-du-Monde	545	100
4	Centre Bell	761	94
5	Jardin botanique	3930	68
6	Jean-Talon Market	636	98
7	Lieu Historique National du Canal-de-Lachine	508	98
8	McGill University	548	99
9	Mont Royal	4462	28
10	Musée des beaux-arts	2099	100
11	Notre-Dame-de-Bonsecours Chapel	681	97
12	Old Montreal	6290	100
13	Pointe-à-Callière	912	98
14	Rue ste. – Catherine	1677	97
15	Rue St-Paul	648	98
16	St Joseph Oratory of Mont Royal	2352	82
17	Underground city	534	100
18	Vieux-Port de Montréal	1026	98

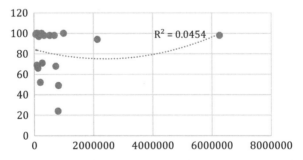

Figure 3.2 The correlation between number of visitors (*x* axis) and Walkscores (*y* axis) based on the Montreal Tourism Organization's list of attractions

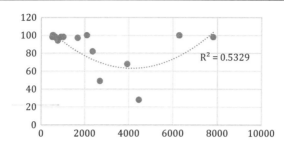

Figure 3.3 The correlation between number of reviews (x axis) and Walkscore (y axis) based on TripAdvisor list of top things to do in Montreal

happening, it does not harm the destination as a whole, because the aggregate number of visitors in the destination remained the same.

Some of the attractions have a resilience to the supposed cannibalisation effect. The Old Port (Vieux-Port), Musée des beaux-arts and Centre Bell lead the Montreal list (Table 3.2) both in walkability points and number of visitors. But, their number of visitors does not necessarily reflect a 'typical' spontaneous walking visitor. Centre Bell is home for many large events, while the Port is the home of the Cirque du Soleil entertainment group and the art museum attracts many organised groups and school field trips.

In the context of TripAdvisor reviews (Table 3.3), Old Montreal and the cathedral of the Notre-Dame are both walkable attractions that lead the number of reviews. The number of visitors to the cathedral (Table 3.2) refers only to guided tours and not to independent visitors. The result is that this number is probably biased downwards and does not reflect the actual number of visitors. In this case, the high number of review is used as a proxy for the 'real' number of visitors. Old Montreal and the Cathedral are both iconic symbols of the city, located in its centre and their walkable advantages are outputs of their importance rather than the cause of their popularity. The city and its services were developed around them, preserving their centrality and strengthening their already high walkability.

These examples demonstrate the shortcomings of existing databases. The number of visitors includes event attendees, school field trips and local visitors. The two former groups are less affected by walkability. The TripAdvisor reviews could possibly be used as a proxy for the number of independent visitors, but they are inaccurate due to the nature of the TripAdvisor application, while other forms of attendees are not precluded from assigning a review. Another weakness deals with the Walkscore application. It was planned for the use of locals and, as a result, focuses on everyday activities which are less relevant to tourists. The case study nevertheless indicates the importance of walkability analysis to urban destinations. The existing databases portrays a partial analysis of the links between walkability and popularity of attractions regarding visitations and number of reviews. Walkability does not always bring popularity for a single attraction. The reasons for these results and the implications for the destinations are require further research and the development of appropriate databases, including the number of independent visitors and a Walkscore index for tourists.

Sources:
Montreal Tourism Organization: http://www.tourisme-montreal.org/Montreal-Tourism/Toolkit
Walkscore.Com, About Walk score: https://www.walkscore.com/about.shtml.

Chapter Summary and Conclusion

This chapter has discussed tourist use of public transport at destinations. Therefore, this is primarily transport for short distances and brief travel periods. The first part of the chapter explored the factors that drive tourist mode choice at destinations. These included: visitor characteristics, trip characteristics, destination features, travel motivations and mode quality evaluations. The chapter then examined various modes of public transport. An important element of this analysis is that there are substantial gaps in the knowledge of visitor use of public transport, with studies often conducted in isolation if they are conducted at all. Most knowledge is instead therefore usually based on individual case studies rather than more detailed statistical analysis.

Other significant and emerging issues include the impact of new technologies and apps on transport behaviour. Companies such as Uber are an obvious example but there are a range of new self-driving technologies that will also likely have considerable impact; some of these will be discussed in Chapter 6. Also of importance from a sustainability perspective is the growing role of cycling and walking as transport options for tourists. As noted, some destinations and hotels are now providing cycle services to guests to encourage usage and act as a point of differentiation. While walkability of destinations is partly a function of design and the nature of the built environment other important factors include perceptions of safety and security and the provision of appropriate information. Indeed, these factors apply to all tourist use of public transport. We will return to several of these issues in Chapter 5 which discusses the marketing, management and planning of public transport for tourists, as well as issues of pricing and potential conflicts between locals and visitors. Prior to that, the next chapter will examine long-haul use of public transport by tourists.

Further Readings

On public transport and tourism at destinations in general see

Antoniou, C. and Tyrinopoulos, Y. (2013) Factors affecting public transport use in touristic areas. *International Journal of Transportation* 1 (1), 91–112.
Le-Klähn, D.-T. and Hall, C. M. (2015) Tourist use of public transport at destinations – a review. *Current Issues in Tourism* 18 (8), 785–803.
Reilly, J., Williams, P. and Haider, W. (2010) Moving towards more eco-efficient tourist transportation to a resort destination: The case of Whistler, British Columbia. *Research in Transportation Economics* 26 (1), 66–73.

On rail and mass transit see

Chang, H.H. and Lai, T.Y. (2009) The Taipei MRT (Mass Rapid Transit) tourism attraction analysis from the inbound tourists' perspective. *Journal of Travel and Tourism Marketing* 26 (5–6), 445–461.

On buses see

Guiver, J., Lumsdon, L., Weston, R. and Ferguson, M. (2007) Do buses help meet tourism objectives? The contribution and potential of scheduled buses in rural destination areas. *Transport Policy* 14 (4), 275–282.
Lumsdon, L.M. (2006) Factors affecting the design of tourism bus services. *Annals of Tourism Research* 33 (3), 748–766.

On cycling see

Gössling, S. (2013) Urban transport transitions: Copenhagen, City of Cyclists. *Journal of Transport Geography* 33, 196–206.

On walking see

Forsyth, A. (2015) What is a walkable place? The walkability debate in urban design. *Urban Design International* 20 (4), 274–292.
Southworth, M. (2005) Designing the walkable city. *Journal of Urban Planning and Development* 131 (4), 246–257.

On potential low carbon transport futures in urban areas see

Corazza, M. V., Guida, U., Musso, A. and Tozzi, M. (2015) A European vision for more environmentally friendly buses. *Transportation Research Part D: Transport and Environment*, doi:10.1016/j.trd.2015.04.001
Kamga, C. (2015) Emerging travel trends, high-speed rail, and the public reinvention of U.S. transportation. *Transport Policy* 37, 111–120.
Mittal, S., Dai, H. and Shukla, P.R. (2016) Low carbon urban transport scenarios for China and India: A comparative assessment. *Transportation Research Part D: Transport and Environment* 44, 266–276.

4 Long-Distance and Inter-Destination Public Transport

Introduction

The term 'public transport' is usually associated more with local transport than with long-distance trips. In Europe, for example, only less than 2% of train trips are international or long distance trips (Eurostat, 2015). The United States National Household of Travel Survey, 2001–2002 (US Department of Transportation, 2002) pointed that 90% of long distance travel (greater than 50 miles) is by car, and the rest by plane (7%), bus (2%) and train (1%). This situation is different in other places. In Japan, for instance, 40% of long distance business trips and 10% of leisure long distance trips are undertaken by train (Ministry of Land, Infrastructure, Transport and Tourism, Japan, 2010). A report in the UK estimates that 30% of adults use long-distance train services each year (Department for Transport, UK, 2015). These figures are significant as they suggest that it is possible to develop more sustainable forms of long-distance tourism mobility away from reliance on place and private vehicles.

One of the reasons for a modal shift towards the use of public transport in long distance travel is the factor of distance itself. In the US, even with its limited use of public transport in this context, the median distance for long distance bus travel was 462 km, compared to the corresponding median distance for car travel (300 km) (US Department of Transportation, 2002). In Japan, the car is preferred until 300 km journeys and then trains to 700 km; for longer distances, the Japanese travellers prefer planes. The distance of travel is related to another explanation for modal shift: time. In Italy, for example, 71.2% of High Speed Rail (HSR) users along the Rome–Naples corridor stated that their main reason for choosing HSR is the reduced travel time (Cascetta *et al.*, 2011). When British users were asked why they prefer trains for their long distance travels, 42% of them claimed that this is the fastest way of travelling (Department for Transport (UK), 2015). This explanation was also used by South Africa as the major reason to prefer trains over other transport modes for long distance travel. 'Even in the poorer provinces of Limpopo and Eastern Cape, travel time was mentioned by more households than costs' (Transport Department, South Africa, 2014: 93).

Nevertheless, as noted below, good infrastructure for public transport that shortens the time of travel as well as providing comfort for the traveller is essential for modal shift over longer distances in which trains are competing with planes. In terms of some of the market characteristics of long distance public transport the UK Department of Transport (2015) reports that 48% of long-distance train travellers live in higher income households. In the US the urban population is more prone to use public transport for long distance travel than those living in rural areas (Department of Transportation (US), 2002), while the Japanese Ministry of Land, Infrastructure, Transport and Tourism (2010) highlights the leading share of business-related trips over other segments of long distance travellers. Public transport therefore already appears to be popular for business tourism, however, its penetration in the long distance leisure tourism is not as strong. In the case of the latter, the cost of travel (Department for Transport (UK), 2015), attitudes towards private vehicles and personal convenience are all major factors in limiting the uptake of public transport.

There are also substantial variations between countries in the use of the train for long-distance travel, for example. In the EU the number of international passenger-kilometres travelled by French passengers in 2009 was, at 9983 million passenger-kilometres, more than double that for Germany (4162 million pkm), which in turn recorded a figure that was more than twice that of the UK (1641 million pkm). When passenger data is normalised to express passenger volumes in relation to population France, Sweden and Denmark register the longest average distances travelled on national railways in 2009, each of these countries averaging more than 1000 pkm per inhabitant, while Austria, France, Luxembourg and Belgium had the highest levels of international travel by train (Eurostat, 2012). These variations are potentially the result of a number of factors: the location of international borders, international business travel and commuting, access to transport infrastructure and the transport culture of each country. This chapter reviews some of the issues that arise with respect to long-distance travel by public transport, primarily in relation to travel to destinations. As with the previous chapter, this is undertaken via a review of the major public transport modes.

Plate 4.1 Eastside entrance to London St. Pancras Station. London St Pancras is the terminus for East Midlands Trains services from London to Derby, Leicester, Nottingham and Sheffield, and for Eurostar's trains to Paris, Brussels and Lille. Thameslink trains call at platforms beneath the main station and travel south to Gatwick Airport and Brighton and north to Luton Airport Parkway for Luton Airport and Bedford. Southeastern high-speed domestic services to Kent also run from the station with the coastal resort of Margate the furthest terminus. The station is unusual for the UK as all signage is in English and French.

Railways

Tourists' choice of transport mode is related to their spatial extent of visit (Duval, 2007; Lumsdon & Owen, 2004). Tourists travelling to multiple regions tend to use a private mode (Masiero & Zoltan, 2013). Worldwide, trains and buses carry only a small portion of total holiday journeys (see Figures 2.2 and 2.3). However, the development and extension of train connections, particularly high-speed rail (HSR) systems, plays an important role in stimulating inter-city travels (Hall, 2009; Masson & Petiot, 2009; Ryder, 2012; Wang *et al.*, 2012; Wang *et al.*, 2013; Xie, 2013) and replacing other modes such as plane and private car. For trips less than 150 km, HSR has little advantage over conventional trains and especially cars, which give greater flexibility and easier door-to-door connectivity. For distances between 150 km and 400 km, passengers reach their end destination faster with HSR than by travel on highways. Between 400 km and 800 km, HSR is the fastest mode for personal travel, being faster than both air and road travel in terms of door-to-door journey times (Yin *et al.*, 2015). Beyond 800 km, air travel is faster (Pepy & Perren, 2006; Chen & Hall, 2011). According to Hall (2009), the competitive range of HSR could even extend up to 1500 km at speeds of 350 km/h. Indeed, time is highly significant no matter what form of long-distance rail travel is selected. For example, time was the main reason given for using the train for long-distance travel in the UK (see Insight 4.1), while in South Africa for 32.6% of households travel time is the biggest determinant of modal choice. Other factors include the cost of travel (26.1% of households), flexibility (9.2% of households) and safety from accidents (8.7% of households) (Transport Department, 2014).

Hall (1991) compared the time differences between HSR and air travel in terms of door-to-door journeys. According to Hall (1991) in a city-centre to city-centre HSR journey, travellers are assumed to be able to reach the train station in 15 minutes and then the train in another five minutes; at the other end, 15 minutes are allowed to reach the final destination. For air, the model is based on a 45 minute journey to the airport and another 60 min for check-in and waiting time; at the destination airport, five minutes are calculated to exit the terminal and another 45 minutes to arrive at the final destination. The total access and waiting time is thus modelled at 35 minutes by rail and 155 minutes by air. On this basis, the break-even distance between HSR and air is 530 km for a 200 km/h high-speed train or 960 km for a 300 km/h service (Hall, 1991; see also Albalate *et al.*, 2015).

The speed of HSR creates a situation in which existing traffic is substituted (there is a shift from other modes to HSR) and new traffic is generated (trips that were previously not taken). Both of these scenarios have implications for sustainability, especially in relation to changes in the structure of transport and other emissions. However, the volume of traffic substituted to and generated by HSR is highly case specific (Yin *et al.*, 2015).

In the case of Spain the modal share of rail on the Madrid to Seville corridor after two years of operation of the Spanish high speed train (AVE: Alta Velocidad Española) rose from 14% to 51% (includes both AVE and traditional rail), while the market share of aviation decreased from 40% to 13%, and road journeys (bus and car) fell from 44% to 36% (Givoni, 2006). Of those who chose HSR, some 32% switched from air, 25% from car, 14% from existing rail services and 26% were new passengers whose journeys were a result of AVE (Vickerman, 1997). In the case of France and Japan, the volume of traffic generated by HSR was far greater than expected (Yin *et al.*, 2015). For example, on France's Paris–Lyon line, passenger numbers reached 19.2 million in 1985, this was an increase of 7 million relative to 1980, and higher than the forecast increase of 5.9 million and, of which, 49% was newly generated traffic. Similarly, in Japan, passenger numbers exceeded forecasts by 20% in the first year of operation of the Sanyo line (Osaka–Hakata) (Yin *et al.*, 2015). In contrast, passenger numbers fell short passenger numbers fell short of expectations in Germany, Taiwan and South Korea for reasons related to spatial and urban structure (Germany); the existence of extensive toll-free inter-city highways (Germany – in comparison France has many tolled highways); poor integration with other transport modes (Taiwan), as well as external factors such as changes in the location of firms over the time of project development (Taiwan) (Vickerman, 1997; Givoni, 2006; Yin *et al.*, 2015).

Compared to other modes, the HSR offers the best compromise between travel time, comfort, safety and reliability and thus makes it attractive to travellers. The competitive range of HSR may be even greater because of its comfort and convenience for business travellers, extending up to a 4.5 hour train journey (Hall, 2009), and in some cases even beyond. In Europe HSR has become an important part of city-to-city travel (Delaplace, 2012; Delaplace & Dobruszkes, 2015). Bullock *et al.* (2014) in a World Bank study of HSR in China reported that as of October 1, 2014, over 2.9 billion passengers are estimated to have taken a trip in a China HSR train, with traffic growing from 128 million in 2008 to 672 million in 2013, which represents about 39% growth per annum since 2008. In 2013, China HSR carried slightly more HSR pkm (214 billion) than the rest of the world combined. This represented about 2.5 times the HSR pkm of Japan, the second largest country in terms of HSR traffic. As Bullock *et al.* (2014: 1) state, 'These are substantial numbers for a system that is still in its early days'. However, somewhat surprisingly, the crossover effects between tourism and HSR have not received as much empirically appraisal as may be expected given the cost of building HSR and their potential impact on tourism and other forms of economic development (Guirao & Campa, 2015).

Insight 4.1: Public Attitudes Towards, and Use of, Long-distance Train Services in the UK

An opinions and lifestyle survey undertaken in February 2015 by the UK Department for Transport (2015), provides some useful insights into

British perceptions of long-distance train travel. The study estimated that 30% of adults had used long-distance train services in the previous 12 months. Of those who had made long-distance journeys and used a train in the previous 12 months, around one in five (18%) said that they had not used a train to make any of those long-distance journeys. Twenty-two percent had used trains for all of their long-distance journeys; 11% had used trains for at least half (but not all) of those journeys; a further 11% had used a train for about half of those journeys and 37% had used a train for less than half of their long-distance journeys (Department for Transport, 2015).

Those aged 75 and older (12%) or those in routine and manual occupations (19%) were less likely to use long-distance rail services, while those living in higher income households were more likely to be long-distance rail users (48%). The most common reason for making long-distance train journeys in the previous 12 months was to visit friends or relatives (54%) a significant increase from 44% in 2012. The second most common reason given in 2015 with 28% was for days out (day trips). Approximately one in five long-distance train users said they had travelled for holidays (22%) or business (19%) (Department for Transport, 2015).

When asked why the respondents had chosen to use the train last time they made a long-distance journey, 42% stated that it was quicker by train. Exactly which mode of transport the train is quicker than was not captured, although it is likely to be in comparison to car use. Forty percent of users said that they had used a train to make their long-distance journey because it was easier and 20% said that they didn't drive, didn't want to drive or don't use a car. Fifteen percent of users said that using the train for long-distance journeys was cheaper than using the car. Ten percent of users said that a reason for using a train for long-distance journeys was that they could do other things while travelling, whilst 14% said that trains are comfortable. Other reasons given by users were that someone else had planned the journey (3%), that there is a railway station close to their home or destination (3%) or that trains were reliable and punctual (2%) (Department for Transport, 2015).

The most popular ways that users passed time on their most recent long-distance train journey included: reading books, magazines and newspapers (58%); looking at the view (52%); sending texts, making calls or sending emails for personal reasons (49%); eating or drinking

(43%); talking to other passengers for personal reasons (39%); and, using an electronic device for films, music, games or the internet (39%). A majority of users (28%) said that they had spent most time reading (Department for Transport, 2015).

When asked what the main reason was for not using a train, a quarter said that it was easier than by car or plane, 17% said that train fares were too high and 12% that it was not convenient. Eight percent of infrequent users said that their main reason for not using the train was because trains do not go where they want, while 7% said that they think it is cheaper by car or plane. When asked what improvements would encourage them to use trains to make long-distance journeys more often, the majority (64%) of infrequent users (including non-users) stated cheaper fares (Department for Transport, 2015).

In China, the HSR has facilitated travel between large cities such as Shanghai and Beijing, improving traffic accessibility and, consequently, the distribution of regional tourism resources. Furthermore, the development of inter-city railways provides accessibility to places, with which follow opportunities for people nearby the stations to open up tourism-supporting businesses (Li et al., 2013). The HSR developments are regarded as contributing to improving the quality of urbanisation in all its ecological and social dimensions has been given high priority in the 12th Five-Year Plan, which is the most important national policy document at the time of writing with respect to spatial planning and transport (Yin et al., 2015). The interrelationships between HSR and spatial structure are considered as a critical factor in urban development and are therefore significant contributors to creating the socio-technical structures within which mobility occurs. However, as noted above, one of the most significant aspects of HSR is that while the direct effects of reductions in travel time are understood, the indirect effects and externalities are not so well appreciated, yet are equally if not even more important for long-term sustainability.

One broader dimension of the contribution of HSR to sustainability is how it might exacerbate the development gap between the connected and the unconnected. Accessibility is a crucial aspect of economic development. A number of studies suggest that the disparity between connected and unconnected cities and regions tends to become larger as HSR acts to create new locational advantages for the cities and regions that are often already well connected. This therefore serves to disadvantage the cities and regions that are not so accessible and are therefore not served by the new economic and transport networks that emerge from HSR (Vickerman *et al.*, 1999). In the case of the Japanese Shinkansen (bullet train), Brotchie (1991) compared population growth, employment and economic activity in cities that had an HSR station versus those that did not and found that cities with a station did better than average, especially with respect to employment in information-based industries. Similarly, Chen and Hall (2011) studied six London-terminating long-distance railway lines two of which were HSR. Cities connected to HSR within one hour of the capital experienced a strong impact on private and knowledge-intensive activities and appeared to benefit from the spill over effects of London-based value-added activities. In contrast, cities not connected with HSR continued to focus on local service activities.

In terms of tourism HSR appears to have had a mainly positive impact on the number of visitors to the cities it serves. However, an examination of the research also suggests that it creates a great deal of turbulence in the marketplace. Table 4.1 suggests that while HSR may bring more visitors, the speed of the service also allows them to return quicker or on the same day. Therefore, the increased speed of the service means that those who may have at one time stayed overnight may now become day-trippers instead because of changes in time-budgets (Hall, 2005). Nevertheless, overall, research suggests that the reduced travel time due to the HSR enables already dominant cities to become even more competitive and further enlarge their area of influence (Yin *et al.*, 2015), especially in the case of conventions and exhibitions type tourism (de Urena *et al.*, 2010).

In China Bullock *et al.* (2014) provide some initial comparisons of passenger profiles on HSR versus ordinary trains. On the two lines studied business trips accounted for 62% of the total trips on Tianjin-Jinan HSR and 45% of the total on Changchun-Jilin HSR, percentages that were substantially higher than on the ordinary trains for the same connection (51% and 28%, respectively). Leisure travel accounted for 28% on the Tianjin-Jinan HSR line and 46% on Changchun-Jilin HSR. In comparison, leisure travel accounted for a higher proportion of passengers on the ordinary long-distance train, 37% and 58% respectively. In the case of Wuhan in China (Zhang, 2010, in Yin *et al.*, 2015) reported that HSR cut the trip time from Guangzhou to Wuhan from 11 to three hours. During Wuhan's 2010 Spring Festival 80% of visitors came from Guangzhou, the first time since 1998 that the number of tourists coming to Wuhan from other cities was higher than the number going in the other direction (Zhang, 2010, in Yin *et al.*, 2015). However, one aspect of the turbulence created by new rail systems such as HSR in a wider regional context is the capacity for switching behaviour by visitors to

Table 4.1 Impact of HSR on tourism

HSR Line	Impact
Madrid–Toledo, Spain	30% of journeys on the HSR are for tourism reasons; 70% of the tourists travelling on the train are international visitors (de Urena et al., 2010)
Paris–Lyon, France	Fewer overnight stays. Winter tourism did not seem to be affected by the TGV (Bonnafous 1987)
Atlantic, France	Several large business tourism development projects occurred in Le Mans. Conventions and trade shows began to attract national and international clients for the first time. Hotel stays increased, but there was a decrease in the average number of nights stayed. The city of Tours experienced a large increase in the number of visitors from Paris when the HSR was implemented although increase in international tourists was marginal (Masson & Petiot, 2009)
Paris–Marseille, France	The southern region benefited from an increase in short-stay travel and from an increase in travel from specific markets (young adults, seniors, high-income professionals and international travellers) (Masson & Petiot 2009)
Sanyo Shinkansen, Japan	Visitor numbers to the three prefectures along the HSR (Hiroshima, Yamaguchi, Fukuoka) increased by 7.9%, 1.3%, and 11.8%, respectively (although overnight stays did not go up proportionately), while for the outer regions, nearly half had a decrease in visitors (Shimane −6.5%; Oha −0.4%; Miyazaki −2.8%). Some cities along the Shinkansen line also saw a big drop in the number of visitors because inter-city trains did not stop there anymore (Okabe, 1980)

Source: Okabe (1980); Bonnafous (1987); Masson and Petiot (2009); de Urena et al. (2010); Yin et al. (2015).

take advantage of the new time budgets that HSR offers (Zhou et al., 2015, 2016). For example, Masson and Petiot (2009) suggested that one of the impacts of an HSR link between Spain and France on tourism activity in Perpignan, France, would be that it risked decline because of the relative attractiveness of Barcelona.

The development of the Qinghai-Tibet railway has made the destination more accessible and affordable for tourists with most claiming that they would not have visited Tibet without the train (Su & Wall, 2009). Tourists appeared to be highly interested in the scenic view along the ride. The physical comfort when travelling by train was also considered important for tourists to adjust to the high altitude. The railway is expected to boost the number of tourists to Tibet and contribute to tourism development at the destination. Similarly, the HSR was also found to influence tourists' destination choice in Spanish cities (Pagliara et al., 2015). Foreign tourists, who were less sensitive to price, preferred the HSR for more convenient access to nearby towns. On the other hand, the implementation of the Spain Pass may have contributed to this yet further studies are needed for confirmation.

The role of a good public transport connection is also essential for city-airport routes (Koo et al., 2010). Public transport, typically train, is recommended as the most suitable mode to link airports with their associated urban destinations (Shafabakhsh et al., 2014) and are integral to the development of integrated transport systems. The availability of such services can facilitate the spatial extent of visit by visitors arriving at airports. For example, over some distances HSR competes with aircraft (as noted above), while over others it is complimentary if not essential to airport success. For example, with respect to competition, the total number of journeys on the 450 km Paris–Lyon route went up by 56% between 1980 and 1985. Over the same time period the number of passengers per train rose by 151% while the number per aeroplane declined by 46% on average (van den Berg & Pol, 1998). However, in terms of integration and cooperation between different transport modes we can note that rail, light rail and HSR are extremely important feeders of airports (Vespermann & Wald, 2011). For example, Stockholm's Arlanda Airport has rail services integrated into its terminals which provide for connections for long-distance (Intercity), regional and commuter train services as well as the Arlanda Express HSR service, which does the trip to central Stockholm in 20 minutes. HSR can also provide a seamless rail–air journey connection possibility where ticketing and security structures are in place. For example, in Germany Deutsche Bahn cooperates with Lufthansa to offer code share ticketing and shared baggage handling on some shorter-distance routes into the main hub of Frankfurt (Grimme, 2007a).

The case of Deutsche Bahn cooperation with Lufthansa is a good example of intermodality, which refers to a characteristic of a transport system, which allows at least two different modes to be used in an integrated manner in a door-to-door transport chain (Grimme, 2007a). Indeed, Frankfurt International Airport receives over 20,000 long-distance train passengers a day and is one of the largest long-distance train stations in Germany by passenger volume. Short-distance trains also play an important role with 3000 passengers, visitors and employees arriving at the airport on local and regional trains during peak hours The percentage of passengers from other major German metropolitan areas using rail to Frankfurt compared to other modes of ground airport access is also significant, varying between 36% for Berlin and 83% for Hamburg (Grimme, 2007a). Some international carriers include Rail&Fly tickets in their airfares, which serves to encourage passengers to use the train for hub airport access, instead of using a feeder flight on a domestic air carrier. Some budget carriers have also included Rail&Fly tickets in their products while Deutsche Bahn have entered into code-sharing agreements with a number of airlines as well. These agreements may also be significant from a passenger's perspective as they may also be eligible to earn air miles! However, Grimme (2007a, 2007b) also notes that short-distance air services have not been completely eliminated with inter-modal products. He noted that at the time he was writing only two to three daily slot pairs had been released for alternative use at Frankfurt Airport due to the reduction in frequencies between Cologne/Bonn and Frankfurt. This compared to the four daily slot pairs that were still in use for this extreme short-distance route while between Stuttgart and Frankfurt, Lufthansa were still operating six daily flights with planes up to 150 seats. As Grimme (2007: 16) noted, 'Although theoretically a considerable amount of airport capacity could be freed up with a shift of short-haul feeder flights to high speed trains... in reality operational complexity, high upfront investments, transaction costs and passenger acceptance seem to limit the scope of the integration of air and rail'.

Furthermore, the loss of short-distance slots as a result of the development of rail/air intermodality may have unexpected rebound effects. While greenhouse gases from short-haul flights could be reduced, the question of how the released airport capacity is used becomes significant. If a slot 'previously used by a short-haul flight is used for an additional intercontinental flight, total greenhouse gas emissions are set to rise, as a long-haul flight typically emits ten to twenty times more carbon dioxide than a short-haul flight' (Grimme, 2007b: 17).

Insight 4.2: The Rail Pass

In countries or regions with well-established rail networks and high-speed rail (HSR) services, where tourists can rely on train for travelling inter-destinations, there has been substantial interest in the development of a rail pass (Bazin *et al.*, 2010). As the name suggested, a rail pass provides holders with largely unlimited access to train travel within a pre-determined period of time at a fixed price. Tourists can choose to have a pass that is valid for a continuous period of time e.g. one calendar month, or for a certain number of days within a fixed time windows e.g. any five days in one month. A rail pass can be in the form of (1) a single country pass e.g. the Spain Rail Pass and Japan Rail Pass, (2) a multi-country pass e.g. the Eurail Global Pass or the Select Pass (for a selected number of neighbouring countries such as France-Germany-Italy) and (3) a regional pass e.g. the JR Hokkaido Pass and the JR West Pass (Japan). The rail pass enables travel on HSR such as the TGV (France), ICE (Germany) or the Shinkansen (Japan); yet often the fastest vehicles are not included. In most countries, the rail pass covers only rail travel. However, in some cases e.g. the Japan Rail Pass and the Swiss Rail Pass, pass holders are also given access to other public transport modes like buses and ferries (Table 4.2).

Table 4.2 Benefits and disadvantages of a rail pass

Benefits	Disadvantages
• Flexible travel dates and routes • Cost savings compared to combined point-to-point tickets • Discounts for group travel and for the young travellers (under 26 years old) • Other benefits include special offers by partner hotels, attractions and other public transport operators	• Need to purchase in advance, before arriving at the destination • Reservations are often required for travelling on high-speed trains (sometimes with fees) • Do not allow rides on the fastest trains: no access to the Eurostar for the Eurail Pass holders or to the Nozomi by the Japan Rail Pass

The pass may not be more economical than the total price of all single trips, if those were bought in advance at promotional fares. However, it does let travellers change their travel dates and routes (within the time frame) at the last minutes. In any cases, travelling by train in Europe has been made easy and convenient by the extensive and highly developed rail networks throughout the continent. Table 4.3 illustrates an example of a train tour through nine cities in five countries (with the fastest option). The prices shown are for full flexible tickets, with which tourists can change the travel dates (with or without fees) (€705.50 in total). Tourists can book the tickets separately or go for a rail pass such as the Eurail Global Pass (e.g. 689€ for 10 days within two months, 28 countries included).

The rail pass has been implemented widely in Europe, yet there is a need for a better integration of the product with related services (Bazin

Table 4.3 Some train routes in Europe and their relative costs

No.	Route	Distance (km)	Duration (hour)*	Operator	Train**	Price (€)***
1	Madrid to Barcelona	620	2:30	Renfe	AVE	125.9
2	Barcelona to Paris	1037	6:30	Renfe-SNCF	Renfe-SNCF HSR	109
3	Paris to Brussels	320	1:42	Thalys International	Thalys	60
4	Brussels to Frankfurt	400	3:05	Deutsche Bahn	ICE	124
5	Frankfurt to Munich	400	3:10	Deutsche Bahn	ICE	101
6	Munich to Venice	530	6:50	Deutsche Bahn	EC	92.6
7	Venice to Florence	260	2:05	Trenitalia	Frecciarossa	49
8	Florence to Milan	275	1:32	Trenitalia	Frecciarossa	44

*Fastest train option.
**All except the EC (route 6) are HSR.
***Full fare (no promotion), standard class, checked in January 2016 for travel in March 2016.

et al., 2010). The HSR can influence tourists' choice of destination with cities served by the HSR network having a higher chance to be visited (Pagliar *et al.*, 2015). Destination management of cities or places along the network should also consider possible ways to promote their attractions and develop supporting services.

Bus and Coach

Buses offer a more flexible form of long-distance transport given that they are able to use the road network and are therefore able to reach a larger number of locations as rail. For example, in Italy long distance coach services have long played a significant role in connecting the most dispersed part of the country to major destinations. In 2012 the industry supplied more than 88 million bus-km, serving about 2.6 billion pkm (Beria *et al.*, 2014). However, the capacity of bus services to move people is often restricted by a range of factors including access restrictions and limitations on competition in some regions, although such limits may be for the purpose of ensuring that other transport modes such as rail can continue to be economic. In the EU the actual passenger occupancy rate is about 20–40% for long-distance bus travel and 25–50% for railway travel (Andersson & Ögren, 2013). Although buses are integral to public transport in most regions of the world their use by tourists is often primarily within destinations rather than for more long-haul travel. Long-distance bus transport tends to be used by the elderly and young people (Gianini, 2012). In a study of long distance bus users in Zibo City, China, convenience had the greatest influence on traffic mode choice. In a study of long-distance bus services in Sri Lanka, Rambukwella and Santoso (2015) report that the five most influential factors influencing customer satisfaction were cleanliness, travel time taken, safety of driving, seat availability and on-board security.

The issue of convenience is also a major theme in Klein's (2009, 2014, 2015) research on inter-city travel in the US. As Klein notes after almost 50 years of decline in ridership as a result of competition with other modes and growing private car ownership, intercity buses have become one of the fastest growing intercity transport modes in the US (see also Fischer & Schwieterman, 2011; Schwieterman & Fischer, 2012). For example, on the Northeast Corridor (between Boston and Washington, DC), intercity bus travel more than doubled between 1997 and 2007 from 3.5 million to over 7 million trips. This growth is attributed to the development of curbside intercity buses, which pick up and drop off passengers on city street corners rather than in bus terminals. The development of curbside long-distance buses also shares some of the characteristics of paratransit (see Chapter 1) as well as highlighting some of the changes that can occur to public transport as a result of technological change.

Between 2010 and 2011 alone, the departures of curbside buses grew 32% in the US although there is also overall growth in the intercity bus sector (American Bus Association (ABA), 2012). The intercity bus industry in the US is recognised as a low-cost means of travel, but is also significant for tourism. However, the relatively lower income levels of bus tourists mean that they tend to be a focus of destinations that tend to compete on price and massification. In Brazil some destinations have even limited or excluded coaches in an effort to attract drive tourism because it is regarded has having higher levels of expenditure (Lohmann et al., 2011). Interestingly, New Zealand, which has long been a focal point for coach based transport (see below), has been increasingly seeking to encourage tourists to use hire vehicles so as to generate higher returns from visitors.

According to Pantuso (2012), CEO and president of the ABA, intercity bus riders usually purchase roundtrip tickets, stay approximately 4–5 days and spend about $92 per day. Curbside intercity bus riders tend to be younger, with 73% under 35 years old: 18 to 25 year olds make up about 48% of passengers, 26 to 35 year olds make up about 25% of passengers (Pantuso, 2012). This profile also highlights the extent of online ticketing in curbside intercity buses. A study in Philadelphia of BoltBus riders found that were about half Philadelphia residents and half visitors. Seventy-seven percent of visitors spent money in restaurants or bars and 55% spent money at retail places; additionally, 44% of residents visited restaurants or bars and 39% of residents went shopping (in Collins, 2013).

One of the interesting dimensions of curbside intercity bus industry is that it is regarded as having its origins within migrant communities. The so-called 'Chinatown buses' were the first curbside carriers to emerge in the late 1990s. These companies initially served an exclusively ethnic population but quickly attracted other passengers. Within 10 years, there were 10 to 15 companies offering service between urban Chinese-immigrant enclaves in more than 25 cities, though the connections from New York to Boston, Philadelphia and Washington, DC, were the most significant routes (Klein 2009, 2015; Klein & Zitcer, 2012). In fact Chatman and Klein (2009) suggest that foreign-born residents are much more likely to use transit, carpool, walk and bicycle, particularly in their first few years of living in the US. In the American context curbside buses are also a response to a highly deregulated market, although some European countries have deregulated their markets, for example StageCoach have interests in both UK and US curbside buses, the European market retains a reasonable degree of regulation.

In the case of Europe International Road Transport Union (IRU) proposals to improve coach tourism include:

- Coherent strategy for integrating high-quality group tourism with other interests.
- Promote the use of bus only lines by tourist coaches.
- Instructions and signs for coach drivers.
- Safe, secure and accessible intermodal coach terminals.
- Safe and secure amenities for drivers and passengers.
- Group tourism marketing plans by cities in partnership with industry.

With respect to the EU a major challenge for long-distance coach travel is the complexity of EU VAT (Value Added Tax/Goods & Services Tax) tax directives under which taxation occurs where the transport takes place, proportionately in terms of distances covered. However, the EU member states have different compliance systems making the tax process extremely complicated for ticketing between countries (Mannaerts, 2014).

Buses and coaches serving integrated bus-aviation terminals offer a flexible means to ensure inter-model transfer (Vespermann & Wald, 2011). A number of cities even offer free airport transfers via public transport as a means of trying to reduce car use. In 1999, the Hotel Ticket system, which allows hotel guests to travel by urban public transport free of charge, was introduced in Basel, Switzerland. More recently, the city, in addition to a Geneva Transport Card for free public transport for hotel guests during their stay, has introduced free transfer for hotel guests from its airport. The Geneva area public transport companies provide a free transfer ticket called 'Geneva Arrival' to all air travellers. The ticket is valid for 80 minutes and can be used to travel by train (SBB), bus, tram or boat (Mouettes Genevoises). Geneva International Airport (GVA) has assumed all the costs of this free transfer ticket, which is obtained simply by pressing a button on a ticket machine in the arrival area with no need to produce proof of hotel reservation.

Tourists that travel by coach, normally in package tours, form a significant part of New Zealand's tourism industry, with around 20–25% of international visitors participating in coach tours (Becken, 2005). In part this is because of the removal of many passenger services from the New Zealand rail network over the years, but especially following deregulation of the bus and rail sector in the 1980s. In such a case coaches and pre-booked tours provide a ready way to see the country. Nevertheless, consumers of the coach tour market are not homogenous; cultural background plays a vital role tourist travel behaviour. Asian tourists tended to limit their visitation to major cities, Australian and Europeans were more geographically dispersed. A typical coach tour is characterised by high level of mobility and large number of locations. Therefore, to effectively manage the tour industry while successfully maintaining sustainability for destination development, in the longer term tourism planners need to identify different tourist segments based on cultural background and address them with corresponding strategies.

Insight 4.3: Double Collective Passenger Land Transport to Tackle Climate Change

In April 2016 the European Citizens Mobility Forum (ECMF) called for a holistic vision to reduce greenhouse gases and tackle climate change. The ECMF is an IRU initiative consisting of representatives from the EU institutions, civil society researchers and stakeholders, trade associations and business representatives from the door-to-door collective land transport chain. The ECMF urged EU decision makers to adopt the objective of doubling the use of collective land transport in the EU as the shortest and cheapest way for society to reduce the carbon footprint of passenger transport. The ECMF argued that that doubling the use of collective land transport modes in the EU would result in at least 500 million tonnes less CO_2 emitted by 2025 and 10% less car traffic less per year. For every European, it would represent only 1 more trip out of 20 made by bus or train instead of the private car.

Gesine Meissner, a coordinator for the Transport Committee of the European Parliament and member of the ECMF, said 'Decarbonising transport is a challenge one has to take up from many different angles, the development of cleaner vehicles or incentives through road pricing for example. But we should not forget obvious instruments like simply transporting passengers together instead of everyone using their private car. A very simple mean of increasing fuel efficiency and reducing emissions'.

Source:
ECMF/IRU Press Release: https://www.iru.org/resources/newsroom/double-collective-passenger-land-transport-to-tackle-climate-change
ECMF Action Programme: https://www.iru.org/sites/default/files/2016-04/I-0336-ECMF-action-program-EN.pdf

Ferries and Waterborne Transport

Ferries are an important means of longer-distance travel and intermodality in a number of regions. The first car ferry is considered to be the Motor Princess, which was built in 1923 for the Canadian Pacific Railway Company's coastal service in British Columbia (Wergeland, 2012). Overtime, ferries have become larger in response to growth in demand for carrying car and freight transport, improved energy efficiencies as a result of oil price increases and the growth of the tourism market. Ferries are often an important part of motor travel circuits. For example, on the DFDS Seaways ferry route linking Kiel, Germany with Klaipeda, Lithuania, survey results reveal the predominant third-country passenger groups (i.e. passengers from countries other than Germany and Lithuania) on ferries sailing from Kiel to Klaipeda and back were Latvian (28%), Dutch (20%), British (14%) and Danish (12%) nationals; 86% of Latvian passengers used the ferry to travel between home in Latvia and work in Western Europe. Western European passengers comprised a diverse segment of motorised tourists using the ferry in summer to reach the Baltic States faster than by land (Povilanskas *et al.*, 2015). However, passenger services are also significant on some routes especially with respect to connecting to rail services. For example, Table 4.4 indicates the EU regions with the highest level of maritime passengers. By far the largest number of maritime passengers (almost 27 million) in 2011 was recorded for the Greek region of Attiki, which includes the port of Piraeus near Athens which is the major terminal for ferries travelling to the Greek Islands. The Italian regions with the highest number of maritime passengers were the islands of Sicilia and Sardegna which have regular ferry services to the mainland. The high numbers for Kent in the United Kingdom and the Nord-Pas-de-Calais in France reflect the high frequency of English Channel ferry crossings between the two regions. The Swedish and Finnish capital city regions of Stockholm and Helsinki-Uusimaa as well as Tallinn in Estonia are major ports for the extensive Baltic Sea ferry network, while there is also an extensive regular ferry service between Helsingborg in Sweden and Helsingør (Elsinore) in Denmark.

The Pacific North West of Canada and the United States is a major hub for tourism related ferry traffic, carrying over 44 million passengers including over 23 million on Washington State Ferries and 19 million on BC Ferries. Washington State Ferries are regarded as the state's most popular tourist attraction and the Alaska Marine Highways operate the longest ferry routes in the world (Wirtz *et al.*, 2015). The Pacific North West Economic Region (PNWER) is seeking to develop a NORPASS Integrated Ferry Pass for foot and car passengers that would allow even greater ease of mobility between the different providers so as to encourage regional interline and multi-modal tourism transportation.

Large numbers of people also use ferry services in Asia, particularly in Bangladesh, China, Japan, the Philippines and Indonesia. However, analyses of these markets are extremely limited even though the extent of ferry use is substantial given the geography of these countries. For example, the World Bank (2013) estimate that about 14 million passengers a year are traveling by inter-island shipping in Indonesia. In 2012 domestic shipping carried over 50 million passengers in the Philippines. Sixty percent of the Philippine domestic merchant fleet in 2012 or 4837 vessels, were registered for passenger service, most of which are motorbancas. In 2012 the primary routes were served by four major shipping lines operating 17 long haul vessels. The secondary routes were served by 183 Roll-on Roll-off (RORO) operated by 34 shipping companies, while there were approximately 1600 tertiary routes served by motorboats/motorbancas (Government of the Philippines, 2013).

Table 4.4 EU-27 regions with highest number of maritime passengers, 2008–11

Region	Ports with more than 200,000 passengers per year	Passengers, 2011 ('000)	Annual rate of change (%)			
			2008	2009	2010	2011
Attiki, Greece	Paloukia Salaminas, Perama, Piraeus, Rafina, Aegina (001), Rio (080), Poros Trizinias (076), Faneromeni Salaminas, Megara, Galatas Trizinias	26,946	–1.6	–3.9	–4.0	–7.2
Kent, UK	Dover	12,879	–3.4	–5.5	0.6	–3.3
Nord-Pas-de-Calais, France	Calais, Dunkerque	12,664	–2.1	–6.2	0.9	–3.1
Sydsverige, Sweden	Helsingborg, Ystad, Trelleborg, Malmö, Karlskrona	12,484	–0.8	–11.1	–6.6	0.5
Campania, Italy	Napoli, Capri, Pozzuoli, Porto D'Ischia, Sorrento, Procida, Casamicciola, Castellammare Di Stabia,Salerno, Amalfi, Positano	12,180	5.6	5.9	–0.9	–2.0
Sicilia, Italy	Messina, Palermo, Trapani, Milazzo, Favignana, Lipari, Vulcano Porto	11,679	5.1	–7.3	4.9	–19.4
Schleswig-Holstein, Germany	Puttgarden, Kiel, Dagebuell, Föhr I., Amrun I., Luebeck, Norstrand I., List/Sylt, Helgoland I., Pellworm I., Buesum, Hoernum/Sylt	11,133	–4.3	–3.1	2.5	–5.1

Stockholm, Sweden	Stockholm, Grisslehamn, Kappelskar	10,964	2.1	3.4	−11.1	0.7
Hovedstaden, Denmark	Helsingør (Elsinore), Københavns Havn, Ronne, Hundested	10,791	−0.8	−11.9	−8.3	−1.9
Sjælland, Denmark	Rødby (Færgehavn), Sjaellands Odde, Gedser, Taars, Rorvig, Kalundborg, Kragenaes	10,605	−4.6	−7.1	−1.9	−3.1
Helsinki-Uusimaa, Finland	Helsinki	10,295	4.6	1.2	8.5	5.0
Eesti, Estonia	Tallinn, Kuivastu, Virtsu, Heltermaa, Rohuküla, Patareisadam	10,108	10.5	-0.4	39.0	6.3
Sardegna, Italy	Olbia, La Maddalena, Palau, Porto Torres, Carloforte, Golfo Aranci, Portovesme, Santa Teresa Di Gallura, Calasetta	8801	−5.7	5.4	−12.0	−4.2
Calabria, Italy	Reggio Di Calabria	7704	−2.1	9.2	−10.5	−22.1
Toscana, Italy	Piombino, Portoferraio, Livorno, Porto Santo Stefano, Isola Del Giglio, Rio Marina	6934	28.5	−9.2	−19.8	3.2

Eurostat Regional Yearbook (2013) http://ec.europa.eu/eurostat/documents/3217494/5784025/KS-HA-13-001-10-EN.PDF/28921853-f4a0-4f2f-80d3-f7d1a9b4021c

Cycling

Cycling tourism can include a variety of activities, ranging from participating in cycling competition or simply an independent cycling trip to the countryside. Lamont and Buultjens (2011) segmented cycling tourists into independent cycle tourists, recreational cyclists, participatory events, passive participants and competitive cycle tourists. However, much cycling activity occurs within a destination context rather than being a form of home to destination transport. These issues are partly illustrated in Table 4.5 which shows the estimated differences between the share of population that use cycling as the main mode of transport and the estimated share of cycle holidays as a percentage of all holidays for European countries. In comparison, countries such as Australia, Canada, Korea and the US would fall in the low to low-medium demand bands (Shin *et al.*, 2011). Indeed, Chen and Cheng (2016) noted that from a sustainable mobility perspective, one major concern is that cycle tourism might generate additional car journeys, as cycle tourists often put their bikes in cars and drive to the location where their cycling will take place. In seeking to encourage use of integrated bike-rail transport services they note that cycle tourists in general are concerned about the service

Table 4.5 Demand bands for cycle tourism in Europe

Demand band	Share of population using cycling as main mode of transport	Estimated share of cycle holidays as percentage of all holidays	Countries attributed to demand band
Very high	>20%	3.7%	Netherlands
High	12–20%	3%	Hungary, Denmark, Sweden, Belgium, Germany, Finland, Austria, Switzerland
Medium-high	8–12%	2%	Slovakia, Poland
Medium	>5<8%	2%	Latvia, Czech Republic, Slovenia, France
Low-medium	>2–5%	1%	Romania, Lithuania, Serbia, Norway, Croatia, Macedonia, Italy, Estonia, Ireland, Greece, United Kingdom
Low	≤2%	0.5%	Turkey, Bulgaria, Luxembourg, Portugal, Malta, Cyprus, Spain

Source: Derived from Weston *et al.* (2012: 35).

attributes of the integrated bike-rail transport service, such as price, type of bike storage, bike storage location and service frequency.

Nevertheless, route-based and long-distance cycling can still be a significant form of tourism related transport for some locations as well as a regional development mechanism, especially in more peripheral areas (Ritchie & Hall, 1999). In North Carolina it was forecast that cycling tourism in the northern Outer Banks coastal area would generate an annual income of at least $60 million as well as 1407 jobs (both direct and indirect) (Meletiou et al., 2005). This figure is nine times greater than the initial investment on building the infrastructure. Similarly, in Ireland, the Great Western Greenway is estimated to generate a profit of over €1 million per year from cyclists (Deenihan et al., 2013), representing a payback period of only six years.

Cycling tourists vary in their background and consequently are very different in their motivations, travel behaviour and behavioural intentions, as well as their socio-demographical profiles and cycling behaviour (Kruger & Saayman, 2014; Ritchie et al., 2010). Cyclists can be grouped into different segments, e.g. based on level of involvement (Ritchie et al., 2010) or level of recreation specialisation (Chen & Cheng, 2016). Although research suggests that the level of experience is not a good criterion for market segmentation as it is not correlated with the duration of cycle trips (Lumsdon et al., 2004). However, in general, frequent or high potential cyclists are well-educated (Kruger & Saayman, 2014; Lee, 2014) and in their middle age (Gibson & Chang, 2012; Lamont & Buultjens, 2011; Lamont & Causley, 2010).

Cycling is an outdoor activity, and thus certain weather conditions may be more favourable to participation than others. Deenihan et al. (2013) reported that temperature is a decisive factor: more people in Ireland cycle when the temperature is high and rainfall is low. The findings however may be only relevant in temperate zone as cycling behaviours are also related to a range of infrastructural and cultural influences as well. Frequency of cycling is also dependent on several individual characteristics. Lee (2014) observed that monthly income was a significant predictor of cycling frequency. The author suggested low-income individual's cycle mainly for work trips and other utilitarian purposes, whereas high-income individuals cycle more for leisure and exercise. Understanding income segments is important as it is positively correlated with tourist expenditure, which is then related to trip duration (Lumsdon et al., 2004). Apparently, the longer the trip is, the more the tourist spends (and the more the destination earns). Those travelling for longer than one day tend to spend more per hour than those on day trips. As trip duration and group size are related, Lumsdon et al. (2004) suggested that increased group sizes can lead to longer trips and more spending.

Another important factor on cycling behaviour is the availability of supporting infrastructure. Lamont (2009) found that the attributes of cycling routes such as surface quality, terrain, safety and supporting infrastructure are determinants of cycle tourists' overall trip satisfaction. Safety is the top concern, thus most cyclists prefer to cycle on segregated facility or on roads with cycle lanes. Only a minority do not mind cycling on roads without any cycling facilities (Deenihan & Caulfield, 2015). Cycle tourists are even willing to make trade-offs (time and cost) to be able to cycle on segregated cycling paths or cycle lanes instead of sharing the road with other vehicles (Deenihan & Caulfield, 2015). For example, tourists are willing to increase their cycling time by approximately 100% to cycle upon a fully segregated cycling lane, and 40–50% to cycle along a road with a cycle lane, rather than along a road without cycling infrastructure. They are also willing to pay 98% and 48% more for a fully segregated lane and a road with cycle lanes respectively than for a road without cycling facilities. Differences in preferences exist between genders, with cycling facilities appearing to be more important to females than to males. Younger and male tourists were found to be more likely to choose a road without cycling facilities than older female tourists, who tend to prefer cycling on cycle lanes or a cycling facility segregated from traffic (Deenihan & Caulfield, 2015).

Insight 4.4: Cycling Tourism: EuroVelo

EuroVelo is a bicycle route network, which aims to link long-distance cycle paths in all European countries. The network has connected more than 45,000 km of existing cycle paths and is expected to cover a total distance of over 70,000 km upon completion in 2020. The EuroVelo project is coordinated by the European Cyclists' Federation (EFC) and its partners at the national and regional levels. Currently the network comprises of 14 cycle routes namely EuroVelo 1 to 13 and EuroVelo 15 with even numbers being used for east-west routes and odd numbers for north-south ones. These paths have an average length of 5373 km with the EV13 – Iron Curtain Trail being the longest (10,400 km) and the EV15 – Rhine Cycle Route being the shortest (1320 km). The network passes through many capitals and connects important historical and cultural centres. As several countries are involved, the EFC provide a guideline on route development process to ensure consistent quality of infrastructure (EuroVelo, 2011).

Potential users of the network can be both daily and holiday cyclists, therefore the roads need to be attractive, safe and comfortable for long cycling. Four principles of route development are: safety, attractiveness, coherence and directness and comfort. Most parts of the routes avoid roads with large traffic volumes and provide connections to tourist attractions in the most possible direct way. Furthermore, accessibility to public transport is important, and connections to public transport interchanges are ensured at intervals of no greater than 150 km. Bike facilities and services, rest areas, restaurants and accommodation are made available throughout the routes within bike-reachable distances.

The European Union co-funded the EuroVelo project as a part of its 'Sustainable Tourism' action and incorporated the network into the Trans-European Transport Networks (TENT-T) in December 2012 for complete and integrated development. There are many challenges to the development of sustainable cycle tourism in Europe such as the lack of high quality tracks in some countries, cost of transporting the bikes and the low participation of tourism services providers (Piket *et al.*, 2012). However, given that the bicycle industry in Europe is growing (over 20 million bicycles and ebikes were sold in 2014) (Confederation of the European Bicycle Industry (CONEBI) (2015)) and the tourism cycle market in Europe is valued at over €44 billion per annum. The EuroVelo network has a considerable economic potential. It is estimated that the network will attract 60 million annual cycle trips and generate over €7 billion of direct revenue from users (Weston *et al.*, 2012).

Sources:
Confederation of the European Bicycle Industry (CONEBI): http://www.conebi.eu/
Eurovelo: eurovelo.com or eurovelo.org

Walking

Walking to or between destinations is not an overly useful mode of transportation. The walker cannot take heavy luggage with them and travels slowly comparing to riding a horse (in pre-mechanised times) or in the contemporary period to traveling by car, train or plane. Apart from the poorest of people who have little choice in walking over long distances, the purpose of a long distance walking is found then in a different domain. Saunders *et al.* (2013) described this purpose as a personal transformation and Solnit (2000) as a search of something intangible. In the present chapter, this transformative and intangible purposes of long distance walking will be discussed by addressing two forms of long-distance walking: pilgrimage and hiking.

Pilgrimage

Pilgrimage is defined as 'a journey resulting from religious causes, externally to a holy site, and internally for spiritual purposes and internal understanding' (Barber, 1993: 1). It is one of oldest types of long-distance walking (Solnit, 2000), and pilgrimage routes have existed for hundreds and even thousands of years all over the world (Timothy & Boyd, 2015). Collins-Kreiner (2010) pointed that despite pilgrimage being a central principle in the world's major religions: Buddhism, Hinduism, Islam, Judaism and Christianity the term 'pilgrimage' could be also used to describe a secular ritual (see Hall, 2006). She claimed that contemporary tourism research has to address both religious and secular pilgrimage phenomenon, because they share the same characteristics and the boundaries between them are blurred.

Solnit (2000) showed how secular and religious pilgrimage alike draw a line between spiritual sphere and a concrete space. Both types of pilgrimage provide the intangible story with the most material details: where Buddha was born, where Jesus was believed to be crucified or alternatively, in a case of a secular pilgrimage, where a famous painter or author lived. Pilgrimage unifies mind and body, thinking and doing. Solnit argues that these materials aspects of the religious pilgrimage made some Protestants, as well as Buddhist and Jews to object pilgrimage as a kind of secular 'icon worship' (Solnit, 2000: 50).

However, religious pilgrims, unlike most secular pilgrims, perceive walking as 'work'. Solnit (2000) recalled the origins of the word 'travel' in 'travail' (French), which means work, effort and even labour pains. She described how Christian pilgrims often travelled in the Middle Ages barefoot, on their knees or with stones in their shoes to make their walking difficult and inconvenient. Other forms of intentional burdens were the carrying of heavy crosses on the backs and/or fasting during the journey. Some contemporary religious pilgrims may moderate the walking challenge and choose to use planes and cars as part of the journey (Solnit, 2000). Muslim pilgrims negotiate exhausting pilgrimage rituals in Mecca mainly by foot, but only after arriving in Mecca by planes and buses (Henderson, 2011). The situation in Jerusalem is similar, where pilgrims also arrive by planes and buses (Solnit, 2000).

One of the famous pilgrimage paths is the Camino de Santiago (also known as the Way of St. James). The primary destination of the path is a church in Santiago de Compostela, Spain, where the remains of St. James, an apostle of Jesus, were supposedly found in the 9th century. During the Middle Ages, Santiago was the third most visited pilgrimage destination in the Roman Catholic world, after Rome and Jerusalem, with a network of roads approaching it. The main road to Santiago starts in France, and takes a month to walk. Secondary routes begin in Switzerland, Belgium, the Netherlands, Germany, Portugal and other countries all over Europe (Timothy & Boyd, 2015).

Until the 1990s the roads to Santiago were relatively neglected. However, the Camino de Santiago has become popular again in recent years. More than 300,000 people now travel to Santiago each year with those travelling at least 100 km on foot, or 200 km if they have come by bicycle or on horseback, being provided with a pilgrimage official certificate for completing the trail (compostela) (Timothy & Boyd, 2015). Lois-González (2013) explained the revival of the Camino de Santiago pilgrimage route as a reaction to the hyper technological era of high-speed transport and intense communication. 'The decision to travel to Santiago on foot is strongly associated with a liminal experience...it also involves returning to the human scale of things, the relaxed contemplation of the landscape and the enjoyment of nature, becoming acquainted with cultural heritage and undergoing a powerful inner experience (whether of a religious, nature or otherwise)' (Lois Gonzales, 2013: 19–20).

Hiking

Di Felice (2014) defined hiking as all kinds of physical activities that involve walking in the countryside, the forest or the mountains along trails. The hiking experience combines both personal-oriented motivations, such as love of nature, self-reflection and happiness and place-oriented motivations such as bonding to the place, national identity and ideology. Collins-Kreiner and Kliot (2015) analysed this double set of motivations as belonging to the universalism-particularism continuum, ranging from formally detached relationships (detached from place – universalism) to personalised relationships (attached to place – particularism). In other words, the slow pace of hiking enables the hiker not only to be close to himself/herself but also to connect more deeply to place.

It is only since the development of national parks and other protected areas since the late 19th century that natural hiking trails have been developed for a range of scenic, ecological, educational, economic and health related purposes (Frost & Hall, 2009). Transportation, therefore, is not of one of the purposes for hiking in natural trails. Nevertheless, more than 100 million people all over the world use them as a mobility choice (Di Felice, 2014).

Natural trails are used to both experience and help form conservation and ecological corridors. The Pacific Crest Trail (PCT), for example, was established by the US *National Trails System Act of 1968* to conserve a strip of land 4265 km long and 1.6 km wide connecting California, Oregon and Washington. Thousand hundreds of hikers use this long trail (the longest in the US) for recreational purposes (Thomas, 2015). Trails are also utilised to formal educational purposes. School field trips and other official instructive programs are direct to develop a sense of respect and care for the environment, especially among children. Informal learning can take place in the natural surroundings via the hikers' experience (Timothy & Boyd, 2015).

Constructing trails and then serving the hikers that use them can bring employment and business opportunities for rural and poor communities along the trails (Hill *et al.*, 2006). However, Timothy and Boyd (2015) pointed out that most trails do not generate much economic impact directly, because the hikers are widely spread and spend relatively little money. This observation is also supported by the findings of Hill *et al.* (2006) on the marginal economic impact of the Mehloding Hiking and Adventure Trail on the population of the rural area in KwaZulu-Natal Province, South Africa.

Health-related issues are another reason for the growing popularity of natural trails (Timothy & Boyd, 2015). Hiking is a recommended physical activity to help improve or maintain health (Di Felice, 2014). Wolf and Wohlfarth (2014) showed how hiking activity improves both health and well-being indicators. Having said that, it is important to note that hiking can be dangerous as well. Mountain sickness, sudden cardiac death, fatigue and injuries due to extreme weather and environmental events are just part of the risks associated with hiking in natural trails (Di Felice, 2014). About half of the reported medical incidents at Yosemite National Park (2000–2009) were related to hiking activities (Boore & Bock, 2013).

Insight 4.5: Walking in the Footsteps of Abraham Through a Tempestuous region: The Abraham Path

The Abraham Path follows the trail of Abraham (also called Ibrahim or Avraham), the founding father of the main three monotheistic religions (Judaism, Christianity and Islam). The route begins in Turkey and ends in Sinai desert or Saudi Arabia. It covers more than 2000 km across 19 walkable regions, and 124 day stages (Abrahampath official website, undated), and is planned to cross eventually nearly 5000 km and ten countries in the Middle East (The World Bank, 2014). The Ibrahim trail is not a unified continuous route but follows a range of regional independent walking trails, developed and maintained by a wide range of local organisations and enthusiasts. Some sections are more readily accessible to independent travellers; others may require the assistance of a local guide (Abrahampath official website, undated).

The most recognised and structured section is located in the region of Israel, Palestine and Jordan where more than 4000 people have hiked the trail since 2008 (World Bank, 2014; Kutulas & Awad, 2016). The National Geographic magazine awarded this section as the best new walking trail (National Geographic, 2014) because it is 'a spirit-lifting hike...Here the smoke from a Bedouin camp, there an Israeli military base. Here a porcupine print, there a sacred mountain. And this sense of immersion is what makes the Abraham Path project so extraordinary – it gives travelers the chance to shape their own perspective'.

The World Bank recognised the economic and social potential of Abraham path and works with local organisations in its development. Over $2 million were invested already to fostering the path, training guides, improving homestays conditions and marketing of the path through a virtual information hub, location-based mapping, and social media. The investment is expected to generate jobs and increase incomes for the people and communities located along the path (The World Bank, 2014).

The Path is also perceived as a leverage for conflict resolution. William Ury, a world leading negotiation expert and one of the founders of the Abraham Path believes that 'the path would connect the world to the Middle East in a new way: through the combined power of Walk, Story and Hospitality'. Furthermore, he argued that when people walk together, shoulder to shoulder, heading the same direction, they cannot confront or fight each other. Hence, the path has a potential to promote understanding between people (William Ury, undated).

However, the utopic vision of the Abraham path initiative also has to face the complicated geo-political situation of Abraham's descendants. At the beginning of 2016, the northern sections of the Abraham path in Turkey, Iraq and Syria are declared as war zones and as a consequence the path is no longer active. In Palestine, travellers are advised to hire a local guide due to current political tension, and when walking in Israel, travellers are urged to use extra caution and avoid public places.

Sources:
Abraham Path official website: http://abrahampath.org/path/.

Chapter Summary and Conclusion

This chapter has discussed tourist use of public transport for long-distance travel to and between destinations. The chapter provided a review of some of the most salient issues with respect to tourist use of the various modes of public transport. As in the previous chapter, an important element of this analysis is that there are substantial gaps in knowledge of tourist use of public transport, this is particularly the case outside of Europe and, to a lesser extent North America and Australasia. China is one area where understanding of use of modes such as HSR is rapidly growing. However, other modes that are important in Asia, such as ferries and long-distance bus transport are vastly under researched despite their significance for VFR travel. Most knowledge is instead therefore usually based on individual case studies rather than more detailed statistical analysis.

The growth of HSR is generally regarded as a positive for long-distance public transport but, as the chapter noted, in some cases this means that market share is being taken from other public transport modes rather than air or car travel. Cycling and walking are not as significant as long-distance transport options for tourists as they are within destinations therefore limiting their overall contribution to sustainable mobility. However, as pointed out, this may change if appropriate intermodal transfers are available especially on rail systems. Several of these issues will be returned to in the following and final chapters. The next chapter discusses the importance of appropriate marketing, management and planning of public transport for tourists.

Further Readings

On intermodality see

Koo, T.T.R., Wu, C.-L. and Dwyer, L. (2010) Ground travel mode choices of air arrivals at regional destinations: The significance of tourism attributes and destination contexts. *Research in Transportation Economics* 26 (1), 44–53.
Vespermann, J. and Wald, A. (2011) Intermodal integration in air transportation: Status quo, motives and future developments. *Journal of Transport Geography* 19 (6), 1187–1197.

On longdistance rail and HSR see

Albalate, D., Bel, G. and Fageda, X. (2015) Competition and cooperation between high-speed rail and air transportation services in Europe. *Journal of Transport Geography* 42, 166–174.
Guirao, B. and Campa, J.L. (2015) The effects of tourism on HSR: Spanish empirical evidence derived from a multi-criteria corridor selection methodology. *Journal of Transport Geography* 47, 37–46.
Ryder, A. (2012) High speed rail. *Journal of Transport Geography* 22, 303–305.

Wang, X., Huang, S., Zou, T. and Yan, H. (2012) Effects of the high speed rail network on China's regional tourism development. *Tourism Management Perspectives* 1 (1), 34–38.

On long-distance bus services see

Capriello, A. (2014) Bus transport service provision and tourism policies: Lessons from Piedmont, Italy. *Tourism Planning & Development* 11 (2), 210–227.
Fischer, L.A. and Schwieterman, J.P. (2011) The decline and recovery of intercity bus service in the United States: A comeback for an environmentally friendly transportation mode? *Environmental Practice* 13 (1), 7–15.
IRU Smart Move Campaign, a global campaign that champions the use of buses and coaches as a clean, safe and sustainable way to travel. See https://www.iru.org/what-we-do/smart-move-campaign

On cycling and walking see

Lamont, M. and Buultjens, J. (2011) Putting the brakes on: Impediments to the development of independent cycle tourism in Australia. *Current Issues in Tourism* 14 (1), 57–78.
Long distance walkers association: https://www.ldwa.org.uk/

5 Tourism and Public Transport, Operational Management and Marketing

Introduction: Integrated Planning and Marketing

Understanding and managing the mobility practices of visitors and tourists are key factors for efficient and successful destination management (Bauder & Freytag, 2015). Public transport is one of the most popular mobility practices used by tourists, especially in urban destinations (Le-Klähn, 2015). Hence, the understanding of public transport practices of visitors and tourists is essential when dealing with tourism management and marketing of tourist destinations.

Planning and marketing of goods and services involve considerations of both demand and supply. In the case of tourism and public transport, the demand is comprised of tourists and visitors to destinations that decide to favour public over private transport. However, tourists are not the only players with demands on public transport. Their segment is added to the already existing and relatively fixed demand for public transport from locals. The supply side is relatively fixed and includes transport networks and infrastructure. Albalate and Bel (2009) pointed out that the current situation, in which the demand of tourists is added to existing supply and demand, often implies negative consequences for local users of public transportation because of congestion. Hence, from a short-term perspective, locals may prefer that tourists choose private transport. From medium and long-term perspectives, tourist selection of high carbon transport modes, such as cars, would have economic and environmental disadvantages as well as meaning that a further source of funding for public transport provision had not been fully explored.

From an economic point of view, tourism demand potentially allows for reductions in transport charges for locals and helps to fund the transportation system and infrastructure. Furthermore, tourists not only coincide with peak times in public transport but may also balance the demand curve of public transport in off-peak hours, weekends and holidays. This extra demand can facilitate the provision of public transport in off-times hours when there are otherwise too few local users to justify maintaining a proper service (Albalate & Bel, 2009). These issues may be particularly important in rural or less populated areas.

The environmental advantages of public transport systems are directed to the population in general, and not focused on the tourism sector alone. Mass transit systems reduce the number of vehicles and as a direct consequence positively contribute to decreasing CO_2 emissions (Scott et al., 2012; Le-Klähn & Hall, 2015; Peeters & Dubois, 2010). The positive effects of public transportation are relevant to all transit contexts, including inter-destination travelling (Filimonau et al., 2014), natural intra-destination travelling (Lin, 2010) and urban intra-destinations travelling (Hoornweg et al., 2011).

The clear advantageous of public transport to sustainable development call for its further implementation by locals and tourists. Le-Klähn (2015) mentioned that any successful implementation requires a proactive and effective transport management by destination authorities alongside the cooperation of tourists. Tourists are not always willing to give up private cars and often do not have enough information regarding public transport options (Le-Klähn, 2015). Additionally, destination managers do not always perceive tourists as a target group for public transport (Albalate & Bel, 2009).

Previous studies have tried to demonstrate a direct link between effective public transport and positive tourist experience and destination satisfaction. Nevertheless, Thompson and Schofield (2007) found that the ease of transport use only marginally influenced the level of the destination satisfaction reported by international tourists to Manchester, UK. Ladki et al. (2014) even found a negative causal link between ease of use of public transportation and the overall satisfaction of tourists to Lebanon. Maunier and Camelis (2013) argued that the link is between transport features and tourist experience dissatisfaction rather than directly to tourist experience satisfaction. They indicated that transportation services are the most frequent source of tourist overall dissatisfaction. In other words, poor public transport may harm the tourist experience but superior public transportation will not necessarily improve it.

Le-Klähn *et al.* (2014b) identified the main factors that form the tourists' appraisal of public transportation. In their study on tourists in Munich, they indicated information, ticket price, service frequency, space on the vehicle and cleanliness as the most important factors. The information factor refers to the clarity, including in English, of the messages in all communication modes (for example, internet sites, tourist information centres and bus stop signage). The ticket price factor includes fares, special schemes as well as the simplicity of the ticketing system. These two factors, clear information and simple ticketing systems contribute together to the ease of use of public transport by tourists. Issues of service frequency were raised by tourists mainly in relation to the services operating during off-peak periods. The final two attributes, space on the vehicle and cleanliness, are related to the comfort that is experienced by tourists when they use the public transport system.

Destination authorities have a clear economic and environmental incentive to promote the public transportation system to tourists. To achieve this goal they have to plan and market the public transport service according to tourists' needs and preferences. The present chapter addresses the main principles of integrated planning and marketing of public transport to tourists, with a detailed discussion regarding service management, distribution channels, ticketing and prices, information and signage, crowdsourcing and smart technologies, safety and security issues, sharing economies challenges and accessibility requirements.

Insight 5.1: Public Transportation for Tourists – a Comparison of Three Urban Destinations

Tourists to urban destinations use public transportation to visit landmarks and attractions. However, since the urban transportation infrastructure was not necessarily built for tourism purposes, tourists have to use a system that does not always match their needs. The outcome can be a less than optimal transportation solution in terms of frequency, connectivity and closeness to the tourist attractions.

Three urban destinations, from three different continents were chosen for the present case study: Vancouver, Copenhagen and Tel Aviv. Each of these destinations has about 100 hotels (according to TripAdvisor, December 2015) and thousands of Airbnb rentals (according to Airdna website, December 2015). For each of the three destinations, the top three landmarks and attractions, according to the TripAdvisor website

Table 5.1 Comparison of public transport and walking times in tourism destinations (December 2015)

Destination	Tourist attractions	Number of lines from central station* in Sunday noon	Frequency (tested Sunday noon)	Walking time to the attraction
Tel Aviv				
95 hotels; 38 B&B				
https://www.tripadvisor.co.il/Hotels-g293984-Tel_Aviv_Tel_Aviv_District-Hotels.html				
6498 Airbnb rentals				
http://www.airdna.co/city/il/tel-aviv				
The best three attractions:	Tayelet/Beach	4	6–15 min	10–15 min
	Old Jaffa port	3	3–12 min	8–16 min
https://www.tripadvisor.co.il/Attractions-g293984-Activities-Tel_Aviv_Tel_Aviv_District.html	Neve – Tzedek	6	5–7 min	10–13 min
Copenhagen				
117 hotels; 47 B&B				
https://www.tripadvisor.co.il/Hotels-g189541-Copenhagen_Zealand-Hotels.html				
7870 rentals				
http://www.airdna.co/city/dk/copenhagen?report=dk_copenhagen				
The best three attractions:	Nyhavn	9	4–12 min	6–14 min
	Church of our Saviour	7	4–6 min	3–6 min
https://www.tripadvisor.co.il/Attractions-g189541-Activities-Copenhagen_Zealand.html	Rosenberg Castle	5	3 min	5 min
Vancouver				
97 hotels; 66 B&B				
https://www.tripadvisor.co.il/Hotels-g154943-Vancouver_British_Columbia-Hotels.html				
3693 rentals				
http://www.airdna.co/city/ca/vancouver?report=ca_vancouver				
The best three attractions:	Granville Island	3	2 min	10–13 min
	Vancouver aquarium	2	12 min	8–22 min
https://www.tripadvisor.co.il/Attractions-g154943-Activities-Vancouver_British_Columbia.html	Downtown Vancouver	4	1 min	2–5 min

*In Tel Aviv, from Savidor train-station.

were selected, and the public transportation from the central station/central train station was tested, using Google Maps. The idea was to demonstrate the route that tourists may take when travelling to visit the most popular tourists attractions.

Table 5.1 presents the results of the comparison, for each city and each attraction. It shows that cities provide frequent public transportation lines to tourist attractions, but the stops are not always at a convenient distance from the attractions. A distance of more than 10 minutes walking can be inconvenient for tourists that do not know the area, and may also carry some heavy bags. All the top attractions in Tel Aviv (the 'Tayelet'/Tel Aviv beach, old Jaffa and Neve Tzedek) may be too remote from public transportation routes and bus stops. Similarly, Granville Island as well as the Aquarium of Vancouver can be too remote for tourists that use motorised public transportation – although there are walkways in place as well as water taxis. Nyhaven in Copenhagen can be too remote, depending on the line that was taken.

Table 5.1 helps illustrate that public transportation lines were not necessarily planned to meet tourists' goals. Stops can be located in inconvenienced distance from main tourist attractions. Even though each attraction can be accessed by more than one line or transportation mode, there is a variance between the different lines and modes in terms of walking distance, which have to be clear to the tourists that use these lines. One of the conclusion that stems from Table 5.1 is that public transportation providers have to pay attention not only to residents' needs, but also to tourists that choose to visit their destinations, and provide proper transportation to central tourist attractions.

Marketing to Tourists

Target customers

To be successful in promoting public transport to tourists, operators first need to identify the target users: those most likely to use public transport for travelling and while at destinations. Lacking data on the user profiles makes it challenging for transport operators to provide good services to tourists (Lumsdon, 2006). Naturally, having limited knowledge of the market restricts the ability to develop and offer appropriate services and qualities. To develop and offer better services, customer information should be included in the tourism transport planning and marketing process. Establishing benchmarks and monitoring programmes is also critical to determine the levels of demand, user profiles, and user motivation (Hall, 2014).

Visitors differ in their transport behaviour, and transport policies need to be customised accordingly to address such complexities (Dallen, 2007b). The visitor users of public transport are different from the local users (Antoniou & Tyrinopoulos, 2013; Thompson, 2004). They tend to be relatively young and have a good educational background (Barr & Prillwitz, 2012; Chang & Lai, 2009; Le, 2014). Younger and better educated people are more likely to be well-travelled and more familiar with public transport systems. It is also more likely that they have used public transport somewhere else (Chang & Lai, 2009). However, it should also be noted that this group of visitors is often more willing to participate in surveys and thus may dominate study samples.

With the car being the most popular transport mode for travelling, users of public transport make up a niche group, which should be appropriately targeted. While any visitor may use public transport, certain visitors are much more likely to adopt a behavioural change than others (Hall, 2014). It is best to focus the marketing efforts on the target segment with greatest potential for a modal shift (Anable, 2005). Examples include the case of visitors to the National Trust sites near Manchester, senior visitors i.e. at least 65 years old with relatively low income were the most likely group to change behaviours and adopt public transport (Anable, 2005). In Munich, the target customers of public transport are overnight international tourists travelling for holiday purposes (Le, 2014). Visitors coming to the city for the first time are also potential users of public transport.

Service improvement

Targeting the right customers is important in marketing public transport services, and so is making the system attractive to visitors. The core of any product or service is its quality and this is especially so in the tourism and transport industries (Chen & Chang, 2005; Erdil & Yıldız, 2011; Tyrinopoulos & Antoniou, 2008). An improvement in public transport services can actually attract more private car users (Redman et al., 2013). On the other hand, poor service delivery can cause passenger dissatisfaction and discourage them from using the services (Guiver et al., 2007). For example, in South Africa in addition to accessibility issues, the 2003 National Household Travel Survey indicated that one-third of households reported that safety from accidents and bad driver behaviour were the most serious transport problems (especially with respect to taxi services) and 20% mentioned that the cost of transport was a serious issue. In particular, 71% of train users were dissatisfied with crowding, 64% were dissatisfied with security on the walk to stations and 63% were dissatisfied with on-board security. With respect to buses, 74% of users were dissatisfied with facilities at bus stops, 54% with crowding on buses and 51% with low off-peak frequencies. Minibus-taxi users were the most dissatisfied overall, but particularly with respect to safety from accidents (67%), a lack of facilities at ranks (64%) and a lack of vehicle roadworthiness (60%) (Walters, 2013).

To attract tourists, a utility public transport network needs to be modified to better accommodate the particular needs of visitors (Lumsdon, 2006). Specifically, public transport operators should consider the dimensions that are important to tourists while developing and improving their services. Examinations of tourists' transport experiences showed that the key to an attractive public transport system is its ease-of-use (Le, 2014; Le-Klähn & Hall, 2015; Thompson & Schofield, 2007). As Thompson and Schofield (2007) indicated, a public transport system's ease-of-use has a stronger influence on tourists' satisfaction with the destination than its efficiency and safety. A complicated system would put off visitors from trying to use it. An important part of making the system user-friendly is the communicating of information to users. As language could be one of the barriers for tourists, information in multiple languages is recommended, especially in signage at interchange stations or stations close to tourist attractions. Having a good map is essential to enhance tourists' cognitive maps and memories (Dziekan, 2008). Providing bus route maps, incorporating bus information in sign boards, and including pictures of tourist sites on the network map are possible ways to make it easier for tourists to find their routes. On-board information such as network maps, next stops, and expected trip duration would also be useful.

Second, a public transport system with an extensive network can be attractive to passengers. Being highly accessible by train is one of the most important attractive factors of Disneyland (Yeung, 2008). However, having a connection does not help if the services are unreliable and infrequent. In rural areas where public transport services are insufficient, not only tourists will be reluctant to come but they will also need to shorten their stay according to the bus schedule. Visitors' expenditure increases with their trip duration (Downward & Lumsdon, 2004); therefore extended stay is preferable for the local economy. Offering acceptable services can motivate people to take the bus instead of the car while at the same time providing more business opportunities for the destination (Guiver et al., 2007). Other quality dimensions contributing to an effective public transport network are reliability, punctuality, and the role of driving staff. In the case of buses, drivers with local knowledge are especially appreciated (Koo et al., 2010).

Third, to offer tourists with more choices and flexibility, public transport services should be combined with other modes such as car and bike in a multimodal package. The combined rail-and-bike for example, is an attractive option. Cycling has become increasingly popular in the last decade with the cycling 'movement' spreading all over Europe to America, Australasia and Asia (Lamont & Buultjens, 2011; Oja *et al.*, 2011). There has been a sharp increase in the number of bikes sold, public bikes, and bike-sharing programs all over the world (Fishman *et al.*, 2013). Offering more public bikes for sharing near public transport stations can potentially attract visitors, especially those who are from countries with cycling cultures. Several bike-sharing programmes have been successful in attracting users such as the Paris's Vélib' and Copenhagen's City Bikes (Gössling, 2013). Public transport operators can consider organising the programme themselves as the German Deutsche Bahn's 'Call-A-Bike'. Alternatively, they can form a partnership with sponsors to implement the bike-sharing programmes for profit.

Insight 5.2: Public Transport, Tourism and the Hosting of Hallmark Events

Events provide a special case of the relationship between tourism and public transport (Robinson *et al.*, 2007). Hallmark tourist events, otherwise referred to as mega or special events are major fairs, festivals, expositions, cultural and sporting events that are held on either a regular or a one-off basis (Hall, 1992). Hallmark events have assumed a key role in international, national and regional tourism marketing strategies, their primary function being to provide the host community with an opportunity to secure high, albeit temporary, prominence in the tourism marketplace. Hallmark events are also extremely significant not just for their immediate tourism component but because they may leave behind legacies that impacts the host community for far longer than the immediate period in which the event actually took place. For example, large-scale public expenditure, the construction of facilities and infrastructure, and the redevelopment of urban areas that have been regarded as requiring 'renewal'. Public transport is integral to the hosting of such events. In many cases, the hosting of large-scale events, such as World Cup football or Olympic Games, provides the justification for large-scale renewal of transport systems (Cornelissen *et al.*, 2011; Gaffney, 2010; Hall & Hodges, 1996; Hiller, 1998). In the case of events such as World Expo and the World Cup, providing efficient public transport services is critical to event success (Jiang *et al.*, 2011; Kim, 2011; Malhado & Rothfuss, 2013). Nevertheless, the temporarily high number of visitors imposes extreme pressure on public transport providers. Kim (2011) recommended that a 'transit-oriented' plan should be initiated at an early stage, which restricts automobile access and allows free PT services for visitors.

The Summer Olympic Games (SOG) presents the largest transport challenge which host cities experience (Currie & Shalaby, 2012). Authorities must operate a transport system for over 40,000 athletes, an even greater number of officials and volunteers and many millions of spectator trips. This is usually provided within cities that already have significant urban 'base load' travel and congested/stressed transport systems. In addition to a number of specific travel capacity and efficiency creation and enhancement measures being applied, a number of public transport specific measures have also been enacted. These measures are indicated for the Summer Olympics since the Sydney 2000 Games (Table 5.2). However, it should also be noted that the transport legacies of hallmark and mega-events are often not as successful as originally hoped for, with long-term viability often depending on post event use of stadia and facilities as well as the extent to which events have enabled the attraction of new populations to districts that will use public transport services (Kassens-Noor, 2010, 2012, 2013).

Table 5.2 Public transport initiatives for the Summer Olympic Games 2000–2016

Measures	Rio 2016	London 2012	Beijing 2008	Athens 2004	Sydney 2000
Spectator public transport use education	Yes	Yes	Yes	Yes	Yes
Resident public transport use education	Limited	Limited	Yes	Yes	Yes
Expanded public transport system	Yes	Yes	Yes	Yes	Yes
Free public transport for Olympic family	Yes	Yes	Yes	Yes	Yes
Public transport for spectators as part of ticketing	Yes	Yes	Yes	Yes	Yes
24 Hours Public transport	Yes	Existing	Some	Some	Yes
Park and Ride	Yes	Yes	Yes	Yes	Yes
Pedestrian focused event sites	No	Yes	No	No	Yes
Public transport only access	Yes	Yes	No	No	Yes

Source: After Currie & Shalaby (2012).

Promoting public transport

Having an excellent transport product does not necessarily guarantee that customers will use it. If tourists are not aware of an efficient public transport system at the destination, they will not be able to use it. As a lack of information is often cited as a reason for non-use of public transport by tourists (Edwards & Griffin, 2013; Kinsella & Caulfield, 2011; Le-Klähn et al., 2014a), ensuring the delivery of information is vital in marketing public transport to tourists.

Tourists require more information than local people (Thompson, 2004), thus it is essential to provide them with accessible and comprehensive information. This is especially important in cities with complex urban structures and public transport networks (Le-Klähn & Hall, 2015). Preferred information channels for tourists include tourist centres, accommodation, word-of-mouth, attraction leaflets, and the internet (Chang & Lai, 2009; Le-Klähn et al., 2014c). Cooperation between public transport operators and tourism service providers can ensure the delivery of accurate, clear and updated information to tourists. Booklets and brochures are traditional information sources for tourists yet real time information is increasingly valued (Dziekan & Kottenhoff, 2007). Information should be easily accessible at train stations, bus stops and through mobile phone applications. An electronic tourist guide that incorporates public transport information is an excellent way to delivery information effectively to tourists (Garcia et al., 2010; Watkins et al., 2011). Such guides should be user-friendly and offer information on departure and arrival time, optimal routes, as well as interactive maps (Pun-Cheng, 2012). However, regardless of forms, information should also be provided in common foreign languages such as in English, Spanish and Chinese or at least be available in the languages of major markets.

As people appeared to be little concerned about the eco-friendly aspect of the mode (see Figure 2.6), marketing strategies for public transport should focus on the passengers' benefits rather than on the mode. It is important to highlight on-board benefits such as relaxing, care-free riding, and comfortable seating as well as the cost-effective benefits of public transport compared to private modes.

In sum, information is the key in promoting public transport to tourists. To encourage a modal shift to public transport, tourism and transport policies should emphasise the benefits of change and the positive aspects of public transport as an alternative mode (Cohen et al., 2014; Miller et al., 2010; Truong & Hall, 2013). However, as noted elsewhere in this book, behavioural change may also require shifts in public transport structures as well as conscious behaviour change.

Pricing and ticketing

Ticket prices have an important influence on public transport customers (Budiono, 2009; Redman *et al.*, 2013) and tourists are no exception (Chang & Lai, 2009; Le-Klähn *et al.*, 2014b). The probability of a tourist choosing a particular public transport mode decreases as its cost increases (Vo, 2013). The cost relative to other forms of transport, including parking fees is also of importance. Therefore, in some cases increases in parking costs and congestion charges can be effective mechanisms to make the relative price of public transport use more attractive (Cervero & Sullivan, 2010; Cervero, 2015).

In general, fare promotion and special ticket schemes are often effective in the case of local residents and could also be applied for visitors. Pricing of public transport is a decision involved multiple stakeholders and depends on several factors. Yet whenever possible, discounts should be considered for special groups of visitors such as students or seniors, who are more price conscious. In urban destinations, such special prices can be in the form of a tourist card such as the 'I Amsterdam City Card' and the 'Paris Pass', which offer the unlimited use of public transport in combination with entrance to attractions for a pre-determined period e.g. one day/24 hours or three days/72 hours. Moreover, promotion could be applied to the use of transport services outside peak hours. Traffic congestion and crowding are a common problem in big cities, especially during peak hours; yet demand during off-peak periods has high elasticity (Paulley *et al.*, 2006). Unlike local commuters, tourists are usually more flexible with time. Applying a different pricing scheme for high/low periods is a common revenue management practice to boost demand in tourism (Talluri & Van Ryzin, 2005), there should also be discounted tickets to motivate tourists to use public transport during off-peak hours.

In rural areas, providing incentives for those who do not arrive by car, as practiced in some regions in the European Alps (Imhof *et al.*, 2009), is recommended. To facilitate public transport use, a multi-modal ticket, which allows transfers between different public transport modes e.g. train, bus and tram is a good option. Additionally, incorporating a smart electronic ticketing system is especially helpful for tourists to avoid confusion and overwhelming of several ticket types (Le-Klähn *et al.*, 2014c). As in the case of Munich's public transport, which still operates a traditional paper ticket system, visitors were confused by the many types of tickets. Given the language barrier, visitors tended to have difficulty to choose the best option for them. In such case, it is essential to provide clear instructions and explanations for visitors in addition to a wide selection. Moreover, beside ticket counters and vending machines, tickets should be made available online for tourists to buy in advance. For those who fly, a discount offer in combination to the flight ticket for example would possibly contribute to encourage more use of public transport at the destination. Perhaps just as importantly local transport planners need to develop strategies to become more tourist friendly and recognise that tourists from other countries may have a different public transport service culture and system. For example, in some countries it is not possible to purchase a ticket once you are on the train (i.e. Denmark), but in others it is a perfectly normal (i.e. in Norway but there may be an extra service charge unless alighting at a stop without a ticket machine) and may even be a positive from a relationship marketing perspective. Similarly, not all travellers have smartphones for information provision or ticketing, therefore other channels need to be available.

Figure 5.1 summarises the marketing strategies to promote public transport use in tourism. An attractive public transport system should offer frequent services, a good connection and most importantly, it should be easy to use. The system should also be reliable and efficient, where constant quality monitoring and customer surveys are necessary. Cost is an important factor on tourist satisfaction with the service. Therefore, planning for pricing strategies should give consideration to certain groups of visitors who are more price-elastic such as students and seniors. Group discount, off-peak

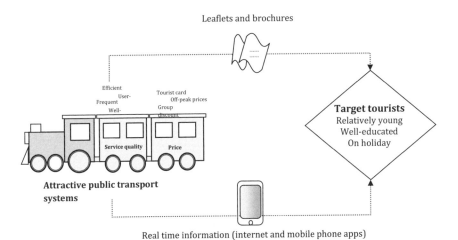

Figure 5.1 Marketing public transport services to tourists

hour tickets, and Tourist Card could also be adopted to motivate more use of public transport. The potential tourist users are likely of younger age group, well-educated, who travel for holiday purposes. To reach out to tourists, information on the transport services should be provided both in traditional channels such as brochures and leaflets, and through the internet and phone apps.

In addition to direct promotional strategies for public transport, transport planners can consider other measures such as incentives, taxation, and emissions quota to encourage sustainable mobility. Integrated land use planning, priority for public transport, and policies to influence attitudinal change could also be applied (D. Hall, 2004; C.M. Hall, 2014). Installing parking restrictions, car closures, and offering alternatives to cars are some other possible measurements.

Information and signage

Information is an essential factor to tourists in moving around a destination, given that they are, by definition, new or infrequent visitors at the places they visit. As a result, the public transportation system is also unfamiliar for them, and they need clear information to learn how to use it effectively. Furthermore, tourist time at a destination is often limited, so they therefore need to adapt to the system quickly, and have only limited opportunity to learn from mistakes. Therefore, Le-Klähn et al. (2014b) pointed identified information as the key predictor of tourists' satisfaction with public transportation in Munich. Tukamushaba and George (2014) also highlighted the importance of clear announcements and communication skills of drivers and staff as predictors of re-use of public transportation modes by tourists to Hong Kong, while Kinsella and Caulfield (2011) showed that lack of information deters visitors from using public transport in Dublin.

In many public transport systems that also aim to serve international tourists, English is the *lingua franca*, a communication platform that served as a contact language among people who do not share a first language (Jenkins et al., 2011). English may be used in oral announcements and is also often utilised in written signs in the public transport system (Backhaus, 2015). Le-Klähn et al. (2014b) pointed out that non-German-speaking tourists reported that English language information was either unavailable or insufficient in the Munich public transport system. Similar findings were found in studies of public transportation in Singapore (Yang et al., 2015) and France (Dubois & Aliaga, 2014). García et al. (2012) recommended using ICT solutions for text-to-speak to face the language problem in public transport systems. This technology allows a voice synthesis from written text, in different languages and accents. Other directions for bridging the language barriers were suggested by Suen *et al.* (2012) that recommended to use signage in universal symbols and also to provide tools to frontline staff to prevent misunderstandings due to cultural differences in verbal and non-verbal communication. Tukamushaba and George (2014) suggested investing in staff training, with a focus on the bus and taxis drivers to improve their communications skills, politeness and honesty. In many countries, staff with multiple language skills can be employed for front office duties at ticketing and information counters. Using a simple device such as a lapel badge that indicates the languages that the server speaks (commonly used in Sweden and Denmark) or having the flags of the countries for which the server speaks the languages is also a simple and straightforward means of improving communication. Importantly, such language skills when combined with service skills can improve customer relations and response and generate positive word-of-mouth.

Plate 5.1 Railway maps in Spanish and English, São Paulo, Brazil

Plate 5.2 Co-location of customer service centre and ticketing machines, Britomart Transportation Centre, Auckland, New Zealand. Britomart is Auckland's major transportation hub and is used for both buses and trains and is adjacent to ferry services.

Insight 5.3: English Travel Information and Twitter on Buses in The Hague

Offering travel in multiple languages can be extremely valuable for international visitors and enable greater confidence in using local public transport. In the Dutch city of The Hague, international travellers can now get travel information in English on buses and trams to help them find their way while travellers can also follow the status of the network in real-time on Twitter. As a city that hosts a number of national and international institutions The Hague receives many foreign visitors for business and tourism. As a result the local public transport operator HTM decided to test a system of English travel information on its buses and trams. The test involved 40 stops where additional information is announced through the speakers, like 'hospital' or 'station' or information on special buildings and attractions in the vicinity. After six months of testing, the account had almost 4200 followers.

Sources:
Eltis The urban mobility observatory: http://www.eltis.org/discover/news/english-travel-information-and-twitter-dutch-buses-netherlands-0#sthash.oeWtZ6B4.dpuf
HTM (English website): https://www.htm.nl/english/

Maps are another form of information that is relatively language free and depends mainly on common and agreed symbols. However, Dubois and Aliaga (2014) pointed out that tourist maps were not readily provided on the main transport services in France. As a result, tourists have to cope with transport networks maps that are often hard to read and use. Kinsella and Caulfield (2011) recommended the use of Spider maps (based on the famous London underground prototype) as these were found to be the most readable public transport maps for tourists. Interestingly, in spite of developments in mobile phone technologies, Dubois and Aliaga (2014) noted that the Paris public transport operator is the only French public transport authority that has developed a downloadable map application specifically for tourists.

Pre-trip information regarding public transport is sometimes more important than on-site information in predicting the use of public transport by tourists as the planning phase shapes the initial mode transport choice, car or public transport (Hall, 2005; Farag & Lyons, 2012). However, Farag and Lyons (2012) also found that previous use of public transport is a significant predictor of pre-trip information use, suggesting that visitors that used public transport in the past tend to consider using it more in future visits. Their findings suggest that public transport use leads to increase in information use, and not the other way around. Hence, improving the public transport information may not result in greater consideration and use of public transport, but useful information is still a necessary tool for tourists in public transport.

One of the potentially most important sources for pre-trip information and for tourist information on public transport in general are destination websites and the websites of public transport agencies. Table 5.3 provides a breakdown of some exemplar national and city destination websites in terms of the information that is available on them with respect to public

Table 5.3 Transportation information on destination websites

Place	Website	Languages	Information on transport	Information on PT	Information on cycling/walking
COUNTRIES					
France	http://france.fr	15	Heading: • About France/Transport What is available: • Brief description of traveling to and in France by different transport modes • Links to transport service providers	Link to train and bus websites within description section. Link to Paris public transport (on side bar).	Link to Vélib', a bike-sharing program in Paris but no other English information on cycling or walking tourism in France.
Spain	http://www.spain.info	15	Heading: • Practical Information/Transport What is available: • List and maps of transport hubs in Spain (airports, train/bus stations, and ports) • Brief description of traveling to and in Spain by different transport modes • Links to transport service providers	Link to train and bus providers or partners within the description section.	Information on cycling, hiking, mountain biking and related activities is listed under Sport Activities. Links to cycling associations, bike rentals, and bike services are provided.
Italy	http://www.italia.it	6	Heading: • Info/How to arrive Wht is available: • How to arrive in Italy by different transport modes, including by bike • Links to transport service providers	Information on High Speed Trains is listed separately under 'Info'. Link to train and bus providers.	Some information on cycling, hiking, mountain biking and related activities is listed under Sports and Wellness. Some links are provided.
Turkey	http://goturkey.com/	5	Little information on transport. Only a list of airports and ports in Turkey	No information.	No information on cycling. Information on trekking or rock climbing is listed under Outdoor Sports.

Britain	https://www.visitbritain.com	11	Heading: • Plan your trip/(1) Entry into Britain and (2) Getting around Britain What is available: • Brief description of transport modes to and around the country • No links to transport providers	General information and tips on travelling by train and bus.	Brief overview of the national cycling network under 'Green Travel'. Information on cycling trails listed under specific destinations.
Germany	http://www.germany.travel	30	Heading: • Travel Information/Along the Way What is available: • Very brief information on travelling within Germany by different modes • Link to transport providers	There is no separate category on public transport. However, there is some news on special offers for travel by the Deutsche Bahn.	Information on cycling and walking under 'Nature and Recreation.'
USA	http://www.visittheusa.com	8	Heading: • Plan/Getting here and around What is available: • Information on travel in the US by different modes • Link to transport providers	Very brief information on bus and train travel with links to service providers.	No dedicated category for cycling and walking. But some news can be found under 'Great Outdoors' or 'See and Do' (using search function).
Mexico	http://www.visitmexico.com	9	Heading: • Visit Mexico/Transportation in Mexico What is available: • Basic information on transport modes in Mexico • Link to transport providers	Only links to bus and train companies.	No information on cycling and walking in Mexico.

(Continued)

Table 5.3 (Continued)

Place	Website	Languages	Information on transport	Information on PT	Information on cycling/walking
COUNTRIES					
Canada	https://www.canada. travel	8	Heading: • Travel info/Getting around What is available: • Information on travelling in Canada by different modes • Links to transport providers	Separate category 'public transportation' provides brief description on public transport at cities and links to transport providers at different states.	No separate information on cycling and walking. However there is some news related to biking under 'Things to do' and 'Trip ideas'.
Australia	http://www.australia. com	10	Heading: • Plan your trip/Book your trip/Transport What is available: • Information on transport modes (bus, car rental, and bike rental) with links to providers' websites	No separate category on travel by public transport in Australia. Description of some train routes is given under suggested itineraries (can be found using the search function).	No dedicated category on cycling and walking. But there are articles on cycling Australia and on cycling trails (keywords search).

			Heading / What is available		
New Zealand	http://www.tourismnewzealand.com	8	**Heading:** • Transport **What is available:** • General information on transport in New Zealand • A search tool to look for a particular mode of transport at a certain city/area and link to providers for booking	Description of coach and rail travel and information on interesting routes. Links to service provides. Filter tool to sort out articles by region and place. Links to booking on side bar.	General information on cycling and some articles on bike tours and bike trails. Hiking information in under 'Activities and Tour'.
Guam	http://www.visitguam.com	6	**Heading:** • Plan your trip/Transportation **What is available:** • Brief information on the two modes of transport (bus and taxi) • Links to car rental companies	Basic information on bus services. No link to local bus provider.	No information on cycling and walking.
China	http://www.travelchina.gov.cn http://www.cnto.org	10	**Heading:** • Plan/ (1) When you arrive and (2) Getting around **What is available:** • Description of the entire transportation network in China • No links to service providers	Brief articles on train and bus in particular city destinations. No links provided.	No information on cycling and walking.

(Continued)

Table 5.3 (*Continued*)

Place	Website	Languages	Information on transport	Information on PT	Information on cycling/walking
COUNTRIES					
Malaysia	http://www.malaysia.travel	10	Heading: • Practical information/Getting here and around What is available: • Brief information on different transport modes and links to providers	No information. Links to providers (mostly for Kuala Lumpur).	Information on bike tours under 'packages'.
Morocco	www.visitmorocco.com	1	No information	No information	Category 'cycling' is listed under 'Experiences', which provides information on cycling activity in different locations
South Africa	http://www.southafrica.net	1	Heading: • Guide to South Africa/Getting around What is available: • Information on travelling around the country by different modes • Links to service providers	Brief information on travel by bus and train with links to providers	No separate category but there articles on bike routes and trails (search function)
Tunisia	http://www.beintunisia.com	5	Heading: • Stay informed/Transport What is available: • Little information on the country's transportation network • No links	No information	No information

CITIES

			Heading / What is available		
Hong Kong	http://www.discoverhongkong.com	14	Heading: • Plan your trip/Traveler Info/Transportation What is available: • Information on travel by different modes • Link to service providers and related activities	Information on different type of public transport modes including prices. Link to providers. Information on tourist card (Tourist Day Pass).	Information (tips and guidelines) on cycling and hiking is under 'Great Outdoors'
London	http://www.visitlondon.com	6	Heading: • Traveler information/Getting around/Transport What is available: • Information on different modes • Link to service providers and related activities	Information on different type of public transport modes including prices and network maps. Link to providers. Information on tourist card (London Pass).	Information on cycle and walk tours company under 'Things to do'
Singapore	http://www.yoursingapore.com	7	Heading: • Know Singapore/Travel Essentials/ (1) Getting to Singapore and (2) While you are here/Getting around What is available: • Brief information on getting to and around Singapore by different modes • No external links to transport providers	Information on the local public transport network. Link to download public subway map (but not to providers)	No information on cycling but there is a shortcut to a separate category on 'walking trails'

(Continued)

Table 5.3 (Continued)

Place	Website	Languages	Information on transport	Information on PT	Information on cycling/walking
CITIES					
Bangkok	http://www.bangkoktourist.com	4	Heading: • Transportation What is available: • Information on different transport modes in the city • No external links to transport providers	Information on the local public transport network, including prices but no link to external websites	No information
Paris	http://parisinfo.com	10	Heading: • Practical Paris/ (1) Getting to Paris and (2) How to get to and around Paris What is available: • Information on different modes • Links to providers	Information on PT network and details on different PT types. Links to PT providers. Info on tourist card (Paris Pass)	Category 'Environmentally friendly travel' includes information on bikes and on foot with links to external websites 'Walks in Paris' describes some popular walking routes
Macau	http://www.macautourism.gov.mo	15	Heading: • Plan your trip/ Before you travel/ (1) Travelling to Macao, and (2) local transportation What is available: • Information on different modes and links to providers	Information on the bus network, bus providers and links to websites	Brief information on cycling under Sports and Recreation
Shenzhen	No official destination marketing website				

New York	http://www.nycgo.com	(not able to select languages)	Heading: • Visitor information/ Transportation What is available: • Information on different modes and links to providers	Information on PT network, prices, maps, and links to websites	Information on NY by bike under transportation with links to bike maps and guides
Istanbul	http://icvb.org.tr	5	(incorporated in the visitors bureau website, no separate destination marketing) Heading: • Explore Istanbul/ Accessibility and Transportation What is available: • Information on different modes and links to providers	Brief information and links to local PT providers	No information on cycling and walking
Kuala Lumpur	http://www.visitkl.gov.my	7	Heading: • Travel What is available: • Information on different modes and links to providers	Information on different PT modes, names of company, contacts, and links to websites on side bar.	Information on walking around KL on foot under 'Travel' but no links to trails and routes. Link on side bar to a brochure on KL by bike

transport availability. Many of the websites, especially at the national level, provide a wide range of language options, although the extent to which public transport information – and connections to providers – is available is highly variable. For purposes of comparison, Table 5.4 provides an overview of the local public transport providers' websites for the city destinations (which were the top 10 city destinations for 2014 according to Euromonitor). As will be noted the range of languages available is less than the destination websites, while only half of them had a specific information section for tourists. Network map, fair information, schedule information and a journey planner were common to all sites, although only four sites provided a live traffic update.

Social Media, Crowdsourcing and Smart Technologies

When appropriately used smart technologies can help spread the availability of information for tourists in general, and also produce knowledge and confidence towards public transportation. Nelson and Mulley (2013) argued that smart technology is the first step for having informed tourists, which are the key to successful future transport service provision. Although this does also assume that tourists, whether domestic or international, also use the smart phones, that enable such access.

This section will explore three types of smart technologies for public transport. The first type of technology is based on top-down knowledge. It is usually developed by governmental and transport authorities and provides official information to public transport users. The second technology uses collective knowledge and GIS technology. It is based on a bottom-up knowledge that is derived from public transport users and is transmitted to other users. The third approach addresses payment systems and offers an approach to ticketing systems by using smart technology.

In their study on Australian public transport services, Nelson and Mulley (2013) portrayed the shared characteristics of governmental internet-based public transport journey planners. The content of these website tools tended to be static and usually did not include online updates and alerts. The most commonly available information were schedules, fares and walking times for local journeys. The authors noted that taking the internet-based journey planners a step forwards to provide real-time updates may be expensive and presented a challenge to transport operators who must balance their investment decisions with a range of different

Table 5.4 Local public transport providers' websites for city destinations

City	Visitors (mil)	Operators	Website	Languages	Network map	Fare	Schedule	Journey planner	Live traffic update	Official mobile apps	Integrated contactless card	Information for tourists	Note
Hong Kong	27.8	MTR Corporation Ltd.	http://www.mtr.com.hk/	2	✓	✓	✓	✓	–	✓	Octopus Card Specially for tourists: Sold Octopus Tourist Card	Heading: • Tourist What is available: • Trip planner by attractions • Suggestions for suitable transport modes • Recommendations for tourists' transport services, where to buy tickets. • Travellers' tips, tourist information, useful links	Informative and user-friendly. One dedicated section for tourists
London	17.4	Transport for London (TfL): London Underground, Rail, Surface Transport	https://tfl.gov.uk	1	✓	✓	✓	✓	✓	✓	Oyster Card For tourists: Visitor Oyster Card	Heading: • Traveller information/ Visiting London What is available: • Guide on getting around London, where to buy tickets, journey planners. • Tourist info and useful links. • Brief information for tourists in 8 languages (complete detailed info is only in English).	Informative and user-friendly. One dedicated section for tourists

(Continued)

Table 5.4 (*Continued*)

City	Visitors (mil)	Operators	Website	Languages	Network map	Fare	Schedule	Journey planner	Live traffic update	Official mobile apps	Integrated contactless card	Information for tourists	Note
Singapore	17.1	SMRT Corporation and SBS Transit	http://www.mytransport.sg	1	✓	✓	✓	✓	–	✓	EZ Link Card For tourists: Singapore Tourist Pass and Singapore Tourist Pass Plus	None	Website of Land Transport Authority. SBS, and SMRT also have their own websites.
Bangkok	16.2	Bangkok Mass Transit Authority (BMTA)	http://www.transitbangkok.com	3	✓	✓	✓	✓	–	✓	Rabbit Card For tourists: none	Heading: • Travel advice What is available: • Some brief advice for using public transport and travelling in Bangkok for tourists.	Has good information on the PT network but tourist information was not incorporated.
Paris	14.97	RATP Group	http://www.ratp.fr	6	✓	✓	✓	✓	✓	✓	Navigo Card For tourists: Paris Visite	Heading: • Practical information/ Visiting Paris What is available: • Type of tickets • Where to buy tickets • Guide to use Paris PT • Guide to visit Paris	Informative and user-friendly. One dedicated section for tourists.
Macau	14.96	Tranmac and TCM	http://www.dsat.gov.mo	3	✓	✓	✓	✓	–	✓	The Macau Pass For tourists: none	None	No trip planner but there is a point-to-point route search

City		Operator	URL							Card	Comments
Shenzhen	13.1	Shenzhen Metro Group Co. ltd.	http://www.szmc.net	2	✓	✓	✓	✓	✓	Shenzhen Tong For tourists: none	None	Website for Metro only.
New York	12.2	Metropolitan Transportation Authority (MTA)	http://www.mta.info/nyct	1	✓	✓	✓	✓	✓	MetroCard For tourists: none	Heading: • Metrocard/Tourism What is available: • Tourist information: attractions, transport advice, maps	Information section for tourists is hidden and can only be found via a search function.
Istanbul	11.9	Istanbul Metropolitan Municipality, IETT	http://www.istanbul-ulasim.com.tr http://www.iett.gov.tr	2	✓	✓	–	✓	–	IstanbulKart For tourists: none	None	Bus and metro operators have different websites, neither has information for tourists.
Kuala Lumpur	11.6	Rapid Rail, Rapid Bus	http://www.myrapid.com.my	1	✓	✓	–	✓	–	MyRapid Card For tourists: none	None	Informative website for commuters. No information specifically for tourists.

Note: Cities were the top 10 city destinations in 2014 in rankings made by Euromonitor, http://blog.euromonitor.com/2016/01/top-100-city-destinations-ranking-2016.html

stakeholder demands. Nevertheless, the authors agreed that new technologies and approaches are needed to increase customer satisfaction of public transport.

When agency or organisational budgets are limited, an alternative method to improve travel information while reducing operational costs is to obtain free real-time knowledge from customers (Nunes *et al.*, 2014). The passengers' mobile devices, their built-in sensors or their active reporting, can generate monitoring data in real-time. The function of the service provider in this approach is to aggregate, clean, analyse and disseminate the live information to the users who are producers and consumers at the same time (Farkas *et al.*, 2015).

The third approach combines the generation of information with a focus on payment opportunities. Di Pietro *et al.* (2015) found that passengers are willing to adopt a mobile ticketing service if it is easy to use, practical, secure and provides online information about timetables, delays and fares. Online payment technologies may therefore be perceived as the next step in the adaptation process of smart technologies to the needs of public transport passengers. Such technologies may also be integrated with online translation services that can translate information into a tourists own language. However, reliable online information is clearly perceived as the basic requirement by passengers before adopting such services, while there is also a need to ensure that other modes of communicating public transport information, such as signage and ticketing/information offices, are retained given their roles as specific information channels.

Tourists, who look for online information and easy ticketing system, may benefit from all these technological developments. However, Neuhofer *et al.* (2015) noted the need for a considered approach in the adoption of such practices and identified several technological constraints that can prevent tourists from fully adopting these communication technologies. The first set of barriers relate to hardware concerns, such a battery deficiencies, which may prevent the ability to use these battery-consuming travel applications. The second type of constraint relate to the availability of free Wi-Fi provision as this barrier restricts the possibility to use travel-related apps during travel. In sum, technological barriers together with the high costs of Wi-Fi access and smartphone access overall may prevent tourists from using practical applications and ICT solutions to smart public transport. As a consequence, the ability of tourists to gain online information on public transport and use online ticketing options is not as great as it could be.

Insight 5.4: Moovit: Bridging the Information Gap in Public Transport?

Moovit, founded in 2012 in Israel, is a free app for smartphones that provides accurate information regarding public transport. It generates a local transit planner, live arrival and departure schedules, local station maps, service alerts and advisories. Moovit uses official transit information and combines it with crowdsourced live updates. Just by using the app the rider turns into a source of live information. As of the beginning of 2016, the app is active in 58 countries, in five continents and 36 languages, providing live information on public transport in more than 700 cities for a community of about 30 million riders. The rate of the reported current growth is more than 1 million new users each month.

In a series of founding rounds the company, which employed only 60 employees, raised more than $80 million, and is now worth as much as $450 million. The list of investors includes capital funds, high-tech giants, as well as more traditional transport firms such as BMW and Keolis, the largest French transportation company (TechCrunch, 2015). Moovit declared it will use the funds to accelerate its growth in developing markets such as India and China as well as make Moovit the main platform for non-car owners, including bike, taxi and car sharing services. Moovit is also integrated with some taxi services. In Israel it is already combined with GetTaxi and in the US it allows people to book on Lyft. Nir Erez, CEO of Moovit stated: 'We believe that once we get hundreds of millions of users we will be able to monetise in multiple ways, such as adding extra services, like connecting to taxis, or value ad advertisement, or selling bus and train tickets' (in TechCrunch, 2015). Other similar apps include Citymapper, which focuses on large cities such as London, Paris and Singapore.

The main strength of Moovit is in filling the gap between the static information that is provided by local transport authorities, which is especially important in places where this information is missing. Its vision is 'building a new transit community' for both developed and developing countries. According to Ashton Kutcher, one of the investors in Moovit, its mission is 'to make public transport a first choice for people across the globe, cutting back on individual car usage and making cities smarter' (Globes, 2015). Kutcher, a high-tech investor and actor, also invested in Airbnb and Uber.

The other gap that Moovit fills is the local-global mobility gap, which is more salient in a tourism context. One of the main challenges in providing public transport to tourists is their familiarity with the local system and language. Tourists are often not familiar with a destination's public transport system and may not have enough time to learn to use it properly. Language barriers can make this task even more difficult. Moovit brings a solution to this problem. Tourists can continue using the app that they already know. All they have to do is to change the place of service. The language and mode of use remains the same, providing a known service in a new location. The Moovit slogan 'Your City, Your Local Transit App' gets new meaning in the context of tourism, when 700 cities become local, at least in terms of public transport use.

Sources:
Moovit website: http://moovitapp.com/
Citymapper website: https://citymapper.com/

Safety and Security

Safety and security are very important considerations in tourist use of public transport (Hall *et al.*, 2004a, 2004b) (see also Insight 2.3). Tourists are target to human and natural risks and hazards in four main circumstances: when they are victims to petty crimes at destinations; when they are perceived as bargaining chips by local criminals; in cases when their nationality or background variables (such as gender) make them targets; and when they are subject to inadequate infrastructure (Dehoorne *et al.*, 2014). In the case of the latter this may include in terms of both security measures as well as the capacity of infrastructure to cope with natural hazards and disasters (Hall *et al.*, 2016). The risk factor of terrorism can also be added to this list of hazards, even if the terror is not directed to tourists but the general local population and the tourists find themselves at the wrong time in the wrong place. However, it is important to stress that the perception of being at risk from a terrorist attack substantially outweighs the realities. Far fewer tourist get killed by terrorists each year, for example, than those killed in traffic accidents while on holiday.

Public transport, as a physical interface between locals and tourists, is a recognised setting for increased tourist risk. All types of hazards can occur in public transport setting. Sometimes these acts are even deliberately directed to public transport services because of their perceived vulnerability in terms of crime and security (Newton *et al.*, 2014). The vulnerability of public transportation settings was significant, for example, in the context of terrorist events, such as the 2005 London bus bombing or the 2004 Madrid train attack.

The perception of security in public transportation is frequently place-dependent (Thompson & Schofield, 2007). In a survey of tourists in Cape Town, South Africa (George, 2003) only 15% of the respondents reported that it is 'very safe' to use public transport in the city. The share of tourists that felt 'very safe' to tour the city by walking (in day time) or driving (day and night time) was more than doubled. However, in two other studies, conducted in Munich, Germany and Manchester, UK, tourists were satisfied with safety and security conditions of the public transportation service (Le-Klähn *et al.*, 2014b; Thompson & Schofield, 2007). The perceived safety of public transport services is therefore often extremely destination dependent and will also likely depend on factors such as word of mouth and media stories as well as the physical realities of travel. In addition, different times of day may require different considerations in communicating and ensuring passenger and tourist security.

Several socio-demographic populations are considered as high-risk groups when using public transport, because of their nationality and personal variables. Female travellers, for example, face additional risks when using public transportation in several destinations. The reoccurring attacks on female tourists on Indian public transport have negatively affected the image of the India as a tourist destination (Chugh, 2015), and the number of arrivals to India has been negatively affected as a result (Mundkur, 2011; Mullen, 2015; Hall & Suntikul, 2016). In some Western countries Muslim travellers or even people perceived to be Arab or Muslim may be racially vilified when travelling on public transport (Noble & Poynting, 2010), although the publicity such events receive together with support from fellow passengers can help limit such incidents. US citizens are another group in high-risk. The US Department of State set a world-wide travel caution warning of a threat of terrorist actions and violence against US citizens and interests: 'U.S. citizens are reminded of the potential for terrorists to attack public transportation systems and other tourist infrastructure. Extremists have targeted and attempted attacks on subway and rail systems, aviation, and maritime services' (US Department of State, 2015).

A perceived physical risk is defined as a concern of personal danger of injury at tourism destinations (Adam, 2015; Sharifpour *et al.*, 2014) and it plays an important role in the decision to visit or not to visit certain destinations (Sönmez & Graefe, 1998). Concerns over criminal and sexual attacks are considered as perceived physical risks for tourists, while feelings of risk that may arise from being perceived as culturally or social different because of religion, race or clothing are also significant barriers for using public transport in some cases. In addition, inadequate public transport infrastructure and the potential for transport accidents pose other physical risks, mainly for tourists who are planning to visits developing and under-developed countries (Adam, 2015). To this can also be noted the potential risks facing some transport infrastructure as a result of natural disasters, e.g. ferry and train services in vulnerable locations, which can also be a significant factor in transport planning (Sakakibara, 2012). In general therefore, if public transport is associated with a potential physical risk, by crime, terror, accidents or sexual attack, this can not only have a significant impact on mode choice, but may even lead to tourists preferring to visit other destinations that are perceived as safer. Indeed, there is substantial evidence that perceptions of personal safety are significant drivers for selection of private cars or taxis as a mode choice (Beirão & Cabral, 2007; Gardner & Abraham, 2007; Spears *et al.*, 2013).

Tourism authorities therefore have to work together with public transport agencies and other stakeholders for improving the safety and security of public transport in the destination. Some of the steps used for securing the safety of public transport passengers include the implementation of customer awareness programs, upgrading of security technologies, setting of sophisticated surveillance devices, tightening of access control, ensuring that there are staff visible on the service and developing methods of screening passengers. Yet, any security scheme has costs, side effects and legal and ethical consequences that should be considered carefully (Hagen *et al.*, 2015).

Sharing Economies

Sharing, as Belk (2014: 1595) argued, is 'as old as mankind', but the so-called 'Sharing Economy' (also referred to as the 'peer' and the 'collaborative' economy) is a new phenomenon of the temporary utilisation of goods and services, without owning them, by relying on Web 2.0 platforms. Peeters *et al.* (2015: 13) defined it as a

> set of practices, models and platforms that, through technology and community, allows individuals and companies, at least partly, to share access to products, services and experiences. It includes non-profit and for-profit platforms that have emerged from an originally pure sharing economy, peer-to-peer and/or non-profit organizations.

The sharing economy is growing fast. On New Year's Day 2016, more than 1 million people were hosted in Airbnb rentals. The short-term rental company that was founded in 2008 reported at the end of 2015 to have more than 2 million rentals worldwide (Airbnb, 2015). Uber, the rideshare platform that was launched at 2009, served its billionth passenger in December 2015 (Bergen, 2015). According to a representative survey of US citizens (PWC, 2015), 8% of Americans engaged in some form of transport sharing and 1% have served as providers under this model. In a British survey (Stokes *et al.*, 2014) 12% of respondents reported taking part in transport sharing activity, but only 5% do it with the internet based platforms.

Many of the sharing economy companies focus on travel services (accommodation, transportation, leisure). Global tourism as a proportion of sharing economy services counts account for about 500 initiatives, with half of these labelled as transport related (2015 data, according to Peeters *et al.*, 2015). Tourism offers a supportive context for the sharing economy. First, most tourists have no ownership on goods and assets (such as accommodation and transportation) at destinations. Second, the tourism industry is heavily depending on information and communication technologies and both suppliers and consumers are early adopters of technological innovations (Gretzel *et al.*, 2015). Third, tourism is also characterised by low levels of unionisation and high levels of casualisation in employment in part as a result of the demand fluctuations for tourism and hospitality services, thereby labour force for short-term and temporary labour practices are a norm in many countries (Hall, 2005).

A number of advantages of the sharing economy for the tourism sector at a destination have been proposed. Juul (2015) noted that the sharing economy may widen high quality and affordable supply of travel options. She indicated on the high personalisation of offers and on the close contact it provides between tourists and locals. Additionally, the flexibility of the sharing economy may assist destinations to cope with the seasonality of the tourism demand. The environmental advantages in terms of saving energy and waste may also be significant (Juul, 2015), at least in the first round of consumption.

Nevertheless, the downside of the sharing economy to the tourist industry is also significant (Dredge & Gyimóthy, 2015), and while sharing economy services may be regarded as a positive by destinations focused on numbers of visitors, the benefits for firms in the sector as a whole, as well as for employees is more doubtful. It harms the job security of already vulnerable workers, it threatens compliance standards of safety, health and disability and it relates to tax evasion. Additionally, the sharing economy produces unfair competition because its hosts and suppliers do not have to comply with the same rules and laws, including with respect to the environment, health and safety, while regulation can be difficult (Juul, 2015; Peeters *et al.*, 2015; Witt *et al.*, 2015). Another example for the negative impact refers to an economic of scale. According to Peeters *et al.* (2015) the Uber rideshare service, backed by global giants such as Google and Goldman Sachs, takes advantage of its size and acts in an anti-competitive manner when recruiting employees from local competitors' under the rhetoric of 'free markets'.

The sharing economy is based heavily on technological innovations. In this situation, there is a clear need for large investments and profit-oriented firms to create a competitive technological edge. The consequences of this are large for-profit businesses that are similar to those of the 'traditional economy'. Peeters *et al.* (2015) described this situation as

> ...the large investment in technology and the competitive edge created by the size of platforms generates an outcome whereby the winner takes all, causing market concentration and failing competition. Through these mechanisms of market concentration and shift to for profit large scale businesses, the original principles of the architects of a pure sharing economy are increasingly compromised. (Peeters *et al.*, 2015: 57)

Peeters *et al.* (2015) summarised a list of the main transport sharing economy business. Some of these aspects of transport and the shared economy have been described as 'new mobility services' (McKinsey Center for Business and Environment, 2015; Ministry of Transport, 2016) (Table 5.5). Peeters *et al.* (2015) noted that many of these companies are peer-to-peer oriented. Examples include Lyft Ride, Blablacar, Carpooling and JoinUpTaxi (ridesharing platforms) or Drivy and Snappcar (car rental). Other peer-to-peer firms of sharing economy transport are focusing in ideas such as rent your car instead of parking it at an airport (Travelercar), rent boats (Boatbound) bikes (Spinlister) and even seats in privet jets (BlackJet). However, all these initiatives are marginal in terms of market share and economic impact in comparison to Uber, the ridesharing and taxi services business. Uber is leading the list of sharing companies with an investment of almost 3 billion dollars. Additionally, Uber is not just a platform for peer-to-peer sharing but also operates as a business that shares its assets. In a similar manner, Zipcar, which was bought by Avis for half a billion dollars, rents its cars to members. Hence, in the cases of both Uber and Zipcar, the sharing is from a business and not from peers (Peeters *et al.*, 2015). Table 5.5 illustrates some of these new mobility services in the context of primarily individual mobility (car sharing: peer to peer through to bicycle sharing); group mobility (ride-share taxi alternatives through to app enabled public transport) and services that

Table 5.5 New mobility services

Service	Characteristics	Examples
Car sharing: peer to peer	Peer-to-peer platform where cars are rented out when not in use. Operator provides technical platform (e.g. website and app) that brings parties together, manages bookings and handles payments.	CarNextDoor, YourDrive, RelayRides
e-hail/taxi alternative	Booking and paying for a ride using an app. The operator provides an app that matches the passenger with a driver, and manages the booking and the payment.	Uber, Lyft
Car sharing: fleet operator	On-demand short-term car rental, with fleet owned and managed by a fleet operator. This is usually app enabled, and urban.	Zipcar, Autolib, Car2Go, Cityhop
Bicycle sharing	On-demand short-term cycle rental. This is usually app enabled and urban.	Velib, BicMAD, Spinlister
App enabled journey planners	App enabled journey planners that show options for a journey (including time, cost, and emissions and which ideally are multi-modal). The app may also act as a booking and payment platform.	CityMapper
Ride-share/Taxi alternative	Offers cheaper ride for those prepared to share a car. Uses technology (e.g. dynamic routing, predictive demand and scheduling) to maximise use.	Uber Pool, Lyft Line
Ride-share	Allows riders travelling in a similar direction to share the ride, thereby splitting costs.	JayRide, Lets Carpool.
On-demand shuttles and minibuses	App enabled demand responsive services – cheaper than a taxi and more tailored than traditional public transport. Uses technology (e.g. dynamic routing) to maximise use.	Kutsuplus, PocketRide, NippyBus, Dynamic shuttle
App enabled public transport	App enabled real time information, journey planning, and payment. Ideally will be multi-modal. Wi-Fi is available on services.	SJ (Swedish Rail)

Sources: After McKinsey Center for Business and Environment (2015); Ministry of Transport (2016).

can be utilised for both individual and group mobility (app enabled journey planners) (McKinsey Center for Business and Environment, 2015; Ministry of Transport, 2016).

The links between sharing economy transport companies and public transport are relatively new and their impacts are not fully revealed. Schur (2014) indicated a possible rebound effect of car and ride sharing on the environment. She argued that the availability of cheap ride services may divert some people from public transportation. That means the platforms result in higher carbon emissions, because their services involved private cars and may inhibit use of public transport, which is more environmental friendly. In order to better understand and cope with the implications of the sharing economy, Peeters *et al.* (2015) argued for the development of EU level guidelines for destinations that would include, among others, recommendations for transport services, with a specific reference to environmental issues, safety, insurance, taxes and licences. They also call for extending the research on economic, environmental, competitive and quality opportunities of the sharing economy in tourism, alongside an investigation of the legal, competitive and financial (taxes) challenges it brings to the tourism industry. However, given the range of philosophical approaches with respect to the regulation of collaborative firms within the various EU countries the likelihood of such initiatives being implemented remains low, while in other jurisdictions with low levels of regulation on passenger transport it is likely that sharing economy platforms will only exacerbate the growth of paratransit operations and the informal sector.

A further issue with respect to the value of new mobility services is that they currently appear to be far more viable in the context of larger cities (McKinsey Center for Business and Environment, 2015) and they also require mobile devices and internet access. This is therefore a significant issue for smaller urban centres and rural areas as well as for people on limited incomes. As of 2014, 60% of the global population did not have access to the internet, and 56% out of this 60% were in developing countries (Valerio, 2016). Chapter 6 provides a further discussion of the significance of urbanisation for the future of public transport.

Accessibility and Disability

Accessible tourism is the process that enables people with mobility, vision, hearing and special cognitive dimensions requirements to function independently and with equity and dignity through the delivery of universally designed tourism products, services and environments (Buhalis & Darcy,

2011; Buhalis & Michopoulou, 2011). Greater accessibility of tourists to public transport will benefit not only the disabled population but also a larger group of consumers, among them, pregnant women, people with temporary transitory disabilities and families with young children (Vila *et al.*, 2015). Transit considerations are an integral part of accessible tourism, as they enable the tourists to reach the destinations, and returning home (Darcy *et al.*, 2011). Furthermore, local transport accessible considerations are also included under the umbrella of accessible tourism (Vila *et al.*, 2015).

In the context of legalisation, accessible tourism is related to the existing set of requirements for accessible transport and mobility. In Argentina, for instance, Law No. 24314 calls for autonomy, self-sufficiency and safety for the disabled population when using transportation (DREDF, undated). In a similar manner the *Canada Transportation Act* (1996) supports 'a safe, economic, efficient and adequate network of viable and effective transportation services accessible to persons with disabilities' (Transport Canada, 2015). The Polish *Charter of Rights of Disabled* lists the rights of disabled people including free access to transportation means (DREDF, undated). The French Law 82-1153 of 1982 refers specifically to urban transportation and states that special measures must be taken to accommodate the special needs of people with limited mobility (Zadra-Veil, 2010). The Japanese 'Barrier-free Transportation Law', stipulates that all newly built transportation facilities and all newly purchased vehicles should meet accessibility standards (Akiyama, 2005).

The UNWTO (2013) has published its own recommendations for accessible tourism and transport. According to the UNWTO all passenger vehicles that serve tourists should be designed to allow safe, comfortable and equitable transport of people with disabilities or reduced mobility. The travel-related information should also be provided in visual and acoustic formats. Stations, passenger terminals, and related facilities should be easy accessed and as simple as possible. Assistance should be available when required and all facilities have to welcome guide dogs and provide the essential items to facilitate their stay (UNWTO, 2013). Nevertheless, the implementation of UNWTO recommendations is often poor (Su *et al.*, 2013). However, it should be noted that in some cases adaption of transport infrastructure built in the early 20th century, or even late 19th century in the case of rail and the earliest metro systems, is both expensive and can have significant logistical constraints. In policy terms there is therefore an important need in many jurisdictions of a wider discussion as to how to best serve disabled passengers and whether there is effective integration of the mainstream public transport system with paratransit transport services (see Chapter 1).

The provision of transportation means to disabled travellers is far from satisfactory. In Queensland, Australia, for example, only 20% of train stations were found to be accessible with ramps, tactile surfaces along the platform and supportive electronic devices for vision-impaired and physically-disabled travellers. However, the links between railway stations and major attractions have been improved, including the use of accessible bus links (Patterson *et al.*, 2012). In their study of the complaints of disabled travellers, Kim and Lehto (2012) found that the land-transit sector is responsible for more than 7% of all complaints of disabled tourists, with a notably high incidents of service failures resulting from service providers' poor attitudes, unprofessional conduct and insufficient knowledge of the disability. The authors recommended that transport authorities and managers should pay special attention to their employees' unsolicited behaviour towards disabled consumers and tourists.

Vila *et al.* (2015) argued that in light of current demographic trends, the competitiveness of tourist destinations also depend on accessible tourism provisions, including transport infrastructure. The World Health Organization (WHO) estimates that over 1 billion people, about 15% of the world's population, have some form of disability, and this rate of disability are increasing due to population ageing and increases in chronic health conditions, such as diabetes and obesity, among other causes (WHO, 2015). Patterson *et al.* (2012) found that improved accessibility represented a competitive advantage for tourism firms when it attracted not only disabled tourists but also elderly people and families with young children. Financial support from city councils or the state government was also identified in this study as an additional motivation to improve the accessibility levels of tourism facilities. Finally, emotional, personal and moral factors were found as further motivations for tourism firms to improve their accessibility and provide a better service for disabled tourists.

Socio-economic Accessibility

Inadequate transport is considered as one of the key factors of social exclusion (Cass *et al.*, 2005). Social exclusion is defined as 'when people or areas suffer from a combination of linked problems such as unemployment, poor skills, low incomes, poor housing, high crime, bad health and family breakdown' (Social Exclusion Unit, 2001: 10). Cass *et al.* (2005) argued that availability of public transport, especially when a private car is unavailable, is crucial in maintaining social inclusion. The most relevant transport aspects were proximity of a bus stop or railway station, directions the buses travel in and their destinations, the cost of travelling by public transport, the quality of the traveling experience, the conditions of waiting and interchange locations and above all the service's frequency, reliability and punctuality. Such considerations may therefore be an important influence on local recreational and tourism behaviour (Hall, 2010).

Suen *et al.* (2012) summarised a list of recommendations to public transport authorities to achieve better social and cultural accessibility to public transport in the EU. Their recommendations for eliminating social exclusion and increase the use of public transport by all population groups include:

- To confirm the conditions for female users especially those travelling with small children and baggage, and focusing on step height and night safety, amongst other requirements.
- To provide adequate service frequency and coverage to locations and neighbourhoods where ethnic minorities are living. Additionally, public transport suppliers are asked to hire more frontline staff from minority groups to improve the communication with these groups.
- To better connect rural areas by using service coordination techniques, innovative funding schemes, flexible routes, taxi subsidy and volunteer-driver programs.
- To minimise racism and improve tolerance to minorities. Public transport management should implement sensitivity training courses on understanding religious and cultural customs. Complaints about abusive or discriminatory behaviours by passengers and staff should be deal immediately.
- To encourage the use of public transport by older adults. Public transport authorities should develop training programs both to the older groups (how to use public transport) and drivers (how to be sensitised to needs of older users).

Public transport enables access to tourist destinations and within destinations to those without a private car, and thus supports the inclusion of various social groups in tourism and travel activities (Lumsdon, 2006). Minnaert and Schapmans (2009) argued that participation of socially excluded groups in tourism can decrease mobility barriers because of the exposure to public transport. According to this perspective, the use of public transport while on holiday is an opportunity to learn and experience public transport, and can encourage more often use after the holiday. But, the links between tourism, public transport and social exclusion are more complicated and bi-directional. McCabe (2009) noted that in the context of tourism and travel, social exclusion is linked, in addition to transport unavailability, to broader constraints and barriers, including lack of information, financial resources, disability, age-related factors and social and time factors (see also Hall, 2010). In other words, accessibility to public transport would marginally increase the participation of social excluded groups in tourism because they experience a multi-faceted system of difficulties and barriers.

Changes in the delivery of public transport may have significant implications for socio-economic accessibility. A study of mobility data from Lisbon in Portugal conducted by the International Transport Forum (ITF) at the OECD, compared existing bus, rail and metro transport modes to a hypothetical scenario where metro and rail services are complemented by fleets of on-demand eight- or 16-seater taxi-buses, which can be summoned using smartphones apps. The study found that in a shared mobility model, the city's transport needs could be met by a car fleet only 3% that of the size of the present fleet. Each vehicle would also be used more intensively, and the greater efficiency would help cut commute prices by half or more, even without subsidies. Switching from current public fixed route and schedule bus services to on-demand shared vehicles could help more people access jobs, healthcare options and education opportunities at a lower cost. The ITF report compared how many transport, health and education opportunities the person who were the 10% best-served had compared to the individual at the bottom 10%, and found that in a traditional public transport system, those at the top 10% had more than 17 times as many opportunities as those at the bottom. However, in a shared transport scenario, the more privileged groups had only just about twice as many opportunities as the bottom segment of society. In the current public transport system access the top segments of society have 39 times as much access to health services as the bottom. Shared mobility would bring this ratio down to 2.5. Similarly, the best-served individuals had almost 30 times as much access to opportunities for secondary education and above within a 30-minute commute in the current transport system, but shared mobility would mean that the top 10% had only twice as many opportunities as the bottom (ITF, 2016). Although not the subject of the study shared mobility may clearly also have implications for tourism and leisure by way of access to sites and recreational areas.

According to McCabe (2009), social excluded groups do not participate in travel and tourism activities because their of lack of access to appropriate resources, including public transport. If so, the travel and tourism context will do little to help them to better use public transport in everyday settings, as Minnaert and Schapmans (2009) argued. Yet, it may be the only way to enable excluded groups to travel.

Insight 5.5: Free Public Transport Services for Tourists

Public transport for tourists is considered in a number of destinations as a leverage for tourism development and marketing. This is the reason that many cities, from Osaka and Singapore to London and Tallinn offer special tourist-cards, for use in public transportation and other tourist attractions. However, in several cities and regions around the world there is even a better deal to tourists, free use of the public transport services. This offer has two main forms, the first form provides an unlimited public transport but stipulates an over-night stay in a local registered accommodation, while the second provides for limited free public transport but with no other requirements.

In several Swiss cities, including Bern, Basel and Geneva, tourists can get a free public transport card if they have an overnight stay in a hotel, a youth hostel or at a campsite. The ticket include free local rides in trams, buses and trains. Other transportation modes are also possible. In Geneva, the ticket can be used in yellow taxi-boats to travel the Geneva-lake. In Bern the free ticket offers two popular local funicular railways. For tourists that are arriving in Geneva by plane, an 80-minute ticket free of charge for a ride to the place of accommodation from the airport is available via a ticket machine in the airport luggage retrieval hall.

Free cards to tourists that stay over-night are also available in regional level. In the Canton of Basel-Landschaft in Switzerland tourists can get a pass for public transport throughout north-western Switzerland, which is also valid for inbound and outbound travels. This pass includes additional offers and it is valid at about 50 tourism facilities in the region. Similarly, all holiday guests in the Black Forest region in Germany receive a special card (the Konus card) that provides free rides on regional public transport as well as hundreds offers for attractions in the region.

Public transport is provided for free to locals and tourists in other countries. The city of Melbourne, Australia, offers a free tram zone that is close to its main tourist attractions (but not necessarily including them). Another free service in Melbourne is the City Circle Tram, taking in many of Melbourne's landmarks and offering a historical tram experience with an automated audio guided tour. In New York, the ferry ride from Manhattan to Staten Island is free and provides great views of the skyline of Manhattan and the Statue of Liberty. However, although the ferry is a significant tourist experience the intention in providing the service is not to promote visits to Staten Island. As stated on the website for the ferry: 'The Staten Island Ferry is run by the City of New York for one pragmatic reason: To transport Staten Islanders to and from Manhattan'. The number of passengers that use the ferry is estimated at 70,000 each weekday and 22 million a year.

Plate 5.3 Staten Island Ferry, New York, USA

Sources:
Bern – Transportation in the City: http://www.bern.com/en/travel-planning/arrival-transport/transportation
Basel Free Public Transport including Visitors' Pass: http://www.myswitzerland.com/en-il/free-public-transport-including-visitors-pass.html
Geneva Transport Card: http://www.geneve-tourisme.ch/en/useful-information/how-to-get-around/geneva-transport-card/
Konus card (Black Forest): http://www.dreisamtal.de/en/service/konus.php?lang=en
Public Transport in Basel: https://www.basel.com/en/public-transport-basel.
Staten Island Ferry: http://www.siferry.com/
Visiting Melbourne: http://ptv.vic.gov.au/getting-around/visiting-melbourne/#p8

Chapter Summary and Conclusion

This chapter has discussed some of the main issues involved in the marketing, management and planning of public transport for tourists by public transport and tourism agencies. The importance of a clear communication strategy is regarded as central to encouraging tourists to use public transport. This requires the use and integration of multiple platforms and embraces not just websites and apps but should also utilise good signage, clear maps and network diagrams, and personal services.

Although the encouragement of tourists to use public transport is clearly of value for the environmental side of sustainability the chapter also notes how public transport impinges on social sustainability because of its role to assist in access. However, it is also noted that some of the impacts of the sharing economy may have potentially negative effects that could impinge on labour conditions and even access in the long-run. These are also issues that will be touched on in the final chapter.

Further Readings

On the overall importance of communication and information to tourists and visitors and their role in management, marketing and planning see

Dziekan, K. and Kottenhoff, K. (2007) Dynamic at-stop real-time information displays for public transport: effects on customers. *Transportation Research Part A: Policy and Practice* 41 (6), 489–501.
Hall, C.M. (2014) *Tourism and Social Marketing*. Abingdon: Routledge.
Kinsella, J. and Caulfield, B. (2011) An examination of the quality and ease of use of public transport in Dublin from a newcomer's perspective. *Journal of Public Transportation* 14 (1), 69–81.
Le-Klähn, D.-T., Hall, C.M. and Gerike, R. (2014) Promoting public transport use in tourism. In S. Cohen, J. Higham, P. Peeters and S. Gössling (eds) *Understanding and Governing Sustainable Tourism Mobility* (pp. 208–222). Abingdon: Routledge.
Lumsdon, L.M. (2006) Factors affecting the design of tourism bus services. *Annals of Tourism Research* 33 (3), 748–766.

On English as Lingua Franca in public transportation in Tokyo see

Backhaus, P. (2015) Attention, please! A linguistic soundscape/landscape analysis of ELF information provision in public transport in Tokyo. In K. Murata (ed.) *Exploring ELF in Japanese Academic and Business Contexts: Conceptualisation, Research and Pedagogic Implications* (pp. 194–209). Abingdon: Routledge.

On pre-trip use of public transportation information

Farag, S. and Lyons, G. (2012) To use or not to use? An empirical study of pre-trip public transport information for business and leisure trips and comparison with car travel. *Transport Policy* 20, 82–92.

On the relationships between smart technologies, the sharing economy and tourism see

Cohen, B. and Kietzmann, J. (2014) Ride on! Mobility business models for the sharing economy. *Organization & Environment* 27 (3), 279–296.

Neuhofer, B., Buhalis, D. and Ladkin, A. (2015) Technology as a catalyst of change: Enablers and barriers of the tourist experience and their consequences. In I. Tussyadiah and A. Inversini (eds) *Information and Communication Technologies in Tourism 2015: Proceedings of the International Conference in Lugano, Switzerland, February 3–6, 2015* (pp. 789–802). Dordtrecht: Springer International.

Rauch, D.E. and Schleicher, D. (2015) Like Uber, but for local governmental policy: The future of local regulation of the "sharing economy". *George Mason Law & Economics Research Paper* 15-01. Washington DC: George Mason University.

On safety and security in transport see

Ceccato, V. and Newton, A. (eds) (2015) *Safety and Security in Transit Environments: An Interdisciplinary Approach*. London: Palgrave Macmillan.

A list of practical safety tips for tourists traveling by public transport

See https://tfl.gov.uk/travel-information/safety/staying-safe\

Transport for London's (TfL) Report It to Stop It campaign after one year. See http://www.theguardian.com/lifeandstyle/2016/apr/04/transport-for-london-found-way-to-stop-you-being-groped-on-tube

French campaign against sexual harassment on public transport. See http://www.thelocal.fr/20151109/france-launches-bid-to-tackle-sexual-harassment

French government site: http://www.familles-enfance-droitsdesfemmes.gouv.fr/harcelement-transports/

On accessible public transport see

Buhalis, D. and Michopoulou, E. (2011) Information-enabled tourism destination marketing: addressing the accessibility market. *Current Issues in Tourism* 14 (2), 145–168.

Suen, L., Simões, A. and Wretstrand, A. (2012) Social, cultural and generational issues in accessible public transport in Europe. In *TRANSED 2012-13th International Conference on Mobility and Transport for Elderly and Disabled People, New Delhi 17–19 September*. See http://www.transed2012.in/Common/Uploads/Poster/279_paper_transedAbstract00160.pdf

The UNWTO recommendations for accessible tourism can be found at: http://www.accessibletourism.org/resources/accesibilityen_2013_unwto.pdf.

On the links between tourism, public transport and social inclusion see

Currie, G. and Stanley, J. (2008) Investigating links between social capital and public transport. *Transport Reviews* 28 (4), 529–547.

Hall, C.M. (2010) Equal access for all? Regulative mechanisms, inequality and tourism mobility. In S. Cole and N. Morgan (eds) *Tourism and Inequality: Problems and Prospects* (pp. 34-48). Wallingford: CABI.

International Transport Forum (ITF) (2016) *Shared Mobility: Innovation for Liveable Cities.* Paris: OECD.

On the transport legacies of major events and accompanying urban regeneration see

Kassens-Noor, E.V.A. (2013) Transport legacy of the Olympic Games, 1992–2012. *Journal of Urban Affairs* 35 (4), 393–416.

6 Futures and Conclusions

Just saying that something is good for you does not mean it will be adopted by people. While sustainability is a vital goal people will not use public transport just because it reduces transport emissions and contributes towards the environment. Instead, consumers want a transport system that meets their needs. This includes not only things such as comfort, safety, security, convenience, and value that are common to all transport users but, as various chapters in this book have indicated, tourists will also require additional dimensions that meet their specific circumstances, such as excellent communication and information services, sufficient luggage space, high levels of punctuality with respect to timetables and ease of connections in terms of both inter-modality and access to accommodation and attractions. However, increases in tourist use of public transport will arise not only from individual preferences but also from the broader structural changes that are part of sustainable transitions. Therefore, this final chapter discusses some of the broader trends and issues that characterise the socio-technical system within which transport is consumed and which will also shape public transport supply and demand in the future. It also provides an outline of the system needs that need to be addressed so as to encourage more tourists to use public transport.

Urbanisation

Urbanisation is one of the most important factors affecting consumption and mobility on the planet today. More than one half of the world population lives now in urban areas, and virtually all countries of the world are becoming increasingly urbanised. Urbanisation is a major driver for public transport both within cities, because of the expansions in population and city size, and between cities, as transport is driven by the point-to-point nature of transport network connectivity (McKinsey Center for Business and Environment, 2015). The growth of urban centres of 500,000 people, for example, demonstrates a higher correlation with international tourism growth than simple population growth for example. As well as encouraging the growth of air routes and motorways, urbanisation is therefore also a major factor in the development of new rail networks, especially such as the high speed rail (HSR) networks discussed in Chapter 4, as well as new mobility services (Chapter 5).

In 2014, 54% of the world's population was residing in urban areas. In contrast, in 1950, 30% of the world's population was urban, and it is estimated that by 2050, 66% of the world's population will be urban. The most urbanised regions are Northern America (82% living in urban areas in 2014), Latin America and the Caribbean (80%) and Europe (73%). In contrast, in Africa only 40% of the population were living in urban areas in 2014, and 48% in Asia. Yet these two areas are currently the fastest growing with respect to urbanisation and it is expected that they will have reached 56% and 64% urban respectively by 2050 (United Nations, Department of Economic and Social Affairs (UNDESA), 2015a). With the expected addition of 2 billion cars globally by 2050, transport-related emissions are projected to grow between 120% and 230% (C40 Cities, 2016).

> Much of this increase will be the result of urban population growth and land cover expansion occurring at rates never seen before. As more and more people move to cities, urban transportation systems will play an increasingly critical role in driving responsible climate action and reducing global emissions. (C40 Cities, 2016: 3)

While today's high-income countries have been highly urbanised for several decades, since 1950 upper-middle-income countries experienced the fastest pace of urbanisation. In Europe 74% of the population lived in urban areas in 2011 and is expected to reach around 82% of urban dwellers by 2050. In 1950, a majority (57%) of the population in high-income countries already lived in urban areas, a figure expected to reach 86% by 2050. In the upper-middle-income countries (e.g. Brazil, China, Mexico), only 20% of the population lived in urban areas in 1950, as compared to 63% in 2014 and an expected figure of 79% urban by 2050 (UNDESA, 2015a). Urban sprawl, relocation of activities to the urban periphery as a result of private car oriented urban planning and design and new mobility habits have resulted in chronic congestion in many cities. For example, in Europe the average delay in minutes for a one-hour journey driven in peak periods is 29 minutes (Corazza et al., 2015).

Aggravating factors for traffic congestion in Europe, as with many places around the world, are the strong dependence on passenger cars for covering small distances (Eurostat, 2013) and a high motorisation rate (cars per head of population). For example, between 2006 to 2011 there was an increase in the motorisation rate in a majority of the EU Member States, and in 10 out of the 28 Member States one car is available per two inhabitants). It is therefore not surprising that passenger cars dominate the modal split across Europe, with the average in the period 2003–2012 being: 7.0% rail, 83.8% passenger cars and 9.2% motor coaches, buses and trolley buses (Eurostat, 2013). At the same time, fuel combustion in transport accounted for 20.2% of the greenhouse gas emissions in the EU 28 Member States in 2011, since 'transport was the only source that presented an increase between 1990 and 2011 (+19%)' (Eurostat, 2013: 147). However, there is some evidence of a decline in the level of personal car ownership in the US, which may be related to the growth of new mobility services (McKinsey Center for Business and Environment, 2015), although such services are primarily based in the larger urban centres.

Clearly, while urbanisation is an important factor in support and use of mass transit, it needs to be placed within the broader context of urban land use planning with respect to how the benefits of public transport and active travel can be best maximised for the economic, social and environmental benefits of individuals and the city and region as a whole. For example, Copenhagen plans to become carbon neutral by 2025 and prioritises bicycles over cars with the city now having more bicycles than people (see Gössling, 2013). The city calculates that one mile on a bicycle is worth $0.42 [27p] to society, while one mile in a car is a $0.20 (15p) loss (Vidal, 2016). Similarly, Helsinki aims to drastically reduce the number of cars on its streets by investing heavily in better public transport, imposing higher parking fees, encouraging bicycles and walking and converting inner city ring roads into residential and walking areas. The city is introducing a 'mobility on demand' system that integrates all forms of shared and public transport in a single payment network (Greenfield, 2014). The idea is to make the city's public transport so good that no one will want a car by 2025 (Vidal, 2016).

Insight 6.1: Shenzhen: New Energy Vehicle Promotion (Winner of the Urban Transportation category in the C40 City Climate Leadership Awards)

In 2010 emissions from Shenzhen's transportation sector accounted for 23 million tonnes of CO_2, or 42% of the city's overall emissions. Although the buses and taxis only accounted for 1.1% of the vehicles in Shenzhen, they were responsible for one-fifth of the city's total emissions. In response to this problem the Shenzhen Development and Reform Commission (SDRC) and the Transportation Commission of Shenzhen jointly launched the New Energy Vehicles (NEV) Promotion which aims to replace traditional vehicles with NEVs across the entire city to reduce CO_2 emissions and improve air quality. The first part of the city's strategy is to prioritise electrified public transportation (buses and taxis). As of December 2013, 3050 units of new energy buses (accounting for 20% of public buses in Shenzhen), and 850 pure electric taxis (accounting for 6% of taxis), were operating in the city, also making it one of the largest 'zero-emissions' public transport fleet in service worldwide. As a result of the initiative it has been estimated that the NEV fleet enabled Shenzhen to reduce CO_2 emissions by 160,000 tonnes between 2009 and 2013, as well as improving air quality.

Source:
http://www.c40.org/profiles/2014-shenzhen

Active Travel and Sustainable Mobility

Car-oriented urbanisation, in which access to shops, employment and services is primarily presumed upon car access rather than public transport, including walking and cycling behaviour, has a major impact upon emissions, quality of life and public health and especially growing levels of obesity and cardio-vascular disease (Booth et al., 2005; Feng et al., 2010; Durand et al., 2011; Sallis et al., 2012). Between April 2008 and April 2009, the US National Household Travel Survey (NHTS) asked the American population 'In the past week, how many times did you take a walk outside including walking the dog and walks for exercise?' Nearly 37% of Americans reported no walk trips at all in the previous week. About 25% of children (5-15 years old) reported taking no walks or bike rides outside for any reason in the previous week. Nearly one-third of younger people (16-65), and almost half of older Americans (65 and over) report taking no walks outside for any purpose in the previous week (Department of Transportation, 2010). The average amount of time spent in active travel each day was just 10 minutes per capita (including people with no active travel). This is a figure well below the minimum 30 minutes per day of activity recommended for good health. Children in middle income African-American families (with household incomes of \$40–\$80,000 per year) and higher income White families (over \$80,000 per year) were more likely to report taking any walks, while 30% of Asian children reported no walk trips in the previous week regardless of income. For children living close to their schools (within two miles/3.21 km), half of the parents thought the amount or speed of traffic was a serious issue in letting their kids walk to school, while less than a quarter thought crime or weather was a serious issue (Department of Transportation, 2010).

The American situation with respect to lack of active travel and health problems is not something that is occurring in isolation and highlights the global epidemic of obesity. For example, if present trends continue half the UK's adult population will be clinically obese by 2050 (Barton, 2009). The obesity problem being further complicated by the impact of aging populations, with the percentage of the global population aged 60 years or over having already increased from 8.5% in 1980 to 12.3% in 2015 and it is projected to rise further to 21.5% in 2050. Europe is projected by UNDESA (2015b) to remain the most aged region over the coming decades, with 34% of the population projected to be aged 60 or over in 2050, followed by North America (27%), Latin America and the Caribbean (25%), Asia (24%) and Oceania (23%). Of those aged 60 or over worldwide, 14% were aged 80 or over in 2015. By 2050, the projected 434 million people aged 80 or over will account for 21% of the global population over age 60 (UNDESA, 2015b).

Growth in the overall number of older persons also produces increases in non-communicable diseases-related disability, including diabetes and cardiovascular diseases related to diet and lack of exercise (Christensen et al., 2009). Therefore active travel is also a major focus of trying to improve the health of aging populations and transportation planners need to recognise the mobility needs of the elderly (Lebel et al., 2011; Moniruzzaman et al., 2013; Annear et al., 2014). As Blocker et al. (2016) noted in the case of the Netherlands, while partaking in fewer and shorter trips than younger generations, today's elderly are increasingly (auto)mobile. Although the elderly benefit from the independence, freedom of movement, and social inclusion of private car based movement, concerns are growing regarding the environmental and accessibility impacts of this induced mobility. As Blocker et al. (2016) concludes, as seniors are becoming increasingly automobile, the results call for strategies to encourage older people to use more physically active and environmentally friendly transport modes such as public transport, walking and cycling.

Encouraging people to be more active is a substantial contributor to both reducing emissions, as a result of less car use, and healthier individuals and communities (Cao & Zhang, 2015). However, to change such mobility behaviour may require substantial interventions and improved urban design. Buehler and Pucher (2012) undertook a detailed analysis of public transport demand in Germany and the US, using comparable national travel surveys from 2001/2002 and 2008/2009 for both countries. Public transport use, as well as cycling and walking participation, is far more successful in Germany than in the US, with much greater growth in overall passenger volumes and trips per capita. In 2001, Americans made 89% of their trips by automobile and 8% on foot, 2% by public transport and less than 1% by bicycle. In contrast, Germans make 40% of their trips by green modes of transport: public transport (8%), bicycle (9%) and foot (23%) (Buehler, 2011). Although there has been growth in car travel in both countries it has not been as great in Germany has it has been in the US. Between 1995 and 2005, per-capita vehicle kilometres of car use increased by 5% in Germany compared to 12% in the US (Buehler, 2011). Partly as a result of these factors per-capita CO_2 emissions from transport in the US were three times the German level in 2005 (3900 vs. 1300 kg CO_2 per year); energy use per capita for transport was also three times higher in the US than in Germany; and between 1999 and 2006, per capita CO_2 emissions and energy use from transport in Germany declined by 7% and 9%, compared to 2% and 4% increases in the US (Buehler, 2011).

Even controlling for differences between the countries in demographics, socio-economics, and land use, Buehler and Pucher (2012) showed that Germans are five times as likely as Americans to use public transport. Moreover, public transport in Germany attracts a much broader cross-section of society for a greater diversity of trip purposes. The success of German public transport is due to a coordinated package of mutually supportive policies that include the following: (1) more and better service, (2) attractive fares and convenient ticketing, (3) full multimodal and regional integration, (4) high taxes and restrictions on car use and (5) land-use policies and planning strategies that promote compact, mixed-use developments (Buehler, 2011; Buehler & Pucher, 2012). Undoubtedly these government interventions are also significant because they also help contribute to a different mobility culture and associated set of behaviours with respect to public transport and non-motorised transport such as cycling and walking (Frank et al., 2007; Buehler, 2011).

Also of importance will be improvements in urban planning and design that encourage public transport and active travel. This is also of extra significance because of the global growth in urbanisation and the extent to which populations are increasingly urban based. For example, in North America 81.5% of the population live in urban areas, Latin America and the Caribbean 79.5% and Europe 73.4% (UNHabitat & UNESCAP 2015). Asia and Africa are currently experiencing massive growth in urbanisation. For example, although urbanisation rates in Asia are significantly lower than the rest of the world, by 2018 the population of Asia is expected to become more than 50% urban. The speed of population increase and urbanisation in Asia is unprecedented. The urban population of the region more than doubled between 1950 and 1975, and doubled again between 1975 and 2000. It is projected to almost double once more between 2000 and 2025. By 2050, nearly two out of three people in Asia will be living in urban areas (UNHabitat & UNESCAP, 2015). In response to these pressures some public transport systems are already changing (Vidal, 2016).

Insight 6.2: Cycle Travel and Public Transport in South Moravia, Czech Republic

South Moravia is in the south-east of the Czech Republic, bordering Austria and Slovakia and is one of the most popular regions of the Czech Republic and is visited by about 1 million visitors each year. Its area of nearly 7200 km² has about 1.17 million inhabitants with one-third of the region's population lives in the capital Brno. The Integrated Public Transport System of the South Moravian Region (IDS JMK) is responsible for local trains, regional buses and local public transport in the cities of Brno, Adamov, Blansko, Břeclav, Bystřice nad Pernštejnem, Hodonín, Kyjov, Vyškov and Znojmo.

Although the railways have offered bicycle transport for some years, in April 2012 South Moravia and IDS JMK launched a project to improve ways for travellers to take their bicycles on public transport. Bus lines on 12 routes were equipped with trailers for the transportation of bicycles on weekends (available from the end of April until end of September) and trains were given additional compartments to transport the bicycles. Two new train connections were added that previously did not have this facility while new tariffs for bicycle transport on railways and buses were also introduced.

The service enables cyclists to travel by public transport to a starting point of a bicycle route, or to use public transport for their return trip. A day ticket for one bike costs 70 CZK (€2.60); a single trip ticket for a bike is equal to a regular passenger ticket. The buses on existing lines had been equipped with external carriers (for six bikes) or trailers (for 20 bikes). Each trailer costs about €2,000. Since the regional buses and trains would be running anyway there were no additional operational costs.

The new bicycle friendly transport connections have proven to be very popular with the number of passengers on some bus lines substantially increasing. Approximately 2500 tourists a year use these buses to transport their bikes while over 20,000 people take their bikes on trains. Even if the use of the 'bike-buses' is comparatively marginal, the systematic approach of introducing cycle-carrying facilities on both modes of transport has increased the numbers of cyclists visiting the region without increasing operational costs, although some route issues arose for buses as not all narrow streets are passable for buses with trailers. Good quality information for travellers about the programme is available via leaflets and a website. According to Herbert Seelmann, a Brno traffic engineer involved in the project, said: 'The service can be applied in other regions with attractive bicycle routes as well. It is a relative low-cost measure which makes a region more attractive for bicycle tourism, being a healthy and sustainable form of recreation'.

Sources:
Eltis The urban mobility observatory: http://www.eltis.org/discover/case-studies/
    helping-cyclists-travel-public-transport-south-moravia-czech-republic#sthash.
    Y9cHjcsZ.dpuf
Brno cycle routes on mapmyride: http://www.mapmyride.com/cz/
    brno-south-moravian-region/
IDSJMK South Moravian Integrated Public Transport System Czech language site
    with information in other languages including English: http://www.idsjmk.cz/
Brno cycling (in Czech): http://www.brnonakole.cz/

Behavioural Change

In the majority of locations tourists, by themselves, are not a sufficient justification for public transport provision. Tourism is instead a valuable 'add-on' to local transport developments that may serve to encourage provision where governments and transport agencies may be unwilling to do so. Tourism is therefore often regarded by government as a means to financially support public transport services that are otherwise uneconomic by many measures, though integral to economic and social well-being. This is especially the case in island communities and peripheral rural areas (Adrianto &

Matsuda, 2004; Baird, 2012; Laird, 2012), but may also apply to some urban routes as well.

There are multiple environmental, economic and social benefits to tourist use of public transport (Le-Klähn & Hall, 2015). In terms of sustainable mobility, train and coach travel are the most carbon efficient travel options as they produce significantly less greenhouse gas emissions than that from car and air travel (Peeters et al., 2007; Gössling, 2010; Filimonau et al., 2014). For example, Lin (2010) found that tourists switching to public transport instead of private cars to access a national park in Taiwan would reduce CO_2 emissions by 22%. Nevertheless, giving up the use of a private car can be difficult whether you are a visitor to a destination or in your home environment. Indeed, the two are arguably inextricably linked because they both require particular sets of behaviour and the provision of services that enable public and non-motorised transport (Gössling et al., 2012a, 2013). The social practices of using public transport, cycling and walking in the home environment may therefore provide a set of attitudes that may increase the likelihood of using public transport to and at destinations should they be of a satisfactory standard. The research of Reilly et al. (2010), in Canada suggests that short-haul tourists tend to have strong preferences for private modes and are less likely to change their behaviour. In contrast, long-haul tourists are more likely to switch modes depending on the options available. As tourists tend to make decision on transport mode well before their arrival, destination managers and public transport agencies need to better communicate to tourists in their planning phase in order to provide the information on public transport at the destination so as to influence mode choice (Reilly et al., 2010; Le-Klähn & Hall, 2015), as well as provide better integration (a) among all modes and routes comprising the multi-modal public transport network, and (b) of the physical and operational elements of each particular mode and service, e.g. cycle, train, bus or ferry.

Figure 1.4 outlined the various elements or segments of a trip on public transport. In order to improve the likelihood of an individual, group or family travelling by public transport these elements need to be as integrated as possible (Rüetschi & Timpf, 2005). Zimmermann and Fang (2015) argued that from a public transport user's perspective a trip involves a number of discrete time segments each time segment is perceived in different ways that need to be considered in public transport planning and design in order to increase use and encourage modal shifts away from private cars. Their approach as well as other features identified in previous chapters in this book and the public transport literature (Le-Klähn & Hall, 2015) are used to modify the model used in Figure 1.4 to highlight the service design issues,

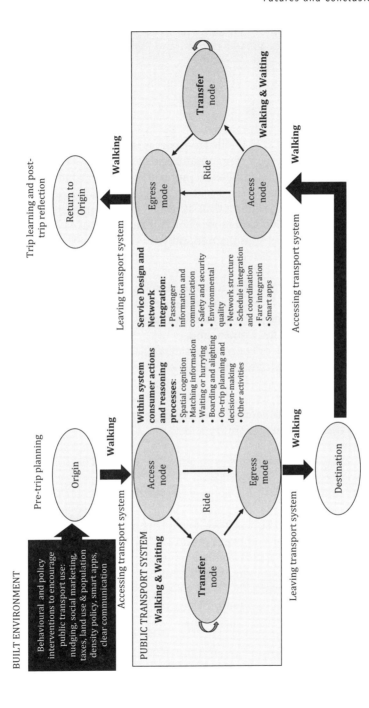

Figure 6.1 Encouraging public transport use via service design, network integration and behavioural and policy interventions

transport network integration issues, and behavioural and policy interventions that may encourage greater tourist (and local) use of public transport (Figure 6.1).

Service design issues

Walking

No matter which type of public transport is used, public transport trips include time spent walking. Zimmermann and Fang (2015: 2) suggest travellers view walking time as significantly more difficult than time spent riding on transport: 'Depending on the situation, walking time can be considered up to twice as onerous as riding time in travel decision making'. Walking therefore has a major impact on mode choice. If the walking environment to public transport is regarded as inappropriate by consumers then it will not be accessed. Key issues include:

- the perceived effort it takes to walk, especially for travellers carrying packages and where level changes via stairs or ramps are required;
- the importance of the perceived safety and security of the walking environment, especially for women; and
- the frequent absence of continuous sidewalks in good condition, free of impediments such as hawkers, parked cars, pot-holes, etc.

Waiting

Waiting time is also perceived by travellers to be much more onerous than riding time. Reasons for this include:

- uncertainty and nervousness as to when the next bus or train will actually arrive;
- the fact that when waiting, no progress is being made in moving to the destination;
- perceived safety and security while waiting, especially at night and/or for women and other vulnerable groups;
- the need to stand in a potentially hostile environment that may be hot or cold and/or without light, weather protection; and
- poor passenger information about routes, schedules, delays, and wayfinding (Zimmermann & Fang, 2015).

Transfers

One or more transfers between different modes, which likely include walking and waiting, is also a negative factor on public transport use.

Furthermore, transfers in off peak periods, including night time, appear to be perceived more negatively than those in peak periods (Guo & Wilson, 2004). The negative perceptions of transfer include:

- the potential unreliability of the service transferred to;
- the possible need to leave a seat on one service to stand on another;
- the quality of the transferring environment in terms of lighting, weather protection, and perceptions of safety and security;
- the need for level and building changes; and
- poor way-finding information guiding new users to the second service (Guo & Wilson, 2004; Rüetschi & Timpf, 2005; Zimmermann & Fang, 2015)

Plate 6.1 Waiting for the Oslo train at Lillehammer Station, Norway. The stress of waiting for the train is lessened by provision of clocks and station announcements.

Plate 6.2 Knutpunkten is the integrated transport centre for bus, train and ferry in Helsingborg, Sweden. The picture shows the link between the upper level (ferry access) with the lower level (bus, taxis, ticketing, information and services). A further level below is Helsingborg central train station. The centre also houses a hotel and meeting facilities.

Network integration

In order to respond to consumer perceptions and experiences with respect trips on to public transport, the public transport network needs to be as integrated as possible. Key dimensions include network structure, schedule integration, transfer points, fare integration, and information for passengers.

Network structure

In the public transport context integration involves making sure that the entire public transport network, including access and departure, supports travel among the entire array of origins and destinations in a minimum of travel time and cost. Zimmermann and Fang (2015: 4) state, 'Public transport networks should be planned, implemented and operated to support door-to-door travel irrespective of the mode or modes, route or routes used'. They suggest that this should therefore consider:

- Individual route alignments and terminals.
- Stop locations.
- Stops added or eliminated.
- Frequencies increased or reduced (see also Rüetschi & Timpf, 2005).

Insight 6.3: Automated Transit Vehicles in Singapore

In late April 2016 Singapore's national public transport operator SMRT announced a joint venture with a partner in the Netherlands, 2getthere, to market, supply and operate automated vehicles in Singapore and the rest of Asia Pacific. The joint venture is targeting both automated and mixed-use transport, and planned to have its third generation rapid transit capabilities on demonstration in Singapore by the end of the year. The autonomous vehicles can carry up to 24 passengers and navigate using artificial landmarks. The system for Singapore is planned to carry up to 8,000 passengers per hour in any single direction. The vehicles are regarded as complementary to SMRT's existing multi-modal transport operations. Colin Lim, managing director of SMRT Services, stated that the development was part of a wider strategy to develop transport capabilities and improve commuter connectivity from home to destination: 'through investments in innovative technologies… There is a growing national push to implement future mobility solutions that can meet our first and last mile connectivity needs' (quoted in Lee, 2016).

Sources:
SMRT: https://www.smrt.com.sg/

Schedule integration/coordination

Schedule integration between different modes or different operators using the same mode has two important implications. The first is to ensure that all routes serving a particular stop or terminal are in operation for the same time period. The second is to coordinate schedules, especially in networks with low frequencies so that the different routes serving an important transfer station are scheduled to arrive and depart at the same time and are 'held' for enough time between or among them so that all applicable transfers can be made (Zimmermann & Fang, 2015).

Transfer points

Although, as noted above, transfers are negatively perceived by customers, it is often more attractive 'to have an alternative available which involves a transfer but is always available, requires a minimum of travel time and travel difficulty, including cost, than a direct travel alternative without a transfer that is long, circuitous, slow and only available in the peak periods' (Zimmermann & Fang, 2015: 5). To enable transfers to occur as easily as possible the following requirements should be fulfilled at transfer points (terminals, stations, stops):

- minimum walking distances and level changes between stopping locations;
- safe, secure level transfer facilities which enable travel by all citizens including the physically challenged (e.g. seniors);
- enhanced lighting and weather protection in walking and waiting areas;
- platforms and passages large enough to accommodate expected flows and numbers of waiting/boarding passengers;
- well lighted, signposted and traffic signal (or more) protected street crossings where required for transfers;
- off-street drop off/pick up facilities for bus transfers at rapid transit stations and at large bus transfer locations; and
- amenities for passengers so that the trip involving public transport through these locations can be made more pleasant and productive, thus presenting a competitive alternative to private vehicles use.

Fare integration

Users of public transport are sensitive not only to the cost of fares, but also the number of times a fare must be paid and the media by which it is purchased. As Zimmermann and Fang (2015: 5–6) observe,

> The objective in fare setting and payment should be to maximise convenience and minimise the perceived cost to the user of public transport. Having to pay for public transport one trip at a time or take a public transport fare card, ticket, pass or cash (the worst) out of a secure pocket or purse multiple times for a trip involving multiple services is very inconvenient. It also increases the negative perception of public transport use compared to driving where the user costs of a single trip are not perceived at all unless tolls are paid or parking is charged for.

Interestingly they go on to suggest that the higher the number of discrete fare media the greater will be the dwell costs and hence operating costs and possibility of non-payment. They therefore suggest greater use of integrated fares paid for by IC cards, which are a rechargeable contactless smart card ticketing system that was originally introduced for public transport in Japan. Although it should be noted that even in Japan while there is considerable overlap between the major IC cards for rail and bus there remain significant gaps (see Japan-guide.com, 2016).

Passenger information

As noted in the previous chapter clear passenger information is critical for encouraging public transport use. The key objective of information provision for public transport is to provide it in one easy to use and understandable format for all services and access/egress and transfer points, irrespective of route and mode to facilitate total trips from origin to destination (Zimmermann & Fang, 2015). The type of information passengers require include:

- schedules and next service arrival times at the first boarding stop;
- way finding information directing travellers between major public transport stops, stations and terminals and major activity centres. This should include walking and transfer times as well as information for disabled travellers;
- way finding information within transfer facilities;
- schedules and next service arrival times at transfer points; and
- information with respect to interruptions to service (Rüetschi & Timpf, 2005; Zimmermann & Fang, 2015).

Behavioural and policy interventions

With respect to the adoption of sustainable mobility behaviour the vast majority of individuals are not yet willing to give up their travel by plane or private car or change their travel markedly, despite enthusiasm by governments and some in industry to encourage voluntary changes in consumer behaviour (Cohen et al., 2014). For the majority of people, issues of climate change, energy, sustainable consumption and sustainable mobility have a relatively low salience in people's day-to-day activities, choices and actions, especially with respect to the selection of transport modes and holidays (Whitmarsh, 2009; Whitmarsh et al., 2011). Even the most environmentally aware tourists might not be more willing to alter their travel behaviour and may even be among the most active travellers (Barr et al., 2010). Indeed, slow travel, which is characterised by greater emphasis on travelling shorter distances, low levels of environmental impact and emissions production, and experience of landscape and culture, has arguably greater potential to contribute to sustainable mobility than notions of slow tourism per se, that are often focussed only on what occurs at the destination. Hall (2012), for example, notes that the Slow Movement appears unaware of the potential contradictions between mobility and sustainability, and quoted its founder Carlo Petrini (2007: 241) who writes:

> It is necessary to move, to meet people, to experience other territories and other tables. If we apply this conviction to the network it is vital to guarantee the circulation within it of people, from one side of the globe to the other, without distinction and without restriction. The right to travel becomes fundamental, a premise on which to base cultural growth and the self-nourishment of the network of gastronomes.

Such a situation reflects the importance of recognising that relevant sustainable consumption information is individually and socially contextualised and actioned (Hall, 2013). 'Concepts and tools do not necessarily motivate behaviour change where individuals are not motivated to change or perceive barriers to doing so' (Whitmarsh et al., 2011: 58), or already perceive that they already *are* behaving in a sustainable fashion.

This is not to suggest that utilitarian (e.g. green labelling, tax incentives, pricing, education) and social/psychological (behavioural economics, nudging, social marketing) approaches to encouraging sustainable mobility are not without value, rather it is to note that their impacts are relatively limited (Hall, 2013, 2014) and need to be undertaken in conjunction with policy interventions that seek to change social practices by virtue of also changing the socio-technical systems within which they emerge. Within such a framework, the potential for change depends on the interplay between three dimensions:

(1) decision-making and cognition of actors (technical, material, and social aspects of knowledge, skills, motivations, understandings, and judgements about the value of public transport);
(2) individual behaviours and social practices (e.g. sustainable travel behaviour, use of public transport); and
(3) broader engagement with socio-technical systems of provision and governance (e.g. creating alternative infrastructures such as cycle ways and walking paths, developing new public transport routes and infrastructure, lobbying for greater provision of public transport, new policies that factor the price of carbon emissions in transport planning) (Hall, 2013).

Critically, all three elements are required over the long-term to develop sustainable mobility behaviours that encourage public transport use and active travel via cycling and walking. In such a situation upstream social marketing that seeks to change the structural dimensions that affect mobility

Table 6.1 Behavioural and policy interventions to encourage greater public transport use

Continuum of habitual behaviour	*Continuum of Intervention*	
	Downstream interventions Focus on individual agency and behaviour	*Upstream intervention* Focus on changing structure and socio-technical regime in order to change individual behaviour
Conscious behaviour Weak or non habitual behaviour	Strong focus on individual decision-making, e.g. knowledge, judgement and skills • Education and provision of information • Green/eco labelling • Tax incentives • Pricing • Using campaigns and volunteering to promote new social norms	Changes to socio-technical system and regime to create new context for behaviours and *generate new* sustainable habits and practices • Environmental design, e.g. changes to built environment to develop denser residential areas with green space and limited car access so as to encourage active travel and public transport use; changes to environmental quality of public transport infrastructure and transfer points • Legislation and regulation • Technological change, e.g. automated transit vehicles • Changes in access to public transport (economic incentives, frequency, pricing, location, transfer points, fare integration)
Moderate habitual behaviour	Growing focus on social practices • Nudging – making choices to encourage public transport use through manipulation of a consumer's environment • Using campaigns and volunteering to promote new social norms of public transport use that reinforce sustainable mobility behaviours	
Strong habits *Unconscious behaviour*	Strong focus on social practices • Lifestyle change via focusing on satisfaction of psychological needs; cultural differentiation; marking social meaning and identity and utilising social norms to reinforce sustainable mobility behaviours	Changes to socio-technical system and regime to create new context for behaviours and *change existing* habits and practices • Environmental design, e.g. changes to built environment to encourage active travel and public transport use by building new cycle ways and walkway and limiting car traffic flows so as to favour public transport network; changes to environmental quality of public transport infrastructure and transfer points • Legislation and regulation • Technological change, e.g. High Speed Rail • Changes in access to public transport (economic incentives, frequency, pricing, location, transfer points, fare integration)

Source: After Verplanken and Wood (2006); Hall (2013, 2014, 2016).

consumption are just as important, and in some cases even more so, than the downstream interventions that focus on individual consumers (Hall, 2014) (see Table 6.1). As Verplanken and Wood (2006: 36) observe, 'Disrupting the environmental cues that trigger and maintain habit performance renders habits open to change'. In addition, in terms of changing organisational thinking about tourist use of public transport and active travel the problem does not always lie with public transport agencies, as Insight 6.4 on the 'Powered by Cycling: Panorama' project in Denmark in which the tourism industry needs to be convinced of the value of the active travel market!

Insight 6.4: Danish Bike Touring: Powered by Cycling

'Powered by Cycling: Panorama' is the title of a project initiated by the Danish Cyclists' Federation in 2012. The project's goal is to respond to a decline in tourism along the Danish coasts by adding a bicycle 'experience' to holiday goers' visits to certain coast destinations. As Project Manager Jesper Pørksen explains:

> The word Panorama was chosen because it describes well what awaits you along the Danish coastline: a splendid view of the seas and of the infinite sky above the flat and bicycle-friendly Danish landscape. Powered by Cycling refers to the more serious part of the project: That bicycle tourism is one of the means for inducing growth in remote coast areas... Our main assets are the North Sea Route and the Berlin-Copenhagen Route, which run along the Danish west and east coasts, respectively. These routes are internationally renowned, and we believe many tourists will find it attractive to cycle on these iconic routes.

Under the project a number of local routes will connect the main cycling routes with local attractions in order to attract non-cycling holiday goers. These route suggestions are also intended to provide touring cyclists with an excuse for making a stop in otherwise quickly-passed coastal towns. As part of the process the Federation is encouraging municipalities and others to build more 'bicycle-friendly' coastal infrastructure. However, according to Pørksen

> What is difficult is to prove to the tourism industry that not only are bicycling opportunities demanded; bicycle tourists are also great customers. The common belief is that cyclists bike all day, eat a pack of toast, and camp in a tent. However, our database shows that most

often tourists on bicycles are 'empty nesters' with money to spend and a huge appetite on the good things in life. We need to change the perception.

Source:
Cycling Embassy of Denmark: http://www.cycling-embassy.dk/
Kristensen, M-B. (2012) Changing the story about bike touring. Cycling Embassy of Denmark, accessed 1 April 2016. http://www.cycling-embassy.dk/2012/08/25/changing-the-story-about-bike-touring/

Plate 6.3 Walking and cycling path Amager Beach Park, Copenhagen, Denmark

Undoubtedly, changes to the design of the built environment are a significant element for the development of sustainable mobility behaviours for public transport and active travel (Frank *et al.*, 2007). Space consumption as a result of the use of passenger cars is substantial. In urban areas, where space is scarcer and scarcer, an automobile consumes 285 m^2 min/pkm (including commuter parking), whereas a bus ranges from 17 m^2 min/pkm (if operating on a reserved lane) to 8 m^2 min/pkm (in mixed traffic), which makes the latter among the most space-efficient modes for travelling within cities (Bayliss, 2000 in Corazza *et al.*, 2015). As a result of such pressures there have been increasing focus on the development of 'compact city' land use models as a means of encouraging more sustainable urban development given that empirical evidence suggests that when density increases, energy use for housing and everyday travel decreases because of efficient infrastructure, proximity to work-places and services, and highly developed public transport (Næss, 2006). Although other factors, such as urban green infrastructure and environmental services, consumption of natural resources, and waster and pollution are also significant for assessment of urban sustainability (Tzoulas *et al.*, 2007; Zapata Campos & Hall, 2013).

However, in the same way that focusing on behavioural interventions in isolation may not lead to sustainable behaviour so just increasing the density of cities, albeit with green infrastructure, may also not encourage the sustainable mobility of individuals by themselves. In particular, after a certain density point the energy consumption or ecological footprint of individuals starts to increase again due to more energy consumption for residents' long leisure-time travel by plane and car, including for second home trips (Holden & Norland, 2005; Muniz *et al.*, 2013; Strandell & Hall, 2015a, 2015b). These results highlight the importance of the need to understand people's leisure mobility over the full range of their consumption, i.e. when they are engaging in tourism and leisure activity, rather than just at their permanent residence. Indeed, a significant issue, even for those who frequently travel from the city to domestic second homes (Adamiak *et al.*, 2016), may be one of hypermobility by which a small number of travellers are responsible for a large share of emissions (Gössling *et al.*, 2009). Arguably, it is this group that most need to change transport modes and/or pay the true environmental cost of their travels (Gössling *et al.*, 2015).

Conclusion: Tourism, Public Transport and Sustainable Mobility

The UITP proposed (Bayliss, 2000; Torode, 2003), an operational definition for sustainable transport and development as that which allows decent living and working conditions in which:

- the majority of citizens should be able to conveniently meet most of their local needs by foot, cycle and public transport;
- public transport services sufficient to meet these needs are available and affordable;

- longer distance journeys between urban centres are adequately served by public transport;
- those journeys which go by private transport, pay their full economic and environmental costs; and
- the capacity and management of the road system is in balance with the demand for highway capacity with full social cost pricing.

These laudable environmental, social and economic goals provide a valuable backdrop to the relationship between tourism and public transport. As this book has highlighted, although relatively under-researched, tourism is a significant user of public transport throughout the world. As a result tourists provide significant economic contributions to regional economies as well as supporting public transport itself, while public transport can also be a vital part of the tourist experience. However, given the backdrop of global environmental change, the potential role that public transport can have in promoting more sustainable forms of mobility, including with respect to tourism, is more vital than ever. The McKinsey Center for Business and Environment (2015) even suggest that mobility is at a 'tipping point', with the convergence of four technological trends: in-vehicle connectivity, electrification, car sharing, and autonomous driving (see also ITF, 2015). Undoubtedly, these trends and their inter-relationships will have profound implications for public transport and sustainable mobility, including directly for tourism and recreation. However, also critical to how these technologies contribute to sustainable mobility is the fact that, in their first wave at least, they are primarily geared to major urban agglomerations and the larger urban centres, and that they require technological access, lack of which may further exacerbate digital, economic and mobility divides. In such a context the notion of a social or common good in the provision of public transport may become more important than ever for sustainable mobility and tourism, especially in rural and peripheral areas.

As noted at the start of this book, transport is essential for tourism. Public transport plays a major role in moving tourists around and within destinations and also carries tourists between destinations. In this volume we have provided an account of how the public transport experience can be improved for tourists so that its value can be maximised and that a greater number of people can be encouraged to shift modes. Significantly, the strategies and interventions by which this occurs are of value to the tourism industry and regional economies, regardless of their environmental benefits. However, the fact that they do have environmental benefits needs to be embraced by government, industry and destinations alike. At a time when their appear to be few genuinely clear ways to both reduce environmental impact while increasing or maintaining economic and personal benefits from tourism, the role of public transport needs far greater recognition and support than ever before. We hope that this book plays a role in travelling that path.

Further Reading

On growth in urbanisation see

United Nations Population Division (urbanization theme): www.un.org/en/development/desa/population/theme/urbanization/

On the role of the built environment in active travel and health see

Sallis, J.F., Floyd, M.F., Rodríguez, D.A. and Saelens, B.E. (2012) Role of built environments in physical activity, obesity, and cardiovascular disease. *Circulation* 125 (5), 729–737.

On innovations in sustainable mobility systems see

International Transport Forum (ITF) (2015) *Urban Mobility System Upgrade: How shared self-driving cars could change city traffic*. Paris: OECD.
International Transport Forum (ITF) (2016) *Shared Mobility: Innovation for Liveable Cities*. Paris: OECD.
Automated people mover systems designed for sustainable mobility: http://www.2getthere.eu/
Japanese IC Cards: http://www.japan-guide.com/e/e2359_003.html
C40 Cities The C40 Low Emission Vehicle Network: http://www.c40.org/networks/low_emission_vehicles

References

Aarhaug, J. (2014) *Taxi as Urban Transport*. Oslo: Institute of Transport Economics, Norwegian Centre of Transport Research. See https://www.toi.no/getfile.php?mmfileid=35880

Abou-Zeid, M., Witter, R., Bierlaire, M., Kaufmann, V. and Ben-Akiva, M. (2012) Happiness and travel mode switching: Findings from a Swiss public transportation experiment. *Transport Policy* 19 (1), 93–104.

Abrahampath official website (n.d.) The Abraham Path is a long-distance walking route across the Middle East. See http://abrahampath.org/path/ (accessed 14 February 2016).

Adam, I. (2015) Backpackers' risk perceptions and risk reduction strategies in Ghana. *Tourism Management* 49, 99–108.

Adamiak, C., Hall, C.M., Hiltunen, M. and Pitkänen, K. (2016) Substitute or addition to hypermobile lifestyles? Second home mobility and Finnish CO_2 emissions. *Tourism Geographies* 18 (2), 129–151.

Adrianto, L. and Matsuda, Y. (2004) Study on assessing economic vulnerability of small island regions. *Environment, Development and Sustainability* 6 (3), 317–336.

Agence France-Presse (2015) Dutch cabinet approves partial ban on Islamic veil in public areas. *The Guardian*, 22 May. See http://www.theguardian.com/world/2015/may/22/netherlands-islamic-veil-niqab-ban-proposal-dutch-cabinet (23 January 2016).

Airbnb (2015) More than one million people will celebrate New Year's Eve in 150 countries on Airbnb. See https://www.airbnb.com/press/news/more-than-one-million-people-will-celebrate-new-year-s-eve-in-150-countries-on-airbnb (accessed 31 December 2015).

Akiyama, T. (2005) Japan's transportation policies for the elderly and disabled. In *Workshop on Implementing Sustainable Urban Travel Policies in Japan and Other Asia-Pacific countries*, 2 March, Tokyo.

Al-Atawi, A. and Saleh, W. (2014) Travel behaviour in Saudi Arabia and the role of social factors. *Transport* 29 (3), 269–277.

Albalate, D. and Bel, G. (2010) Tourism and urban public transport: Holding demand pressure under supply constraints. *Tourism Management* 31 (3), 425–433.

Albalate, D., Bel, G. and Fageda, X. (2015) Competition and cooperation between high-speed rail and air transportation services in Europe. *Journal of Transport Geography* 42, 166–174.

Alfonzo, M.A. (2005) To walk or not to walk? The hierarchy of walking needs. *Environment and Behavior* 37, 808–836.

American Bus Assocation (ABA) (2012) American Bus Association supports National Tourism Week, Motorcoach travel is leading the way. Press Release, 4 May. Washington DC: ABA. See http://www.buses.org/news-publications/press-releases

Anable, J. (2005) "Complacent car addicts" or "aspiring environmentalists"? Identifying travel behaviour segments using attitude theory. *Transport Policy* 12 (1), 65–78.

Andersson, H. and Ögren, M. (2013) Charging the polluters: A pricing model for road and railway noise. *Journal of Transport Economics and Policy* 47 (3), 313–333.

Annear, M., Keeling, S., Wilkinson, T., Cushman, G., Gidlow, B. and Hopkins, H. (2014) Environmental influences on healthy and active ageing: A systematic review. *Ageing & Society* 34 (4), 590–622.

Antoniou, C. and Tyrinopoulos, Y. (2013) Factors affecting public transport use in touristic areas. *International Journal of Transportation* 1 (1), 91–112.

Ashworth, G. and Page, S.J. (2011) Urban tourism research: Recent progress and current paradoxes. *Tourism Management* 32 (1), 1–15.

Backhaus, P. (2015) Attention, please! A linguistic soundscape/landscape analysis of ELF information provision in public transport in Tokyo. In K. Murata (ed.) *Exploring ELF in Japanese Academic and Business Contexts: Conceptualisation, Research and Pedagogic Implications* (pp. 194–209). Abingdon: Routledge.

Banister, D. (2005) *Unsustainable Transport: City Transport in the New Century*. London: Routledge.

Bansal, H. and Eiselt, H.A. (2004) Exploratory research of tourist motivations and planning. *Tourism Management* 25 (3), 387–396.

Barber, R. (1993) *Pilgrimages*. London: The Boydell Press.

Baird, A. (2012) Comparing the efficiency of public and private ferry services on the Pentland Firth between mainland Scotland and the Orkney Islands. *Research in Transportation Business & Management* 4 (1), 79–89.

Barr, S. and Prillwitz, J. (2012) Green travellers? Exploring the spatial context of sustainable mobility styles. *Applied Geography* 32 (2), 798–809.

Barr, S., Shaw, G., Coles, T. and Prillwitz, J. (2010) "A holiday is a holiday": Practicing sustainability, home and away. *Journal of Transport Geography* 18, 474–481.

Barter, P.A. (2008) Public planning with business delivery of excellent urban public transport. *Policy and Society* 27 (2), 103–114.

Barton, H. (2009) Land use planning and health and well-being. *Land Use Policy* 26, S115–S123.

Bauder, M. and Freytag, T. (2015) Visitor mobility in the city and the effects of travel preparation. *Tourism Geographies* 17 (5), 682–700.

Bayliss, D. (2000) Urban development and its implications for mobility. UITP Mexico Conference, April.

Bazin, S., Beckerich, C. and Delaplace, M. (2010) High speed rail service, specific resources activation, and tourist development: The case of Rheims. *Desserte Ferroviaire à Grande Vitesse, Activation Des Ressources Spécifiques et Développement Du Tourisme: Le Cas de L'agglomération Rémoise* (1–2), 65–77.

Becken, S. (2005) Towards sustainable tourism transport: An analysis of coach tourism in New Zealand. *Tourism Geographies* 7 (1), 23–42.

Beirão, G. and Cabral, J. S. (2007) Understanding attitudes towards public transport and private car: A qualitative study. *Transport Policy* 14 (6), 478–489.

Belk, R. (2014) You are what you can access: Sharing and collaborative consumption online. *Journal of Business Research* 67 (8), 1595–1600.

Bergen, M. (2015) *Uber: Now one billion served*, re/code article, December 30 2015. See http://recode.net/2015/12/30/uber-now-one-billion-served.html (accessed 31 December 2015).

Beria, P., Grimaldi, R., Debernardi, A., Ferrara, E. and Laurino, A. (2014) *Spatial and Scenario Analyses of Long Distance Coach Transport in Italy* (No. 54739). University Library of Munich, Germany.

Blackman, R.A. and Haworth, N.L. (2013) Tourist use of mopeds in Queensland. *Tourism Management* 36, 580–589.

Böcker, L., van Amen, P. and Helbich, M. (2016) Elderly travel frequencies and transport mode choices in Greater Rotterdam, the Netherlands. *Transportation*, DOI: 10.1007/s11116-016-9680-z.

Bonnafous, A. (1987) The regional impact of the TGV. *Transportation* 14, 127–137.

Boore, S.M. and Bock, D. (2013) Ten years of search and rescue in Yosemite National Park: Examining the past for future prevention. *Wilderness & Environmental Medicine* 24 (1), 2–7.

Booth, K.M., Pinkston, M.M. and Poston, W.S.C. (2005) Obesity and the built environment. *Journal of the American Dietetic Association* 105 (5), 110–117.

Bovaird, T. (2004) Public–private partnerships: From contested concepts to prevalent practice. *International Review of Administrative Sciences* 70, 199–215.

Brotchie, J. (1991) Fast rail networks and socio-economic impacts. In J.F. Brotchie, M. Batty, P. Hall and P. Newton (eds) *Cities of the 21st Century: New Technologies and Spatial Systems* (pp.25–37). Melbourne: Longman Cheshire.

Brändli, H. (1984) *Angebote des öffentlichen Verkehrs [Offers of Public Transport]*. Skriptum, Institut für Verkehrsplanung und Transporttechnik. Zurich: Swiss Federal Institute of Technology.

Budiono, O.A. (2009) Customer satisfaction in public bus transportation: A study of travelers' perception in Indonesia. Masters thesis, Karlstad University.

Buehler, R. (2011) Determinants of transport mode choice: a comparison of Germany and the USA. *Journal of Transport Geography* 19 (4), 644–657.

Buehler, R. and Pucher, J. (2012) Demand for public transport in Germany and the USA: An analysis of rider characteristics. *Transport Reviews* 32 (5), 541–567.

Buhalis, D. and Darcy, S. (eds) (2011) *Accessible Tourism: Concepts and Issues*. Bristol: Channel View Publications.

Buhalis, D. and Michopoulou, E. (2011) Information-enabled tourism destination marketing: addressing the accessibility market. *Current Issues in Tourism* 14 (2), 145–168.

Bullock, R.G., Jin, Y., Ollivier, G.P. and Zhou, N. (2014) *High-speed Railways in China: A look at traffic*. China transport topics no. 11. Washington, DC: World Bank Group. See http://documents.worldbank.org/curated/en/2014/12/23031378/high-speed-railways-china-look-traffic (accessed 1 April 2016).

Burke, M. (2016) Problems and prospects for public transport planning in Australian cities. *Built Environment* 42 (1), 37–54.

Butler, R. (2011) Sustainable tourism in high-latitude islands: Shetland Islands. In J. Carlsen and R. Butler (eds) *Island Tourism: Sustainable Perspectives* (pp. 140–154). Wallingford: CABI.

C40 Cities (2016) *Good Practice Guide: Low-Emission Vehicles*. London: C40 Cities.

Candela, G. and Figini, P. (2012) *The Economics of Tourism Destinations*. Berlin: Springer.

Cantwell, M., Caulfield, B. and O'Mahony, M. (2009) Examining the factors that impact public transport commuting satisfaction. *Journal of Public Transportation* 12 (2), 1–21.

Cao, J. and Zhang, J. (2015) Built environment, mobility, and quality of life. *Travel Behaviour and Society*, doi:10.1016/j.tbs.2015.12.001

Capriello, A. (2014) Bus transport service provision and tourism policies: Lessons from Piedmont, Italy. *Tourism Planning & Development* 11 (2), 210–227.

Caragliu, A. and Del Bo, C. (2012) Smartness and European urban performance: Assessing the local impacts of smart urban attributes. *Innovation: The European Journal of Social Science Research* 25 (2), 97–113.

Carvalho, L., Mingardo, G. and Van Haaren, J. (2012) Green urban transport policies and cleantech innovations: Evidence from Curitiba, Göteborg and Hamburg. *European Planning Studies* 20 (3), 375–396.

Cascetta, E., Papola, A., Pagliara, F. and Marzano, V. (2011) Analysis of mobility impacts of the high speed Rome–Naples rail link using within day dynamic mode service choice models. *Journal of Transport Geography* 19, 635–643.

Cass, N., Shove, E. and Urry, J. (2005) Social exclusion, mobility and access. *The Sociological Review* 53 (3), 539–555.

Castillo-Manzano, J.I. (2010) The city-airport connection in the low-cost carrier era: Implications for urban transport planning. *Journal of Air Transport Management* 16 (6), 295–298.

Cervero, R. (1997) *Paratransit in America: Redefining Mass Transportation*. Westport: Praeger.

Cervero, R. (2000) *Informal Transport in the Developing World*. Geneva: United Nations.

Cervero, R. (2015) Transit-oriented development and the urban fabric. In B.P.Y. Loo and C. Comtois (eds) *Sustainable Railway Futures. Issues and Challenges* (pp. 75–94). Cheltenham: Ashgate.

Cervero, R. and Golub, A. (2007) Informal transport: A global perspective. *Transport Policy* 14, 445–457.

Cervero, R. and Sullivan, C. (2010) *Toward Green TODs*. Berkeley: Institute of Transportation Studies, University of California, Berkeley.

Chang, H.H. and Lai, T.Y. (2009) The Taipei MRT (Mass Rapid Transit) tourism attraction analysis from the inbound tourists' perspective. *Journal of Travel and Tourism Marketing* 26 (5–6), 445–461.

Chapman, L. (2007) Transport and climate change: A review. *Journal of Transport Geography* 15 (5), 354–367.

Chatman, D.G. and Klein, N. (2009) Immigrants and travel demand in the United States: Implications for transportation policy and future research. *Public Works Management & Policy* 13 (4), 312–327.

Chen, C.-F. and Cheng, W.-C. (2016) Sustainability SI: Exploring heterogeneity in cycle tourists' preferences for an integrated Bike-Rail transport service. *Networks and Spatial Economics* 16 (1), 83–97.

Chen, C.L. and Hall, P. (2011) The impacts of high-speed trains on British economic geography: a study of the UK's InterCity 125/225 and its effects. *Journal of Transport Geography* 19 (4), 689–704.

Chen, F.-Y. and Chang, Y.-H. (2005) Examining airline service quality from a process perspective. *Journal of Air Transport Management* 11 (2), 79–87.

Christensen, K., Doblhammer, G., Rau, R. and Vaupel, J.W. (2009) Ageing populations: The challenges ahead. *The Lancet* 374 (9696), 1196–1208.

Chugh, S. (2015) Risk perceptions of international female tourists in India. In S. Kumar, M.C. Dhiman and A. Dahiya (eds) *International Tourism and Hospitality in the Digital Age* (pp. 220–233). Hershey, Pennsylvania: IGI Global.

City of Munich (2014) Facts and figures. See http://www.muenchen.de/rathaus/home_en/Tourist-Office/Salesguide/Facts-and-Figures (accessed 1 April 2016).

Clayton, W., Ben-Elia, E., Parkhurst, G. and Ricci, M. (2014) Where to park? A behavioural comparison of bus Park and Ride and city centre car park usage in Bath, UK. *Journal of Transport Geography* 36, 124–133.

Cohen, S., Higham, J.E.S., Peeters, P.M. and Gössling, S. (eds) (2014) *Understanding and Governing Sustainable Tourism Mobility: Psychological and Behavioural Approaches*. Abingdon: Routledge.

Coles, T.E., Duval, D.T. and Hall, C.M. (2004) Tourism, mobility and global communities: New approaches to theorising tourism and tourist spaces. In W. Theobold (ed.) *Global Tourism* (3rd edn, pp. 463–481). Oxford: Heinemann.

Collins, E.M. (2013) The Curb Side Bus Industry: A New Era of Bus Travel. Analytical Paper, Degree of Master of Arts in Urban Affairs and Public Policy, Faculty of the School of Public Policy and Administration, University of Delaware.

Collins-Kreiner, N. (2010) Researching pilgrimage: Continuity and transformations. *Annals of Tourism Research* 37 (2), 440–456.

Collins-Kreiner, N. and Kliot, N. (2015) Particularism vs. universalism in hiking tourism. *Annals of Tourism Research*. See http://dx.doi.org/10.1016/j.annals.2015.10.007

Confederation of the European Bicycle Industry (CONEBI) (2015) *European Bicycle Market: Industry and Market Profile – 2014 Statistics*. Brussels: CONEBI.

Cooper, C. and Hall, C.M. (2016) *Contemporary Tourism: An International Approach* (3rd edn). Oxford: Goodfellow Publications.

Corazza, M. V., Guida, U., Musso, A. and Tozzi, M. (2015) A European vision for more environmentally friendly buses. *Transportation Research Part D: Transport and Environment*. doi:10.1016/j.trd.2015.04.001

Cornelissen, S., Bob, U. and Swart, K. (2011) Towards redefining the concept of legacy in relation to sport mega-events: Insights from the 2010 FIFA World Cup. *Development Southern Africa* 28 (3), 307–318.

Cortés-Jiménez, I. (2008) Which type of tourism matters to the regional economic growth? The cases of Spain and Italy. *International Journal of Tourism Research* 10 (2), 127–139.

Cortes-Jimenez, I. and Pulina, M. (2010) Inbound tourism and long-run economic growth. *Current Issues in Tourism*, 13 (1), 61–74.

Cullinane, S. (2003) Attitudes of Hong Kong residents to cars and public transport: Some policy implications. *Transport Reviews* 23 (1), 21–34.

Currie, G. and Shalaby, A. (2012) Synthesis of transport planning approaches for the world's largest events. *Transport Reviews* 32 (1), 113–136.

Dallen, J. (2007a) Sustainable transport, market segmentation and tourism: The Looe Valley Branch Line Railway, Cornwall, UK. *Journal of Sustainable Tourism* 15 (2), 180–199.

Dallen, J. (2007b) The challenges of diverse visitor perceptions: Rail policy and sustainable transport at the resort destination. *Journal of Transport Geography* 15 (2), 104–115.

Dann, G. (1981) Tourist motivation an appraisal. *Annals of Tourism Research* 8 (2), 187–219.

Darcy, S., Amrose, I., Scheinsberg, S. and Buhalis, D. (2011) A call for universal approaches to accessible tourism. In D. Buhalis and S. Darcy (eds) *Accessible Tourism: Concepts and Issues* (pp. 390–415). Bristol: Channel View Publications.

Darcy, S. and Dickson, T.J. (2009) A whole-of-life approach to tourism: The case for accessible tourism experiences. *Journal of Hospitality and Tourism Management* 16 (1), 32–44.

Deenihan, G. and Caulfield, B. (2015) Do tourists value different levels of cycling infrastructure? *Tourism Management* 46, 92–101.

Deenihan, G., Caulfield, B. and O'Dwyer, D. (2013) Measuring the success of the Great Western Greenway in Ireland. *Tourism Management Perspectives* 7, 73–82.

Dehoorne, O., Depault, K., Ma, S.Q. and Cao, H.H. (2014) International tourism: Geopolitical dimensions of a global phenomenon. In B.-Y. Cao, S.-Q. Ma and M.-H. Cao (eds) *Ecosystem Assessment and Fuzzy Systems Management* (pp. 389–396). Berlin: Springer.

Delaplace M. (2012) TGV, développement local et taille des villes: Une analyse en termes d'innovation de services. *Revue d'économie régionale et urbaine* 2, 265–292.

Delaplace M. and Dobruszkes F. (2015) From low-cost airlines to low-cost high-speed rail? The French case. *Transport Policy* 38, 73–85.

Dellaert, B.G., Ettema, D.F. and Lindh, C. (1998) Multi-faceted tourist travel decisions: A constraint-based conceptual framework to describe tourists' sequential choices of travel components. *Tourism Management* 19 (4), 313–320.

Department for Transport (UK) (2015) *Public attitudes towards train services: results from the February 2015 Opinions and Lifestyle Survey.* London: Department for Transport. See https://www.gov.uk/government/uploads/system/uploads/attachment_data/file/486598/public-attitudes-towards-train-services-2015-report.pdf (accessed 1 April 2016).

Department of Transportation (US) (2002) *National Household Travel Survey, 2001-2002.* Washington DC: Department of Transportation. See https://www.rita.dot.gov/bts/sites/rita.dot.gov.bts/files/subject_areas/national_household_travel_survey/long_distance.html (accessed 1 April 2016).

Department of Transportation (2010) *NHTS Brief National Household Travel Survey: Active Travel. December.* Washington DC: Department of Transportation.

de Urena, J.M., Garmendia, M., Coronado, J.M., Vickerman, R.W. and Romero, V. (2010) New metropolitan processes encouraged by high-speed rail: The cases of London and Madrid, 12th WCTR, July 11–15, 2010, Lisbon, Portugal. See http://www.wctrsociety.com/wp/wp-content/uploads/abstracts/lisbon/selected/01788.pdf (accessed 1 April 2016).

Di Felice, P. (2014) A method to support hikers in natural areas in the selection of paths tailored for them. *Asian Journal of Information Technology* 13 (7), 382–388.

Di Pietro, L., Mugion, R.G., Mattia, G., Renzi, M.F. and Toni, M. (2015) The Integrated Model on Mobile Payment Acceptance (IMMPA): An empirical application to public transport. *Transportation Research Part C: Emerging Technologies* 56, 463–479.

Diana, M. (2012) Measuring the satisfaction of multimodal travelers for local transit services in different urban contexts. *Transportation Research Part A: Policy and Practice* 46 (1), 1–11.

Dickinson, J.E., Calver, S., Watters, K. and Wilkes, K. (2004) Journeys to heritage attractions in the UK: A case study of National Trust property visitors in the south west. *Journal of Transport Geography* 12 (2), 103–113.

Dickinson, J.E. and Dickinson, J.A. (2006) Local transport and social representations: Challenging the assumptions for sustainable tourism. *Journal of Sustainable Tourism* 14 (2), 192–208.

Dickinson, J. E. and Lumsdon, L. (2010) *Slow Travel and Tourism.* London: Earthscan.

Dickinson, J.E. and Robbins, D. (2007) Using the car in a fragile rural tourist destination: A social representations perspective. *Journal of Transport Geography* 15 (2), 116–126.

Dickinson, J.E. and Robbins, D. (2008) Representations of tourism transport problems in a rural destination. *Tourism Management* 29 (6), 1110–1121.

Dickinson, J.E., Robbins, D. and Fletcher, J. (2009) Representation of transport: A rural destination analysis. *Annals of Tourism Research* 36 (1), 103–123.

Dijk, M., de Haes, J. and Montalvo, C. (2013) Park-and-Ride motivations and air quality norms in Europe. *Journal of Transport Geography* 30 (1), 49–160.

Dijk, M. and Parkhurst, G. (2014) Understanding the mobility-transformative qualities of urban park and ride polices in the UK and the Netherlands. *International Journal of Automotive Technology and Management* 14 (3/4), 246–270.

Dolsak, N. and Ostrom, E. (2003) The challenges of the commons. In N. Dolsak and E. Ostrom (eds) *The Commons in the New Millennium* (pp. 3–34). Cambridge, MA: MIT.

Downward, P. and Lumsdon, L. (2004) Tourism transport and visitor spending: A study in the North York Moors, National Park, UK. *Journal of Travel Research* 42 (4), 415–420.

Disability Rights Education and Defense Fund (DREDF) (nd) International laws. http://dredf.org/legal-advocacy/international-disability-rights/international-laws/ (accessed 1 January 2016).

Dredge, D. and Gyimóthy, S. (2015) The collaborative economy and tourism: Critical perspectives, questionable claims and silenced voices. *Tourism Recreation Research* 40 (3), 286–302.

Dubois, D. and Aliaga, A. (2014) Tourism and public transport: A winning team? How French and European transport authorities manage tourist flows. In *European Transport Conference 2014*, Frankfurt, Germany. London: Association for European Transport.

Durand, C.P., Andalib, M., Dunton, G.F., Wolch, J. and Pentz, M.A. (2011) A systematic review of built environment factors related to physical activity and obesity risk: implications for smart growth urban planning. *Obesity Reviews* 12 (5), e173–e182.

Duval, D.T. (2007) *Tourism and Transport: Modes, Networks and Flow.* Clevedon: Channel View Publications.

Dziekan, K. (2008) *Ease-of-use in Public Transportation.* Stockholm: Department of Transport and Economics, Royal Institute of Technology.

Dziekan, K. and Kottenhoff, K. (2007) Dynamic at-stop real-time information displays for public transport: Effects on customers. *Transportation Research Part A: Policy and Practice* 41 (6), 489–501.

Eaton, B. and Holding, D. (1996) The evaluation of public transport alternatives to the car in British National Parks. *Journal of Transport Geography* 4 (1), 55–65.

Edwards, D. and Griffin, T. (2013) Understanding tourists' spatial behaviour: GPS tracking as an aid to sustainable destination management. *Journal of Sustainable Tourism* 21 (4), 580–595.

Erdil, S.T. and Yıldız, O. (2011) Measuring service quality and a comparative analysis in the passenger carriage of airline industry. *Procedia - Social and Behavioral Sciences* 24, 1232–1242.

Eurostat (2012) *Europe in figures – Eurostat yearbook 2012.* Luxembourg: Publications Office of the European Union.

Eurostat (2013) *Energy, Transport and Environment Indicators.* Luxembourg: Publications Office of the European Union.

Eurostat (2015) Railway passenger transport statistics – quarterly and annual data. See http://ec.europa.eu/eurostat/statistics-explained/index.php/Railway_passenger_ transport_statistics_-_quarterly_and_annual_data (accessed 1 April 2016).

EuroVelo (2011) *Guidance on the route development process.* ECF. See http://www.eurovelo. org/wp-content/uploads/2011/08/Guidance-on-the-Route-Development-Process.pdf (accessed 14 Febraury 2016).

Ewing, R., Handy, S., Brownson, R.C., Clemente, O. and Winston, E. (2006) Identifying and measuring urban design qualities related to walkability. *Journal of Physical Activity and Health* 3 (1), S223–S240.

Fang, K. and Zimmerman, S.L. (2015) *Public transport service optimization and system integration*. China transport topics; no. 14. Washington, DC: World Bank Group. See http://documents.worldbank.org/curated/en/2015/03/24271681/public-transport-service-optimization-system-integration (accessed 1 April 2016).

Farag, S. and Lyons, G. (2012) To use or not to use? An empirical study of pre-trip public transport information for business and leisure trips and comparison with car travel. *Transport Policy* 20, 82–92.

Farkas, K., Feher, G., Benczur, A. and Sidlo, C. (2015) Crowdsending based public transport information service in smart cities. *IEEE Communications Magazine* 53 (8), 158–165.

Fellesson, M. and Friman, M. (2008) Perceived satisfaction with public transport service in nine European cities. *Journal of the Transportation Research Forum* 47 (3), 93–104.

Feng, J., Glass, T.A., Curriero, F.C., Stewart, W.F. and Schwartz, B.S. (2010) The built environment and obesity: a systematic review of the epidemiologic evidence. *Health & Place* 16 (2), 175–190.

Fesenmaier, D.R. and Jeng, J.-M. (2000) Assessing structure in the pleasure trip planning process. *Tourism Analysis* 5 (1), 13–27.

Filimonau, V., Dickinson, J. and Robbins, D. (2014) The carbon impact of short-haul tourism: A case study of UK travel to Southern France using life cycle analysis. *Journal of Cleaner Production* 64, 628–638.

Fischer, L.A. and Schwieterman, J.P. (2011) The decline and recovery of intercity bus service in the United States: A comeback for an environmentally friendly transportation mode? *Environmental Practice* 13 (1), 7–15.

Fishman, E., Washington, S. and Haworth, N. (2013) Bike share: A synthesis of the literature. *Transport Reviews* 33 (2), 148–165.

Fodness, D. (1994) Measuring tourist motivation. *Annals of Tourism Research* 21 (3), 555–581.

Forsyth, A. (2015) What is a walkable place?; The walkability debate in urban design. *Urban Design International* 20 (4), 274–292.

Frank, L.D., Saelens, B.E., Powell, K.E. and Chapman, J.E. (2007) Stepping towards causation: do built environments or neighborhood and travel preferences explain physical activity, driving, and obesity? *Social Science & Medicine* 65 (9), 1898–1914.

Freedman, S. (2009) Factions clash over Israel's buses. *The Guardian*, 16 December. See. http://www.theguardian.com/commentisfree/belief/2009/dec/16/israel-buses-gender-segregation-orthodox (accessed 23 January 2016).

Frost, W. and Hall, C.M. (eds) (2009) *Tourism and National Parks: International Perspectives on Development, Histories and Change*, London: Routledge.

Frost, W. and Laing, J. (2015) Natural heritage, parks and protected areas. In C.M. Hall, S. Gössling and D. Scott (eds) *The Routledge Handbook of Tourism and Sustainability* (pp. 374–383). Abingdon: Routledge.

Gaffney, C. (2010) Mega-events and socio-spatial dynamics in Rio de Janeiro, 1919–2016. *Journal of Latin American Geography* 9 (1), 7–29.

Garcia, A., Arbelaitz, O., Linaza, M.T., Vansteenwegen, P. and Souffriau, W. (2010) Personalized tourist route generation. In F. Daniel and F.M. Facca (eds)

Current Trends in Web Engineering, ICWE 2010 Workshops (pp. 840–845). Berlin: Springer.

García, C.R., Candela, S., Ginory, J., Quesada-Arencibia, A. and Alayón, F. (2012) On route travel assistant for public transport based on Android technology. In *Innovative Mobile and Internet Services in Ubiquitous Computing (IMIS), 2012 Sixth International Conference,* 4–6 July 2012. IEEE.

Gardner, B. and Abraham, C. (2007) What drives car use? A grounded theory analysis of commuters' reasons for driving. *Transportation Research Part F: Traffic Psychology and Behaviour* 10 (3), 187–200.

George, R. (2003) Tourist's perceptions of safety and security while visiting Cape Town. *Tourism Management* 24 (5), 575–585.

Giannini, M. (2012) ITS for long distance bus passenger transport. *Procedia-Social and Behavioral Sciences* (Transport Research Arena 2012), 48, 3153–3158.

Gibson, H. and Chang, S. (2012) Cycling in mid and later life: Involvement and benefits sought from a bicycle tour. *Journal of Leisure Research* 44 (1), 23–51.

Givoni, M. (2006) Development and impact of the modern high speed train: A review. *Transport Reviews* 26, 593–612.

Globes (2015) Ashton Kutcher fund invests in Israeli co Moovit. Globes Israel's Business Arena, 3 November. See http://www.globes.co.il/en/article-ashton-kutcher-fund-invests-in-moovit-1001078466 (accessed 1 April 2016).

Glover, L. (2011) Public transport as a common pool resource. Conference paper delivered at the 34th Australasian Transport Research Forum (ATRF) Proceedings, 28–30 September 2011, Adelaide, Australia.

Gordon, C., Mulley, C., Stevens, N. and Daniels, R. (2013) Public–private contracting and incentives for public transport: Can anything be learned from the Sydney Metro experience? *Transport Policy* 27, 73–84.

Gorter, C., Nijkamp, P. and Vork, R. (2000) Analysis of travelers' satisafction with transport chain. *Transportation Planning and Technology* 23, 237–258.

Government of the Philippines (2013) *The Philippine Maritime Industry: Prospects and Challenges in 2013 and Beyond.* Planning and Policy Office, 29 May 2013. See http://www.marina.gov.ph/reports/other_reports/Philippine%20Maritime%20Industry.Prospects%20and%20Challenges.pdf (accessed 1 April 2016).

Gossling, S. (2010) *Carbon Management in Tourism: Mitigating the Impacts on Climate Change.* Abingdon: Routledge.

Gössling, S. (2013) Urban transport transitions: Copenhagen, City of Cyclists. *Journal of Transport Geography* 33, 196–206.

Gössling, S., Ceron, J-P., Dubios, G. and Hall, C.M. (2009) Hypermobile travellers. In S. Gössling and P. Upham (eds) *Climate Change and Aviation* (pp. 131–149). London: Earthscan.

Gössling, S., Hall, C.M., Ekström, F., Engeset, A.B. and Aall, C. (2012a) Transition management: A tool for implementing sustainable tourism scenarios? *Journal of Sustainable Tourism* 20 (6), 899–916.

Gössling, S. and Peeters, P. (2015) Assessing tourism's global environmental impact 1900-2050. *Journal of Sustainable Tourism* 23 (5), 639–659.

Gössling, S., Scott, D. and Hall, C.M. (2013) Challenges of tourism in a low-carbon economy. *Wiley Interdisciplinary Reviews: Climate Change* 4 (6), 525–538.

Gössling, S., Scott, D. and Hall, C.M. (2015) Inter-market variability in CO_2 emission-intensities in tourism: Implications for destination marketing and carbon management. *Tourism Management* 46, 203–212.

Gössling, S., Scott, D., Hall, C.M., Ceron, J.-P. and Dubois, G. (2012b) Consumer behaviour and demand response of tourists to climate change. *Annals of Tourism Research* 39 (1), 36–58.
Greenfield, A. (2014) Helsinki's ambitious plan to make car ownership pointless in 10 years. *The Guardian*, 10 July. See https://www.theguardian.com/cities/2014/jul/10/helsinki-shared-public-transport-plan-car-ownership-pointless (accessed 1 April 2016).
Gretzel, U., Sigala, M., Xiang, Z. and Koo, C. (2015) Smart tourism: Foundations and developments. *Electronic Markets* 25 (3), 179–188.
Grimme, W.G. (2007a) Air/rail passenger intermodality concepts in Germany. *World Review of Intermodal Transportation Research* 1 (3), 251–263.
Grimme, W. (2007b) Experiences with advanced air–rail passenger intermodality – The case of Germany. In 11th ATRS World Conference, Berkeley, June. See http://www.dlr.de/fw/en/Portaldata/42/Resources/dokumente/paper/GRIMME-NR206.pdf (accessed 1 April 2016).
Gronau, W. and Kagermeier, A. (2007) Key factors for successful leisure and tourism public transport provision. *Journal of Transport Geography* 15 (2), 127–135.
Grünig, M. (2012) Sustainable urban transport planning. In F. Zeman (ed.) *Metropolitan Sustainability* (pp. 55–76). Oxford: Elsevier.
Guillen, M.D.V. and Ishida, H. (2004) Motorcycle-propelled public transport and local policy development: The case of "tricycles" and "habal-habal" in Davao City Philippines. *IATSS Research* 28 (1), 56–66.
Guirao, B. and Campa, J.L. (2015) The effects of tourism on HSR: Spanish empirical evidence derived from a multi-criteria corridor selection methodology. *Journal of Transport Geography* 47, 37–46.
Guiver, J., Lumsdon, L. and Weston, R. (2008) Traffic reduction at visitor attractions: The case of Hadrian's Wall. *Journal of Transport Geography* 16 (2), 142–150.
Guiver, J., Lumsdon, L., Weston, R. and Ferguson, M. (2007) Do buses help meet tourism objectives? The contribution and potential of scheduled buses in rural destination areas. *Transport Policy* 14 (4), 275–282.
Guo, Z. and Wilson, N. (2004) Assessment of the transfer penalty for transit trips geographic information system-based disaggregate modeling approach. *Transportation Research Record: Journal of the Transportation Research Board* 1872, 10–18.
Hadlaw, J. (2003) The London underground map: Imagining modern time and space. *Design Issues* 19 (1), 25–35.
Hagen, J.M., Valdal, A.K., Pettersen, K. and Gjerstad, B. (2015) Evaluation of comprehensive security systems for public transport - a methodological approach. *Journal of Risk Research* 18 (7), 822–839.
Hall, C.M. (1992) *Hallmark Tourist Events*. London: Belhaven.
Hall, C.M. (2005) *Tourism: Rethinking the Social Science of Mobility*. Harlow: Pearson.
Hall, C.M. (2006) Travel and journeying on the sea of faith: Perspectives from Religious Humanism. In D. Timothy and D. Olsen (eds) *Tourism, Religion and Spiritual Journeys* (pp. 64–77). London: Routledge.
Hall, C.M. (2010) Equal access for all? Regulative mechanisms, inequality and tourism mobility. In S. Cole and N. Morgan (eds) *Tourism and Inequality: Problems and Prospects* (pp. 34–48). Wallingford: CABI.
Hall, C.M. (2012) The contradictions and paradoxes of slow food: Environmental change, sustainability and the conservation of taste. In S. Fullagar, K. Markwell and E. Wilson (eds) *Slow Tourism: Experiences and Mobilities* (pp. 53–68). Bristol: Channel View Publications.

Hall, C.M. (2013) Framing behavioural approaches to understanding and governing sustainable tourism consumption: Beyond neoliberalism, "nudging" and "green growth"? *Journal of Sustainable Tourism* 21 (7), 1091–1109.

Hall, C.M. (2014) *Tourism and Social Marketing*. Abingdon: Routledge.

Hall, C.M. (2015) On the mobility of tourism mobilities. *Current Issues in Tourism* 18 (1), 7–10.

Hall, C.M. (2016) Intervening in academic interventions: Framing social marketing's potential for successful sustainable tourism behavioural change. *Journal of Sustainable Tourism* 24 (3), 350–375.

Hall, C. M. and Hodges, J. (1996) The party's great, but what about the hangover?: The housing and social impacts of mega-events with special reference to the 2000 Sydney Olympics. *Festival Management and Event Tourism* 4 (1–2), 13–20.

Hall, C.M. and Page, S. (2014) *The Geography of Tourism and Recreation*, 4th edn. Abingdon: Routledge.

Hall, C.M. and Suntikul, W. (2016) Tourism policies and politics in Asia. In C.M. Hall and S. Page (eds) *The Routledge Handbook of Tourism in Asia*. Abingdon: Routledge.

Hall, C.M., Duval, D. and Timothy, D. (eds) (2004a) *Safety and Security in Tourism: Relationships, Management and Marketing*, New York: Haworth Press.

Hall, C.M., Timothy, D. and Duval, D. (2004b) Security and tourism: towards a new understanding? *Journal of Travel and Tourism Marketing* 15 (2–3), 1–18.

Hall, C.M., Malinen, S., Vosslamber R. and Wordsworth, R. (eds) (2016) *Business and Post-Disaster Management: Business, Organisational and Consumer Resilience and the Christchurch Earthquakes*. Abingdon: Routledge.

Hall, D. (2004) Transport and tourism: Equity and sustainability issues. In L. Lumsdon and S.J. Page (eds) *Tourism and Transport* (pp. 45–55). Oxford: Pergamon.

Hall, P. (1991) Moving information: A tale of four technologies. In J.F. Brotchie, M. Batty, P. Hall and P.W. Newton (eds) *Cities of the 21st Century: New Technologies and Spatial Systems* (pp. 1–24). Melbourne: Longman Cheshire.

Hall, P. (2009) Magic carpets and seamless webs: opportunities and constraints for high-speed trains in Europe. *Built Environment* 35 (1), 59–69.

Halsall, D.A. (2001) Railway heritage and the tourist gaze: Stoomtram Hoorn–Medemblik. *Journal of Transport Geography* 9 (2), 151–160.

Hamid, S.A. (2014) Walking in the city of signs: Tracking pedestrians in Glasgow. *Current Urban Studies* 2 (3), 263.

Haughton, G. and McManus, P. (2012) Neoliberal experiments with urban infrastructure: The Cross City Tunnel, Sydney. *International Journal of Urban and Regional Research* 36 (1), 90–105.

Henderson, J.C. (2011) Religious tourism and its management: The hajj in Saudi Arabia. *International Journal of Tourism Research* 13 (6), 541–552.

Hergesell, A. and Dickinger, A. (2013) Environmentally friendly holiday transport mode choices among students: The role of price, time and convenience. *Journal of Sustainable Tourism* 21 (4), 596–613.

Herrschel, T. (2013) Competitiveness and sustainability: Can 'smart city regionalism' square the circle? *Urban Studies* 50 (11), 2332–2348.

Hill, T., Nel, E. and Trotter, D. (2006) Small-scale, nature-based tourism as a pro-poor development intervention: Two examples in Kwazulu-Natal, South Africa. *Singapore Journal of Tropical Geography* 27 (2), 163–175.

Hiller, H.H. (1998) Assessing the impact of mega-events: a linkage model. *Current Issues in Tourism* 1 (1), 47–57.

Hockey, A., Phillips, J. and Walford, N. (2013) Planning for an ageing society: Voices from the planning profession. *Planning Practice and Research* 28 (5), 527–543.

Holden, E. and Norland, I. (2005) Three challenges for the compact city as a sustainable urban form: Household consumption of energy and transport in eightresidential areas in the greater Oslo region. *Urban Studies* 42, 2145–2166.

Hong Kong Tourism Board (2015) Visitor arrivals. See http://partnernet.hktb.com/en/research_statistics/index.html (accessed 1 April 2016).

Hoornweg, D., Sugar, L. and Gomez, C.L.T. (2011) Cities and greenhouse gas emissions: Moving forward. *Environment and Urbanization* 23 (1), 207–227.

Howard, R.W. (2009) Risky business? Asking tourists what hazards they actually encountered in Thailand. *Tourism Management* 30 (3), 359–365.

Hsu, T.-K., Tsai, Y.-F. and Wu, H.-H. (2009) The preference analysis for tourist choice of destination: A case study of Taiwan. *Tourism Management* 30 (2), 288–297.

Hwang, Y.H. and Fesenmaier, D.R. (2003) Multidestination pleasure travel patterns: Empirical evidence from the American Travel Survey. *Journal of Travel Research* 42 (2), 166–171.

Ilan, S. (2015) An ultra-orthodox woman who refuses to sit at the back of the bus. There's no such rule in Jewish law, Chani Weiser notes, but Israel still has dozens of gender-segregated bus lines. *Haaretz*, 16 July.

Imhof, R., Vogel, M. and Ruiz, G. (2009) Mobility and protected areas in the Alps. *Eco.mont* 1 (1), 57–62.

International Transport Forum (ITF) (2015) *Urban Mobility System Upgrade: How shared self-driving cars could change city traffic.* Paris: OECD.

International Transport Forum (ITF) (2016) *Shared Mobility: Innovation for Liveable Cities.* Paris: OECD.

Japan-guide.com (2016) IC Cards. See http://www.japan-guide.com/e/e2359_003.html (accessed 24 April 2016).

Jeng, J. and Fesenmaier, D.R. (2002) Conceptualizing the travel decision-making hierarchy: A review of recent developments. *Tourism Analysis* 7 (1), 15–32.

Jenkins, J., Cogo, A. and Dewey, M. (2011) Review of developments in research into English as a lingua franca. *Language Teaching* 44 (3), 281–315.

Jiang, S., Du, Y. and Sun, L. (2011) Analysis of mode choice performance among heterogeneous tourists to Expo Shanghai 2010. In P. Chen (ed.) *Intelligent Computing Information Science* (pp. 154–164). Berlin: Springer.

Journeys (2014) Passenger transport mode shares in world cities. *Journeys* November, 54–64.

Juul, M. (2015) The sharing economy and tourism. Tourist accommodation. *European Parliamentary Research Service (EPRS)*, briefing, September. See http://www.europarl.europa.eu/RegData/etudes/BRIE/2015/568345/EPRS_BRI(2015)568345_EN.pdf (accessed 31 December 2016).

Kagermeier, A. and Gronau, W. (2015) Identifying key factors for the successful provision of public transport for tourism. In F. Orsi (ed.) *Sustainable Transportation in Natural and Protected Areas* (pp. 228–238). Abingdon: Earthscan by Routledge.

Kamga, C. (2015) Emerging travel trends, high-speed rail, and the public reinvention of U.S. transportation. *Transport Policy* 37, 111–120.

Kassens-Noor, E. (2010) Sustaining the momentum: Olympics as potential catalyst for enhancing urban transport. *Transportation Research Record: Journal of the Transportation Research Board* 2187, 106–113.

Kassens-Noor, E. (2012) *Planning Olympic Legacies: Transport Dreams and Urban Realities.* Abingdon: Routledge.

Kassens-Noor, E. (2013) Transport legacy of the Olympic Games, 1992–2012. *Journal of Urban Affairs* 35 (4), 393–416.

Kelly, J., Haider, W. and Williams, P.W. (2007) A behavioral assessment of tourism transportation options for reducing energy consumption and greenhouse gases. *Journal of Travel Research* 45 (3), 297–309.

Khadaroo, J. and Seetanah, B. (2007) Transport infrastructure and tourism development. *Annals of Tourism Research* 34 (4), 1021–1032.

Khisty, C.J. and Lall, B.K. (2003) *Transportation Engineering: An Introduction* (3rd edn). Upper Saddle River: Prentice Hall/Pearson.

Khosla, E.G. (2015) Here's everywhere Uber is banned around the world. *Business Insider*, 8 April. See http://www.businessinsider.com/heres-everywhere-uber-is-banned-around-the-world-2015-4?IR=T&r=US&IR=T

Kim, K.S. (2011) Exploring transportation planning issues during the preparations for EXPO 2012 Yeosu Korea. *Habitat International* 35 (2), 286–294.

Kim, S.E. and Lehto, X.Y. (2012) The voice of tourists with mobility disabilities: Insights from online customer complaint websites. *International Journal of Contemporary Hospitality Management* 24 (3), 451–476.

Kinsella, J. and Caulfield, B. (2011) An examination of the quality and ease of use of public transport in Dublin from a newcomer's perspective. *Journal of Public Transportation* 14 (1), 69–81.

Klein, N. (2009) Emergent curbside intercity bus industry: Chinatown and beyond. *Transportation Research Record: Journal of the Transportation Research Board* 2111, 83–89.

Klein, N. (2014) Curbside buses and the transformation of the intercity bus industry. Doctoral dissertation, Rutgers University-Graduate School-New Brunswick.

Klein, N. (2015) Get on the (curbside) bus: The new intercity bus. *Journal of Transport and Land Use* 8 (1), 155–169.

Klein, N. and Zitcer, A. (2012) Everything but the chickens: Cultural authenticity onboard the Chinatown bus. *Urban Geography* 33 (1), 46–63.

Knowles, R.D. and Ferbrache, F. (2015) Evaluation of wider economic impacts of light rail investment on cities. *Journal of Transport Geography.* http://doi.org/10.1016/j.jtrangeo.2015.09.002

Koo, T.T.R., Wu, C.-L. and Dwyer, L. (2010) Ground travel mode choices of air arrivals at regional destinations: The significance of tourism attributes and destination contexts. *Research in Transportation Economics* 26 (1), 44–53.

Koo, T.T.R., Wu, C.-L. and Dwyer, L. (2012) Dispersal of visitors within destinations: Descriptive measures and underlying drivers. *Tourism Management* 33 (5), 1209–1219.

Kozak, M. (2001) Comparative assessment of tourist satisfaction with destinations across two nationalities. *Tourism Management* 22, 391–401.

Kruger, M. and Saayman, M. (2014) How do mountain bikers and road cyclists differ? *South African Journal for Research in Sport, Physical Education and Recreation* 36 (2), 137–152.

Kutulas, Y. and Awad, M. (2016) Bike and hike in Palestine. In R. Isaac, C.M. Hall and F. Higgins-Desboilles (eds) *The Politics and Power of Tourism in Palestine.* Abingdon: Routledge.

Künneke, R. and Finger, M. (2009) The governance of infrastructures as common pool resources. In *Workshop on the Workshop 4*, Indiana University, Bloomington, 2–7 June, 4, 3–6.

Kübler, D. and Schwab, B. (2007) New regionalism in five Swiss metropolitan areas: An assessment of inclusiveness, deliberation and democratic accountability. *European Journal of Political Research* 46 (4), 473–502.

Kyle, G., Graefe, A., Manning, R. and Bacon, J. (2003) An examination of the relationship between leisure activity involvement and place attachment among hikers along the Appalachian Trail. *Journal of Leisure Research* 35 (3), 249–273.

Ladki, S., Shatila, F. and Ismail, S. (2014) The effect of Lebanese public transport on visitor's satisfaction. *Journal of Tourism Challenges and Trends* 7 (2), 87–96.

Lai, W.-T. and Chen, C.-F. (2011) Behavioral intentions of public transit passengers – The roles of service quality, perceived value, satisfaction and involvement. *Transport Policy* 18 (2), 318–325.

Laird, J. (2012) Valuing the quality of strategic ferry services to remote communities. *Research in Transportation Business & Management* 4 (1), 97–103.

Lamont, M.J. (2009) *Independent bicycle tourism in Australia: a whole tourism systems analysis.* PhD Thesis. Southern Cross University. Lismore, NSW.

Lamont, M. and Buultjens, J. (2011) Putting the brakes on: Impediments to the development of independent cycle tourism in Australia. *Current Issues in Tourism* 14 (1), 57–78.

Lamont, M. and Causley, K. (2010) Guiding the Way: Exploring cycle tourists' needs and preferences for cycling route maps and signage. *Annals of Leisure Research* 13 (3), 497–522.

Langer, S. and Car, A. (2014) GIS-based decision support for public toilet site selection: A case study of South Batinah Region ih Oman. In R. Vogler, A. Car, J. Strobl and G. Griesebner (eds) *GI Forum 2014. Geospatial Innovation for Society* (pp. 135–139). Berlin: Herbert Wichmann Verlag.

Laperrouza, M. and Finger, M. (2009) Regulating Europe's single railway market: Integrating performance and governance. In *Second Annual Conference on Competition and Regulation in Network Industries, 20 November, No. MIR-CONF-2009-001.* See http://infoscience.epfl.ch/record/142562/files/laperrouza.pdf

Lave, R. and Mathias, R. (2000) State of the art of paratransit. In *Transportation in the New Millennium*, Washington, DC: Transportation Research Board.

Le, D.-T.T. (2014) Tourist use of public transport at destinations – the case of Munich, Germany. PhD thesis, Technische Universität München. See https://mediatum.ub.tum.de/doc/1221950/1221950.pdf

Lee, C.-F. (2014) An investigation of factors determining cycling experience and frequency. *Tourism Geographies* 16 (5), 844–862.

Lee, J. (2016) Singapore goes Dutch on driverless shuttles. *Nikkei Asian Review*, 21 April. See http://asia.nikkei.com/Business/Companies/Singapore-goes-Dutch-on-driverless-shuttles (accessed 21 April 2016).

Le-Klähn, D-T. (2015) Public transportation. In C.M. Hall, S. Gössling and D. Scott (eds) *The Routledge Handbook of Tourism and Sustainability* (pp. 440–449). Abingdon: Routledge.

Le-Klähn, D.-T. and Hall, C.M. (2015) Tourist use of public transport at destinations – a review. *Current Issues in Tourism* 18 (8), 785–803.

Le-Klähn, D.-T., Gerike, R. and Hall, C.M. (2014a) Visitor users vs. non-users of public transport: The case of Munich, Germany. *Journal of Destination Marketing & Management* 3 (3), 152–161.

Le-Klähn, D.-T., Hall, C.M. and Gerike, R. (2014b) Analysis of visitor satisfaction with public transport in Munich, Germany. *Journal of Public Transportation* 17 (3), 68–85.

Le-Klähn, D.-T., Hall, C.M. and Gerike, R. (2014c) Promoting public transport use in tourism. In S. Cohen, J. Higham, P. Peeters and S. Gössling (eds) *Understanding and governing sustainable tourism mobility* (pp. 208–222). Abingdon: Routledge.

Le-Klähn, D.-T., Roosen, J., Gerike, R. and Hall, C.M. (2015) Factors affecting tourists' public transport use and areas visited at destinations. *Tourism Geographies* 17 (5), 738–757.

Lew, A. and McKercher, B. (2006) Modeling tourist movements: A local destination analysis. *Annals of Tourism Research* 33 (2), 403–423.

Li, G., Luan, X., Yang, J. and Lin, X. (2013) Value capture beyond municipalities: Transit-oriented development and inter-city passenger rail investment in China's Pearl River Delta. *Journal of Transport Geography* 33, 268–277.

Lebel, A., Cantinotti, M., Pampalon, R., Thériault, M., Smith, L.A. and Hamelin, A.M. (2011) Concept mapping of diet and physical activity: Uncovering local stakeholders perception in the Quebec City region. *Social Science & Medicine* 72 (3), 439–445.

Lin, T.P. (2010) Carbon dioxide emissions from transport in Taiwan's national parks. *Tourism Management* 31 (2), 285–290.

Lohmann, G., Santos, G. and Allis, T. (2011) 'Los hermanos' visiting the south region of Brazil: a comparison between drive tourists and coach tourists from Argentina, Paraguay and Uruguay. In B. Prideaux and D. Carson (eds) *Drive Tourism: Trends and emerging Markets* (pp. 49–60), Abingdon: Routledge.

Lois González, R.C. (2013) The Camino de Santiago and its contemporary renewal: Pilgrims, tourists and territorial identities. *Culture and Religion* 14 (1), 8–22.

Lumsdon, L.M. (2006) Factors affecting the design of tourism bus services. *Annals of Tourism Research* 33 (3), 748–766.

Lumsdon, L., Downward, P. and Cope, A. (2004) Monitoring of cycle tourism on long distance trails: the North Sea Cycle Route. *Journal of Transport Geography* 12 (1), 13–22.

Lumsdon, L., Downward, P. and Rhoden, S. (2006) Transport for tourism: Can public transport encourage a modal shift in the day visitor market? *Journal of Sustainable Tourism* 14 (2), 139–156.

Lumsdon, L. and Owen, E. (2004) Tourism transport: The green key initiatives. In L. Lumsdon and S. Page (eds) *Tourism and Transport. Issues and Agenda for the New Millenium* (pp. 157–169). New York: Elsevier.

Lumsdon, L. and Tolley, R. (2004) Non-motorised transport and tourism: A case study – cycle tourism. In L. Lumsdon and S. Page (eds) *Tourism and Transport* (pp. 147–156). Oxford: Pergamon.

Malhado, A.C.M. and Rothfuss, R. (2013) Transporting 2014 FIFA World Cup to sustainability: Exploring residents' and tourists' attitudes and behaviours. *Journal of Policy Research in Tourism, Leisure and Events* 5 (3), 252–269.

Mandeno, T.G. (2011) Is tourism a driver for public transport investment? Master of Planning thesis, University of Otago, Dunedin.

Mannaerts, Y. (2014) Streamlining regulatory and administrative framework, European Tourism Day, 1 December, Brussels: IRU. See https://www.iru.org/apps/cms-filesystem-action?file=mix_presentations/coachtourism.pdf (accessed 1 April 2016).

Marjavaara, R. (2007) The displacement myth: Second home tourism in the Stockholm Archipelago. *Tourism Geographies* 9, 296–317.

Masiero, L. and Zoltan, J. (2013) Tourists intra-destination visits and transport mode: A bivariate model. *Annals of Tourism Research* 43, 529–546.

Masson, S. and Petiot, R. (2009) Can the high speed rail reinforce tourism attractiveness? The case of the high speed rail between Perpignan (France) and Barcelona (Spain). *Technovation* 29 (9), 611–617.

Maunier, C. and Camelis, C. (2013) Toward an identification of elements contributing to satisfaction with the tourism experience. *Journal of Vacation Marketing* 19 (1), 19–39.

McCabe, S. (2009) Who needs a holiday? Evaluating social tourism. *Annals of Tourism Research* 36 (4), 667–688.

McKercher, B., Wong, C. and Lau, G. (2006) How tourists consume a destination. *Journal of Business Research* 59 (5), 647–652.

McKinsey Center for Business and Environment (2015) *Urban Mobility at a Tipping Point*. Detroit: McKinsey Center for Business and Environment. http://www.mckinsey.com/business-functions/sustainability-and-resource-productivity/our-insights/urban-mobility-at-a-tipping-point

McManus, P. (2005) *Vortex Cities to Sustainable Cities: Australia's Urban Challenge*. Sydney: UNSW Press.

Meletiou, M.P., Lawrie, J.J., Cook, T.J., O'Brien, S.W. and Guenther, J. (2005) Economic impact of investments in bicycle facilities: Case study of North Carolina's Northern Outer Banks. *Transportation Research Record* 1939, 15–21.

Mendel, S. and Brudney, J. (2012) Putting the NP in PPP: The role of nonprofit organizations in public-private partnerships. *Public Performance & Management Review* 35, 617–642.

Merriman, P. (2009) Automobility and the geographies of the car. *Geography Compass* 3 (2), 586–599.

Miller, G., Rathouse, K., Scarles, C., Holmes, K. and Tribe, J. (2010) Public understanding of sustainable tourism. *Annals of Tourism Research* 37 (3), 627–645.

Ministry of Land, Infrastructure, Transport and Tourism (Japan) (2010) Inter-regional travel survey in Japan. See http://www.mlit.go.jp/common/001005633.pdf (accessed 1 April 2016).

Ministry of Transport (New Zealand) (2016) *PT2045 Definitions and Frameworks*. Wellington: Ministry of Transport.

Minnaert, L. and Schapmans, M. (2009) Tourism as a form of social intervention: The Holiday Participation Centre in Flanders. *Journal of Social Intervention: Theory and Practice* 18 (3), 42–61.

Mittal, S., Dai, H. and Shukla, P.R. (2016) Low carbon urban transport scenarios for China and India: A comparative assessment. *Transportation Research Part D: Transport and Environment* 44, 266–276.

Moniruzzaman, M., Páez, A., Habib, K.M.N. and Morency, C. (2013) Mode use and trip length of seniors in Montreal. *Journal of Transport Geography* 30, 89–99.

Montreal Tourism Organization (2015) *Annual Report 2014*. Montreal: Montreal Tourism Organization. See http://documents.tourisme-montreal.org/Montreal-Tourism/R-and-D/Statistics/EN/ra-2014-en.pdf (accessed 20 March 2016).

Montreal Tourism Organization (2016) Tourist attraction. Montreal: Montreal Tourism Organization. See http://www.tourisme-montreal.org/Montreal-Tourism/Toolkit (accessed 20 March 2016).

Moore, K., Smallman, C., Wilson, J. and Simmons, D. (2012) Dynamic in-destination decision-making: An adjustment model. *Tourism Management* 33 (3), 635–645.

Mullen, R.D. (2015) India's soft power. In D.M. Malone, C.R. Mohan and S. Raghavan (eds) *The Oxford Handbook of Indian Foreign Policy* (pp. 188–201). Oxford: Oxford University Press.

Mundkur, B. (2011) Incredible India: the inconvenient truth. *Asian Affairs* 42 (1), 83–97.

Muniz, I., Calatayud, D. and Dobano, R. (2013) The compensation hypothesis in Barcelona measured through the ecological footprint of mobility and housing. *Landscape and Urban Planning* 113, 113–119.

Næss, P. (2006) *Urban Structure Matters: Residential Location, Car Dependence and Travel Behaviour*. Abingdon: Routledge.

National Geographic Traveller (2014) Cover story: 10 of the best new walking trails. *National Geographic Traveller*. See http://www.natgeotraveller.co.uk/smart-travel/features/cover-story-10-of-the-best-new-walking-trails/ (accessed 14 February 2016).

Nelson, J.D. and Mulley, C. (2013) The impact of the application of new technology on public transport service provision and the passenger experience: A focus on implementation in Australia. *Research in Transportation Economics* 39 (1), 300–308.

Neuhofer, B., Buhalis, D. and Ladkin, A. (2015) Technology as a catalyst of change: Enablers and barriers of the tourist experience and their consequences. In I. Tussyadiah and I. Alessandro (eds) *Information and Communication Technologies in Tourism 2015* (pp. 789–802). Berlin: Springer.

Newton, A.D., Partridge, H. and Gill, A. (2014) Above and below: Measuring crime risk in and around underground mass transit systems. *Crime Science* 3 (1), 1–14.

Nguyen, C. (2015) Cab drivers in San Jose expand strike calling for equal regulation on Uber, Lyft, *ABC Inc., KGO-TV San Francisco*, 10 November. See http://abc7news.com/news/cab-drivers-expand-strike-calling-for-equal-regulation-on-uber-lyft/1077733/

Niedomysl, T. (2008) Residential preferences for interregional migration in Sweden: Demographic, socioeconomic, and geographical determinants. *Environment and Planning A* 40 (5), 1109–1131.

Noble, G. and Poynting, S. (2010) White lines: The intercultural politics of everyday movement in social spaces. *Journal of Intercultural Studies* 31 (5), 489–505.

Nunes, A.A., Galvão, T. and Cunha, J.F. (2014) Urban public transport service co-creation: Leveraging passenger's knowledge to enhance travel experience. *Procedia-Social and Behavioral Sciences* 111, 577–585.

Oja, P., Titze, S., Bauman, A., de Geus, B., Krenn, P., Reger-Nash, B. and Kohlberger, T. (2011) Health benefits of cycling: A systematic review. *Scandinavian Journal of Medicine & Science in Sports* 21 (4), 496–509.

Okabe, S. (1980) Impact of the Sanyo Shinkansen on local communities. In A. Straszak and R. Tuch (eds) *The Shinkansen High-speed Rail Network of Japan* (pp. 11–20). Oxford: Pergamon Press.

Orsi, F. (ed.) (2015) *Sustainable Transportation in Natural and Protected Areas*. Abingdon: Earthscan by Routledge.

Orski, C.K. (1975) Paratransit: The coming of age of a transportation concept. *Transportation* 4 (4), 329–334.

Ostrom, E. (1990) *Governing the Commons: The Evolution of Institutions for Collective Action*. Cambridge: Cambridge University Press.

Osei–Kyei, R. and Chan, A.P. (2016) Developing transport infrastructure in Sub-Saharan Africa through public–private partnerships: Policy practice and implications. *Transport Reviews* 36 (2), 170–186.

Page, S. (1999) *Transport and Tourism* (2nd edn). Harlow: Prentice Hall.

Page, S. and Connell, J. (2014) Transport and tourism. In A. Lew, C.M. Hall and A. Williams (eds) *The Wiley Blackwell Companion to Tourism* (pp. 155–167). Chichester: Wiley.

Pagliara, F., La Pietra, A., Gomez, J. and Manuel Vassallo, J. (2015) High speed rail and the tourism market: Evidence from the Madrid case study. *Transport Policy* 37, 187–194.

Pan, S. and Ryan, C. (2007) Mountain areas and visitor usage–motivations and determinants of satisfaction: The case of Pirongia Forest Park, New Zealand. *Journal of Sustainable Tourism* 15 (3), 288–308.

Pantuso, P. (2012) *Intercity curbside buses: An industry perspective*. Newark, Delaware: Institute for Public Administration, Curbside Intercity Bus Transportation Policy Forum. See http://www.ipa.udel.edu/transportation/intercitybus/Pantuso.pdf (accessed 1 April 2016).

Parkhurst, G. and Meek, S. (2014) The effectiveness of park-and-ride as a policy measure for more sustainable mobility. In S. Ison and C. Mulley (eds) *Parking Issues and Policies* (pp. 185–211). Bingley: Emerald Insight.

Patterson, I., Darcy, S. and Mönninghoff, M. (2012) Attitudes and experiences of tourism operators in Northern Australia towards people with disabilities. *World Leisure Journal* 54 (3), 215–229.

Paulley, N., Balcombe, R., Mackett, R., Titheridge, H., Preston, J., Wardman, M., Shires, J. and White, P. (2006) The demand for public transport: The effects of fares, quality of service, income and car ownership. *Transport Policy* 13 (4), 295–306.

Pearce, D.G. (2001) Tourism, trams and local government policy-making in Christchurch, New Zealand. *Current Issues in Tourism* 4 (2–4), 331–354.

Peeters, P., Dijkmans, C., Mitas, O., Strous, B. and Vinkensteijn, J. (2015) Tourism and the sharing economy: Challenges and opportunities for the EU. *European Parliament's Committee on Transport and Tourism*. Brussels: EU.

Peeters, P. and Dubois, G. (2010) Tourism travel under climate change mitigation constraints. *Journal of Transport Geography* 18 (3), 447–457.

Peeters, P., Szimba, E. and Duijnisveld, M. (2007) Major environmental impacts of European tourist transport. *Journal of Transport Geography* 15 (2), 83–93.

Peeters, P., van Egmond, T. and Visser, N. (2004) European tourism, transport and environment. *Report for the DG-ENTR project 03-27 MuSST*. Breda, the Netherlands: NHTV Centre for Sustainable Tourism and Transport.

Pepy, G. and Perren, B. (2006) 25 Years of the TGV. *Modern Railways* October, 67–74.

Peter, J.P. and Olson, J.C. (2009) *Consumer Behaviour and Marketing Strategies* (9th edn). New York: McGraw-Hill/Irwin.

Petrini, C. (2007) *Slow Food Nation. Why Our Food Should be Good, Clean, and Fair*. New York: Rizzoli International.

Pettebone, D., Newman, P., Lawson, S.R., Hunt, L., Monz, C. and Zwiefka, J. (2011) Estimating visitors' travel mode choices along the Bear Lake Road in Rocky Mountain National Park. *Journal of Transport Geography* 19 (6), 1210–1221.

Phuket-Travel-Secrets.com (2016) Phuket Songthaew and Microbus http://www.phuket-travel-secrets.com/phuket-songthaew.html

Phun, V. K. and Yai, T. (2015) State of the art of paratransit literatures in Asian developing countries. *Proceedings of the 13th Eastern Asia Society for Transportation Studies*, 11–14. <http://www.dynamicglobalsoft.com/easts2015/program/pdf_files/1169.pdf>

Piket, P., Eijgelaar, E. and Peeters, P. (2012) European cycle tourism: a tool for sustainable regional rural development. *Applied Studies in Agribusiness and Commerce* 7 (2-3), 115–119.

Pikora, T.J., Giles-Corti, B., Bulla, F., Jamrozika, K. and Donovan, R. (2003) Developing framework for assessment of the environmental determinants for walking and cycling. *Social Science & Medicine*, 56, 1693–1703.

Plantsch, M., Ferber-Herbst, G. and Hole, F. (2010) Touristen im Nahverkehr: Ein unterschätztes Potenzial? *Der Nahverkehr* 28 (3), 38–41.

Povilanskas, R., Armaitiene, A., Jones, E., Valtas, G. and Jurkus, E. (2015) Third-country tourists on the ferries linking Germany with Lithuania. *Scandinavian Journal of Hospitality and Tourism* 15 (4), 327–340.

Prideaux, B. (2000) The role of the transport system in destination development. *Tourism Management* 21 (1), 53–63.

Pucher, J. and Buehler, R. (2008) Making cycling irresistible: Lessons from the Netherlands, Denmark and Germany. *Transport Reviews* 28 (4), 495–528.

Pun-Cheng, L.S.C. (2012) An interactive web-based public transport enquiry system with real-time optimal route computation. *IEEE Transactions on Intelligent Transportation Systems* 13 (2), 983–988.

PWC (2015) 'The sharing economy', *Consumer Intelligence Series*. See https://www.pwc.com/us/en/technology/publications/assets/pwc-consumer-intelligence-series-the-sharing-economy.pdf (accessed 31 December 2015).

Quak, H.J. and de Koster, M.R.B. (2009) Delivering goods in urban areas: how to deal with urban policy restrictions and the environment. *Transportation Science* 43 (2), 211–227.

Rambukwella, D.K.K. and Santoso, D.S. (2015) Customer satisfaction analysis of the luxury long distance bus service in Sri Lanka. *Journal of the Eastern Asia Society for Transportation Studies* 11, 1272–1290.

Rayle, L., Dai, D., Chan, N., Cervero, R. and Shaheen, S. (2016) Just a better taxi? A survey-based comparison of taxis, transit, and ridesourcing services in San Francisco. *Transport Policy* 45, 168–178.

Redman, L., Friman, M., Gärling, T. and Hartig, T. (2013) Quality attributes of public transport that attract car users: A research review. *Transport Policy* 25, 119–127.

Regnerus, H.D., Beunen, R. and Jaarsma, C.F. (2007) Recreational traffic management: The relations between research and implementation. *Transport Policy* 14 (3), 258–267.

Reilly, J., Williams, P. and Haider, W. (2010) Moving towards more eco-efficient tourist transportation to a resort destination: The case of Whistler, British Columbia. *Research in Transportation Economics* 26 (1), 66–73.

Ritchie, B.W. and Hall, C.M. (1999) Bicycle tourism and regional development: A New Zealand case study. *Anatolia* 10 (2), 89–112.

Ritchie, B.W., Tkaczynski, A. and Faulks, P. (2010) Understanding the motivation and travel behavior of cycle tourists using involvement profiles. *Journal of Travel and Tourism Marketing* 27 (4), 409–425.

Robbins, D., Dickinson, J. and Calver, S. (2007) Planning transport for special events: A conceptual framework and future agenda for research. *International Journal of Tourism Research* 9 (5), 303–314.

Rodrigue, J.P., Comtois, C. and Slack, B. (2013) *The Geography of Transport Systems*. Abingdon: Routledge.

Rotem-Mindali, O. and Shemesh, I. (2013) Mobility and accessibility concerns for tourists in Tel Aviv-Jaffa area. *Turizam* 61 (3), 259–276.

Rüetschi, U.J. and Timpf, S. (2005) Modelling wayfinding in public transport: Network space and scene space. In C. Freksa, M. Knauff, B. Krieg-Brückner, B. Nebel and T. Barkowsky (eds) *Spatial Cognition IV. Reasoning, Action, Interaction* (pp. 24–41). Berlin: Springer.

Ryder, A. (2012) High speed rail. *Journal of Transport Geography* 22, 303–305.

Sakakibara, Y. (2012) Social change and future transport policy in the Japanese context. *IATSS Research* 35 (2), 56–61.

Sallis, J.F., Floyd, M.F., Rodríguez, D.A. and Saelens, B.E. (2012) Role of built environments in physical activity, obesity, and cardiovascular disease. *Circulation* 125 (5),
729–737.

Samarasekara, G.N., Fukahori, K. and Kubota, Y. (2011) Environmental correlates that
provide walkability cues for tourists: An analysis based on walking decision narra-
tions. *Environment and Behavior* 43 (4), 501–524.

Saunders, R.E., Laing, J. and Weiler, B. (2013) Personal transformation through long-
distance walking. In S. Filep and P. Pearce (eds) *Tourist Experience and Fulfilment:
Insights from Positive Psychology* (pp. 127–146). Abingdon: Routledge.

Schor, J. (2014) Debating the sharing economy. *Grassroots Economic.* http://www.geo.coop/
sites/default/files/schor_debating_the_sharing_economy.pdf

Schwieterman, J. and Fischer, L. (2012) Competition from the curb. *Transportation Research
Record: Journal of the Transportation Research Board* 2277 (1), 49–56.

Scott, D., Amelung, B., Becken, S., Ceron, J-P., Dubois, G., Gossling, S., Peeters, P. and
Simpson, M. (2008) Technical report. In *United Nations World Tourism Organization,
United Nations Environment Programme, and World Meteorological Organization, Climate
Change and Tourism: Responding to Global Challenges* (pp. 23–250). Madrid: UNWTO;
Paris: UNEP; Geneva: WMO.

Scott, D., Gössling, S. and Hall, C.M. (2012) *Tourism and Climate Change: Impacts,
Adaptation and Mitigation,* London: Routledge.

Scott, D., Hall, C.M. and Gössling, S. (2016a) A review of the IPCC 5th Assessment and
implications for tourism sector climate resilience and decarbonization. *Journal of
Sustainable Tourism* 24 (1), 8–30.

Scott, D., Hall, C.M. and Gössling, S. (2016b) A report on the Paris Climate Change
Agreement and its implications for tourism: Why we will always have Paris. *Journal
of Sustainable Tourism* 24 (7), 933–948.

Scott, D., Gössling, S., Hall, C.M. and Peeters, P. (2016c) Can tourism be part of the
decarbonized global economy?: The costs and risks of carbon reduction pathways.
Journal of Sustainable Tourism 24 (1), 52–72.

Scott, K.E., Anderson, C., Dunsford, H., Benson, J.F. and MacFarlane, R. (2005) *An
Assessment of the Sensitivity and Capacity of the Scottish Seascape in Relation to Offshore
Windfarms.* Scottish Natural Heritage Commissioned Report No. 103 (ROAME No.
F03AA06). Inverness: Scottish Natural Heritage.

Seddighi, H.R. and Theocharous, A.L. (2002) A model of tourism destination choice: A
theoretical and empirical analysis. *Tourism Management* 23 (5), 475–487.

Shafabakhsh, G., Hadjihoseinlou, M. and Taghizadeh, S.A. (2014) Selecting the appropriate public transportation system to access the Sari International Airport by fuzzy
decision making. *European Transport Research Review* 6 (3), 277–285.

Sharifpour, M., Walters, G. and Ritchie, B.W. (2014) Risk perception, prior knowledge,
and willingness to travel investigating the Australian tourist market's risk perceptions towards the Middle East. *Journal of Vacation Marketing* 20 (2), 111–123.

Sherwin, H., Parkhurst, G., Robbins, D. and Walker, I. (2011) Practices and motivations of
travellers making rail-cycle trips. *Proceedings of Institute of Civil Engineers* 164 (3),
189–197.

Shimazaki, T. and Rahman, M. (1996) Physical characteristics of paratransit in developing countries of Asia. *Journal of Advanced Transportation* 30 (2), 5–24.

Shin, H.C., Namkung, O., Kim, D.J. and Cho, I.J. (2011) Plan and Implementation of
Korea Bicycle Infrastructure. *Proceedings of the Eastern Asia Society for Transportation
Studies* 8. See https://www.jstage.jst.go.jp/article/eastpro/2011/0/2011_0_27/_pdf.

Singapore Land Transport Authority (2011) Passenger transport mode shares in world cities, *Journeys* 7. See http://www.lta.gov.sg/ltaacademy/doc/JOURNEYS_ Nov2011%20Revised.pdf (accessed 15 January 2016).

Singapore Land Transport Authority (2014) *Land Transport Master Plan 2013*. See https://www.lta.gov.sg/content/dam/ltaweb/corp/PublicationsResearch/files/Report Newsletter/LTMP2013Report.pdf (accessed 15 January 2016).

Singapore Tourism Board (2015) *Annual Report on Tourism Statistics 2014*. See https://www. stb.gov.sg/statistics-and-market-insights/marketstatistics/stb%20tourism%20statistics_ fa%20(low%20res).pdf (accessed 15 January 2016).

Skytrax (2016) Global benchmark of airport quality excellence. See http://www. worldairportawards.com/main/about_skytrax.html (accessed 7 January 2016).

Social Exclusion Unit (2001) *Preventing Social Exclusion*. London: Cabinet Office.

Solnit, R. (2000) *Wanderlust: A History of Walking*. New York: Penguin.

Sommers, K. (2015) Women only public transport in Japan, Malaysia and other countries spares women harassment. *Huffington Post*, 26 August. See http://www.huffington-post.co.uk/2015/08/26/women-only-public-transport-jeremy-corbyn_n_8043506. html (accessed 23 January 2016).

Song, H., van der Veen, R., Li, G. and Chen, J.L. (2012) The Hong Kong tourist satisfaction index. *Annals of Tourism Research* 39 (1), 459–479.

Sönmez, S.F. and Graefe, A.R. (1998) Influence of terrorism risk on foreign tourism decisions. *Annals of Tourism Research* 25 (1), 112–144.

Southworth, M. (2005) Designing the walkable city. *Journal of Urban Planning and Development* 131 (4), 246–257.

Spears, S., Houston, D. and Boarnet, M.G. (2013) Illuminating the unseen in transit use: A framework for examining the effect of attitudes and perceptions on travel behavior. *Transportation Research Part A: Policy and Practice* 58, 40–53.

Starr, S. (2015) Istanbul shows ferries have a future. *The Guardian*, 28 May.

Statista (2014) *Number of Participants in Hiking in the United States from 2006 to 2014 (in millions)*. http://www.statista.com/statistics/191240/participants-in-hiking-in-the-us-since-2006/

Statista (2015). *Number of Persons Going Hiking in their Spare Time in Germany from 2010 to 2015, by frequency (in millions)*. See http://www.statista.com/statistics/413018/ frequency-of-recreational-hiking-germany/ (accessed 4 January 2014).

Statistics Austria (2013) *1969-2013: Reisegewohnheiten der Österreichischen Bevölkerung*. See http://www.statistik.at/web_de/statistiken/wirtschaft/tourismus/reisege-wohnheiten/index.html

Stokes, K., Clarence, E., Anderson, L. and Rinne, A. (2014) *Making Sense of the UK Collaborative Economy*. London: Nesta/Collaborative Lab. http://www.collaboriamo. org/media/2014/10/making_sense_of_the_uk_collaborative_economy_14.pdf

Stradling, S., Carreno, M., Rye, T. and Noble, A. (2007) Passenger perceptions and the ideal urban bus journey experience. *Transport Policy* 14 (4), 283–292.

Strandell, A. and Hall, C.M. (2015a) Impact of the residential environment on second home use in Finland – testing the compensation hypothesis. *Landscape and Urban Planning* 133, 12–33.

Strandell, A. and Hall, C.M. (2015b) Corrigendum to "Impact of the residential environment on second home use in Finland – Testing the compensation hypothesis" [*Landsc. Urban Plan.* 133 (2015) 12–23]. *Landscape and Urban Planning* 137, 165–167.

Su, M.M. and Wall, G. (2009) The Qinghai-Tibet railway and Tibetan tourism: Travelers' perspectives. *Tourism Management* 30 (5), 650–657.

Su, Y.-P., Hall, C.M. and Ozanne, L. (2013) Hospitality industry responses to climate change: A benchmark study of Taiwanese tourist hotels. *Asia Pacific Journal of Tourism Research* 18 (2), 92–107.

Suen, L., Simões, A. and Wretstrand, A. (2012) Social, cultural and generational issues in accessible public transport in Europe. In *TRANSED 2012-13th International Conference on Mobility and Transport for Elderly and Disabled People*, http://www.transed2012.in/Common/Uploads/Poster/279_paper_transedAbstract00160.pdf

Talluri, K.T. and Van Ryzin, G.J. (2005) *The Theory and Practice of Revenue Management.* New York: Springer.

Tangphaisankun, A., Nakamura, F. and Okamura, T. (2010) Influences of paratransit as a feeder of mass transit system in developing countries based on commuter satisfaction. *Journal of the Eastern Asia Society for Transportation Studies* 8, 1341–1356.

Tay, D. (2014) GrabTaxi raises a record-breaking $250M, plans to leave other regional players in the dust. *Tech in Asia*, 4 December. https://www.techinasia.com/grabtaxi-raises-250m

TechCrunch (2015) Moovit raises $50M to scale its public transit app, goes up against CityMapper, *TechCrunch*, 14 January. See http://techcrunch.com/2015/01/14/moovit-raises-50m-to-scale-its-public-trans-app-goes-up-against-citymapper/ (accessed 1 April 2016).

Thomas, E. (2015) Conserving trail corridors: The Pacific Crest National Scenic Trail. In S.G. Clark, A.M. Hohl, C.H. Picard and E. Thomas (eds) *Large-Scale Conservation in the Common Interest* (pp. 115–138). Berlin: Springer.

Thompson, K. (2004) Tourists' use of public transportation information: What they need and what they get. Paper from *The Association for European Transport Conference* held in Strasbourg, France on 4–6 October 2004. http://www.etcproceedings.org/paper/tourists-use-of-public-transport-information-what-they-need-and-what-they-get

Thompson, K. and Schofield, P. (2007) An investigation of the relationship between public transport performance and destination satisfaction. *Journal of Transport Geography* 15 (2), 136–144.

Thrasher, S.A., Hickey, T.R. and Hudome, R.J. (2000) Enhancing transit circulation in resort areas: Operational and design strategies. *Transportation Research Record* 1735, 79–83.

Timothy, D.J. and Boyd, S.W. (2015) *Tourism and Trails: Cultural, Ecological and Management Issues.* Bristol: Channel View Publications.

Torode, R. (2003) A vision of sustainable urban transport. In World Health Organisation and United Nations Economic Commission for Europe Transport, Health and Environment Pan-European Programme (THE PEP) *Workshop on Sustainable and Healthy Urban Transport and Planning*, 16–18 November 2003, Nicosia, Cyprus. See http://www.thepep.org/en/workplan/urban/documents/UITP.pdf (accessed 1 April 2016).

Transport Canada (2015) *Canada Transportation Act (1996, c. 10).* See https://tc.gc.ca/eng/acts-regulations/acts-1996c10.htm (accessed 1 January 2016).

Transport Department (South Africa) (2014) National Household Travel Survey (2013). See http://www.statssa.gov.za/publications/P0320/P03202013.pdf (accessed 1 April 2016).

Tribe, J. and Snaith, T. (1998) From SERVQUAL to HOLSAT: Holiday satisfaction in Varadero, Cuba. *Tourism Management* 19 (1), 25–34.

Truong, V.D. and Hall, C.M. (2013) Social marketing and tourism: What is the evidence? *Social Marketing Quarterly* 19 (2), 110–135.

Tukamushaba, E.K. and George, B.P. (2014) Service quality assessment of transportation and government services: A study of the Hong Kong tourism industry. *International Journal of Hospitality and Event Management* 1 (1), 2−43.

Tyrinopoulos, Y. and Antoniou, C. (2008) Public transit user satisfaction: Variability and policy implications. *Transport Policy* 15 (4), 260–272.

Tsamboulas, D., Verma, A. and Moraiti, P. (2013) Transport infrastructure provision and operations: Why should governments choose private–public partnership?. *Research in Transportation Economics* 38 (1), 122−127.

Tzoulas, K., Korpela, K., Venn, S., Yli-Pelkonen, V., Kazmierczak, A., Niemela, J. and James, P. (2007) Promoting ecosystem and human health in urban areas using green infrastructure: A literature review. *Landscape and Urban Planning* 81, 167–178.

UITP (International Association of Public Transport) (2009) Metro, light rail and tram systems in Europe. European Rail Research Advisory Council. Brussels: UITP. See http://www.uitp.org/sites/default/files/cck-focus-papers-files/errac_metrolr_tramsystemsineurope.pdf

UITP (International Association of Public Transport) (2014a) *Public Transport, a Lever for Local Economic Development and Wealth Creation.* Contribution to the Transport Business Summit "Transport: Driving Europe's Economy", Brussels, 27 March. Brussels: UITP.

UITP (International Association of Public Transport) (2014b) *Statistics Brief: Local public transport trends in the European Union, June.* Brussels: UITP. See http://www.ceec.uitp.org/sites/default/files/Local_PT_in_the_EU_web (2).pdf

UITP (International Association of Public Transport) (2015) World Metro Figures: Statistics Brief, October. Brussels: UITP. See http://www.uitp.org/sites/default/files/cck-focus-papers-files/UITP-Statistic Brief-Metro-A4-WEB_0.pdf

Ujang, N. and Muslim, Z. (2014) Walkability and attachment to tourism places in the City of Kuala Lumpur, Malaysia. *Athens Journal of Tourism* (March), 53−65.

United Nations, Department of Economic and Social Affairs (UNDESA), Population Division (2015a) World Urbanization Prospects: The 2014 Revision (ST/ESA/SER.A/366). New York: United Nations.

United Nations, Department of Economic and Social Affairs (UNDESA), Population Division (2015b) Population Facts (No. 2014/4/Rev.1), October. New York: United Nations.

United Nations, Department of Economic and Social Affairs (UNDESA) and United Nations World Tourism Organisation (UNWTO) (2010) *International Recommendations for Tourism Statistics. ST/ESA/STAT/SER.M/83/Rev.1.* New York: UNDESA & UNWTO.

United Nations Human Settlements Programme (UNHabitat) and United Nations Economic and Social Commission for Asia and the Pacific (UNESCAP) (2015) *The State of Asian and Pacific Cities 2015: Urban Transformations Shifting from Quantity to Quality.* Bangkok: UNESCAP.

United Nations World Tourism Organization (UNWTO) (2006) *International Tourist Arrivals, Tourism Market Trends, 2006 Edition − Annex.* Madrid: UNWTO.

United Nations World Tourism Organization (UNWTO) (2011) *Tourism Towards 2030 Global Overview, UNWTO General Assembly 19th Session, Gyeongju, Republic of Korea, 10 October 2011.* Madrid: UNWTO.

United Nations World Tourism Organization (UNWTO) (2012) *UNWTO Tourism Highlights, 2012 Edition − Annex.* Madrid: UNWTO.

United Nations World Tourism Organization (UNWTO) (2013) *Recommendations on Accessible Tourism*. See http://www.accessibletourism.org/resources/accesibili-tyen_2013_unwto.pdf (accessed 1 January 2016).

United Nations World Tourism Organization (UNWTO) (2015) *UNWTO Tourism Highlights, 2015 Edition*. Madrid: UNWTO.

United Nations World Tourism Organization (UNWTO) (2016) International tourist arrivals up 4% and reach a record 1.2 billion in 2015, *UNWTO Tourism Barometer* (advance release), 14 (January). Madrid: UNWTO.

United Nations World Tourism Organization (UNWTO), United Nations Environmental Programme (UNEP) and World Metereological Organisation (WMO) (2008) *Climate Change and Tourism: Responding to Global Challenges*. Madrid: UNWTO, UNEP, WMO.

Ury, W. (nd) The story of the Abraham Path. See http://www.williamury.com/projects/story/ (accessed 23 January 2016).

Urry, J. (2002) *The Tourist Gaze* (2nd edn). London: Sage.

US Department of State (2015) Worldwide caution, *US Passports and International Travel*. See http://travel.state.gov/content/passports/en/alertswarnings/worldwide-caution.html (accessed 27 December 2016).

Valerio, P. (2016) How IoT helps to bridge the digital divide. *Cities of the Future*, 12 January. http://www.citiesofthefuture.eu/how-iot-helps-to-bridge-the-digital-divide/

van de Velde, D.M. (2015) Local public transport. In M. Finger and C. Jaag (eds) *The Routledge Companion to Network Industries* (pp. 241–253). Abingdon: Routledge.

van den Berg, L. and Pol, P. (1998) *The European High-speed Train and Urban Development: Experiences in Fourteen European Urban Regions*. Cheltenham: Ashgate.

van Goeverden, C.D. (2009) Explaining factors for train use in European long-distance travel. *Tourism and Hospitality, Planning and Development* 6 (1), 21–37.

Van Middelkoop, M., Borgers, A. and Timmermans, H. (2003) Inducing heuristic principles of tourist choice of travel mode: A rule-based approach. *Journal of Travel Research* 42 (1), 75–83.

Veeneman, W.W. (2002) *Mind the Gap: Bridging Theories and Practice for the Organisation of Metropolitan Public Transport*. TU Delft, Delft University of Technology.

Verplanken, B. and Wood, W. (2006) Interventions to break and create consumer habits. *Journal of Public Policy & Marketing* 25 (1), 90–103.

Vickerman, R. (1997) High-speed rail in Europe: Experience and issues for future development. *Annals of Regional Science* 31, 21–38.

Vidal, J. (2016) How are cities around the world tackling air pollution? *The Guardian*, 17 May.

Vila, T.D., Darcy, S. and González, E.A. (2015) Competing for the disability tourism market – A comparative exploration of the factors of accessible tourism competitiveness in Spain and Australia. *Tourism Management* 47, 261–272.

Vespermann, J. and Wald, A. (2011) Intermodal integration in air transportation: status quo, motives and future developments. *Journal of Transport Geography* 19 (6), 1187–1197.

Vickerman, R., Spiekermann, K. and Wegener, M. (1999) Accessibility and economic development in Europe. *Regional Studies* 33, 1–15.

Vo, V.C. (2013) Estimation of travel mode choice for domestic tourists to Nha Trang using the multinomial probit model. *Transportation Research Part A: Policy and Practice* 49, 149–159.

Walters, J. (2013) Overview of public transport policy developments in South Africa. *Research in Transportation Economics* 39 (1), 34–45.

Wang, D., Qian, J., Chen, T., Zhao, M. and Zhang, Y. (2013) Influence of the high-speed rail on the spatial pattern of regional tourism – taken Beijing-Shanghai High-Speed Rail of China as example. *Asia Pacific Journal of Tourism Research* 19 (8), 890–912.

Wang, W., Pan, L., Yuan, N., Zhang, S. and Liu, D. (2015) A comparative analysis of intra-city human mobility by taxi. *Physica A: Statistical Mechanics and Its Applications* 420, 134–147.

Wang, X., Huang, S., Zou, T. and Yan, H. (2012) Effects of the high speed rail network on China's regional tourism development. *Tourism Management Perspectives* 1 (1), 34–38.

Watkins, K.E., Ferris, B., Borning, A., Rutherford, G.S. and Layton, D. (2011) Where is my bus? Impact of mobile real-time information on the perceived and actual wait time of transit riders. *Transportation Research Part A: Policy and Practice* 45 (8), 839–848.

Wergeland, T. (2012) Ferry passenger markets. In W.K. Talley (ed) *The Blackwell Companion to Maritime Economics* (pp. 161–183). Oxford: Wiley-Blackwell Publishing.

Weston, R., Davies, N., Peeters, P., Eijgelaar, E., Lumsdon, L., McGrath P. and Piket, P. (2012) *The European Cycle Route Network EuroVelo: Challenges and Opportunities for Sustainable Tourism. Update of the 2009 Study.* Brussels: European Parliament, Directorate General for Internal Policies, Policy Department B: Structural and Cohesion Policies, Transport and Tourism.

Whitmarsh, L. (2009) Behavioural responses to climate change: Asymmetry of intentions and impacts. *Journal of Environmental Psychology* 29, 13–23.

Whitmarsh, L., Seyfang, G. and O'Neill, S. (2011) Public engagement with carbon and climate change: To what extent is the public "carbon capable"? *Global Environmental Change* 21, 56–65.

Wirtz, G., Malane, R. and Schrappen, P. (2015) PNWER Marine Tourism Panel. In *Pacific NorthWest Economic Region Summit*, 15 July. See www.pnwer.org/uploads/2/3/2/9/23295822/full_marine_tourism_panel_(wirtz_malane_schrappen).pdf (accessed 1 April 2016).

Witt, A., Suzor, N. and Wikström, P. (2015) Regulating ride-sharing in the peer economy. *Communication Research and Practice* 1 (2), 174–190.

Wolf, I.D. and Wohlfarth, T. (2014) Walking, hiking and running in parks: A multidisciplinary assessment of health and well-being benefits. *Landscape and Urban Planning* 130, 89–103.

World Bank (2013) Transport in Indonesia. See http://go.worldbank.org/PF2AFG64V0 (accessed 1 April 2016).

World Bank (2014) Abraham Path: Can Tourism Alleviate Poverty and Boost Shared Prosperity? See http://www.worldbank.org/en/news/feature/2014/06/19/can-tourism-alleviate-poverty-and-boost-shared-prosperity (accessed 14 February 2016).

World Economic Forum (WEF) (2009) *Towards a Low Carbon Travel and Tourism Sector.* Davos: WEF.

World Health Organization (WHO) (2015) *Disability and Health, Fact sheet N°352,*. See http://www.who.int/mediacentre/factsheets/fs352/en/ (accessed 1 January 2016).

World Tourism Organization (WTO) (1991) *Resolutions of International Conference on Travel and Tourism, Ottawa, Canada.* Madrid: WTO.

World Tourism Organization (WTO) (1997) *Tourism 2020 Vision.* Madrid: WTO.

Wynen, J. (2013) Explaining travel distance during same-day visits. *Tourism Management* 36, 133–140.

Xie, M. (2013) The impact of high speed rail between wuhan and shenzhen to tourism along the line. In *2nd International Conference on Civil Engineering and Transportation, ICCET 2012* (Vol. 253–255, pp. 282–286). Guilin, China.

Yang, Y. (2010) Analysis of public transport for urban tourism in China. Master of Arts in Transport Policy and Planning, The University of Hong Kong.

Yang, Y., Currie, G., Peel, V. and Liu, Z. (2015) A new index to measure the quality of urban public transport for international tourists. In *Transportation Research Board 94th Annual Meeting* (No. 15-0626).

Yeung, W. (2008) MTR disneyland resort line – A tourism railway. *Railway Engineering - Challenges for Railway Transportation in Information Age 2008,* 25–28 March, Hong Kong, 1st edn Vol. 2008 (pp. 100–103). ICRE 2008.

Yin, M., Bertolini, L. and Duan, J. (2015) The effects of the high-speed railway on urban development: International experience and potential implications for China. *Progress in Planning* 98, 1–52.

Zadra-Veil, C. (2010) *Urban Transport in France* (No. 6). CIRIEC Working Paper.

Zapata Campos, M.J. and Hall, C. M. (eds) (2013) *Organising Waste in the City. International Perspectives on Narratives and Practices.* Bristol: Policy Press.

Zhang, M. (2010) High-speed railway's prospective impact on Chinese tourism and consideration of countermeasures [in Chinese]. *Value Engineering* 29 (11), 227–228.

Zhou, N., Bullock, R.G., Jin, Y., Lawrence, M.B. and Ollivier, G.P. (2016) *High-speed Railways in China: An update on passenger profiles.* China transport topics no. 15. Washington, DC: World Bank Group. See http://documents.worldbank.org/curated/en/2016/01/25804591/high-speed-railways-china-update-passenger-profiles (accessed 1 April 2016).

Zhou, X., Jia, X. and Du, H. (2015) Travel mode choice based on perceived quality of bus service. In *15th COTA International Conference of Transportation Professionals* (CICTP 2015), Beijing, China, July 24–27, 2015 (pp. 1534–1545). Washington, DC: American Society of Civil Engineers.

Zimmerman, S. and Fang, K. (2015) *Public Transport Service Optimization and System Integration,* China Transport Topics No. 14. Washington, DC: The World Bank.

Index